CW01483607

# AN ILLUSTRATED HISTORY OF AUSTRALIAN BUSHRANGERS

# AN ILLUSTRATED HISTORY OF AUSTRALIAN BUSHRANGERS

GEORGE BOXALL

VIKING

Opposite title page: Portrait of Ned Kelly

Viking
Penguin Books Australia Ltd
487 Maroondah Highway, PO Box 257
Ringwood, Victoria 3134, Australia
Penguin Books Ltd
Harmondsworth, Middlesex, England
Viking Penguin, A Division of
Penguin Books USA Inc.
375 Hudson Street, New York, New York
10014, USA
Penguin Books Canada Limited
10 Alcorn Avenue, Toronto, Ontario,
Canada M4V 3B2
Penguin Books (N.Z.) Ltd
182-190 Wairau Road, Auckland 10,
New Zealand

First published by John Currey, O'Neil
Publishers Pty Ltd 1975
as *Australian Bushrangers An Illustrated History*
Reprinted 1976, 1978
New edition 1981

This edition published by Penguin Books
Australia Ltd 1988

10 9 8 7 6 5 4 3

Copyright © Penguin Books Australia, 1988

All rights reserved. Without limiting the rights
under copyright reserved above, no part of this
publication may be reproduced, stored in or introduced into a retrieval system, or transmitted, in
any form or by any means (electronic, mechanical,
photocopying, recording or otherwise), without
the prior written permission of both the copyright
owner and the above publisher of this book.

Printed and bound through
Bookbuilders Limited, Hong Kong

National Library of Australia
Cataloguing-in-Publication data

Boxall, George E. (George Eedes).
   An illustrated history of Australian
   bushrangers.

   Includes index.
   ISBN 0 670 90070 2.

   1. Bushrangers - Australia. 2. Bushrangers -
Australia - Pictorial works. I. Title.
II. Title: Australian bushrangers, an illustrated
history.

364.1'55'0994

Martin Cash at sixty
Captain Melville's death mask

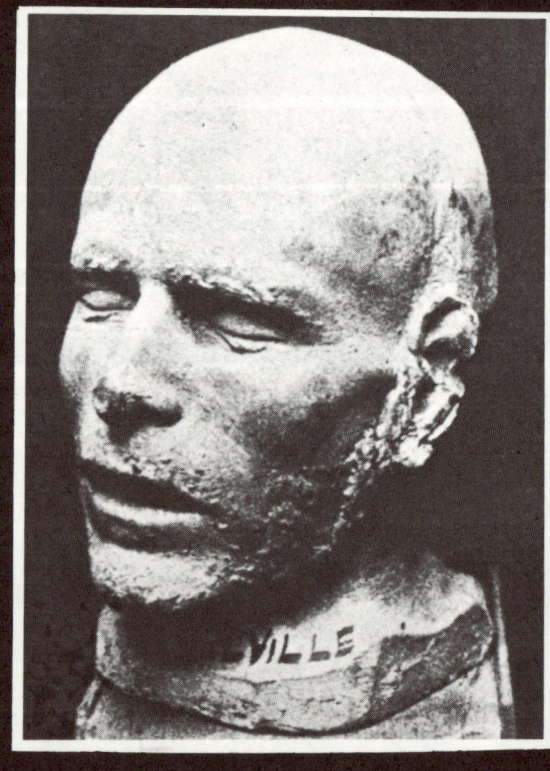

Walhalla gold escort
Morgan's killer, John Quinlan

Mounted trooper
Captain Moonlite

# Contents

Superintendent Hare
Dan Kelly

Steve Hart
Joe Byrne's body displayed

Constable Scanlon
The Kelly home at Greta

# 1 Convict bolters

**The convict system in Australia; conditions of the prisoners; the desperation of despair; some terrible revelations; beginnings of bushranging in Australia; origin and meaning of the term; the Bushranging Act and its abuses.**

The type of brigandage known in Australia as bushranging without doubt evolved more or less directly from the convict system established as the basis of the early settlements. The first bushrangers were simply men who took to the bush to escape work and enjoy freedom of action. Under the harsh laws of the Georgian era the worst criminals were hanged; the convicts sent to Botany Bay in the eighteenth and the earlier years of the nineteenth centuries, were generally men to whom the confinements of the civilization of their day were irksome. Many of them were political agitators, industrial rioters, and machine-breakers. The others were poachers and similarly comparatively mild offenders against the laws who, under present laws, would be sufficiently punished with a few months' imprisonment. Many of these men, when they were removed to a new land where the social conditions did not press so heavily on them, became honest and reputable citizens. If it had not been for the harsh treatment they were subjected to, others who were driven to continue their fight against authority might also have lived quiet and useful lives.

Under the operation of a new humanitarian force the criminal law of England was rapidly softened and ameliorated, and with every advance in this direction the character of the convicts sent out to Australia steadily deteriorated. With every alteration in the law a fresh class of criminal was transported. At first, pickpockets were sent; then sheep and horse-stealers, forgers and others, who had previously only escaped the gallows in rare instances when they could find some influential friend to take sufficient interest in them to plead their cause, were transported as a matter of course. This process continued until transportation ceased. As the last batch of prisoners sent out was presumably the worst, having been guilty of more heinous crimes than their predecessors, we are too apt to judge the early convicts harshly from our knowledge of the later ones. The general effect was that while, with the amelioration of the laws, crime steadily decreased in England, it just as steadily

increased in Australia. Without doubt the worst criminals were transported to Van Diemen's Land after transportation to New South Wales had ceased in 1842. The laws of England prior to the great changes made after 1870 seem to have operated to clear the country of the dissaffected and the discontented, rather than the criminal. It may be interesting to study how far the introduction of large numbers of this class into Australia may have paved the way for modern advances in liberal government in Australia, but it only relates to the bushrangers so far as it enables us to account for the large number of men who 'took to the bush'.

The earlier bushrangers seem to have been idle and dissolute, rather than criminal, characters. They watched for an opportunity to escape into a patch of scrub whenever the eye of the sentry in charge of them was turned away, and the nature of the country was so favourable to this method of evasion that it constituted a continuous challenge to them to run away. Incredible as it may appear now, numbers of men started northward or westward in hopes of reaching the Dutch or English settlements at Batavia, Singapore, Hong Kong, or some other place in that direction. It must be remembered that the majority of the working classes at the beginning of the nineteenth century could not read and had no knowledge of geography. They had heard sailors speak of these settlements and had no idea that hundreds of miles of sea flowed between them and Australia. How many of these poor ignorant men lost their lives in the attempt to achieve the impossible cannot be said, but some terrible stories of cannibalism have been related in connection with this phase of bushranging. The majority of the 'runaways' however, had no definite ideas. They hoped to be able to live in freedom in the bush and to subsist on fruits, roots, or other native plants. A few joined a tribe of blacks and stayed longer or shorter times with them; others simply wandered about until hunger drove them back; many remained at large until they were captured, and these lived by stealing from farmers and other settlers any articles which could be eaten or sold. When one of these early bushrangers grew tired of his freedom he gave himself up at the nearest police station and received fifty lashes. The penalty for a second offence was twelve months in a chain gang.

There was no adequate system of classifying the convicts. It was the custom in advertising runaways to give the name of the man and that of the ship in which he was transported. Then followed the personal description, and that was all. It was admitted to be inconvenient, but no attempt appears to have been made to improve it. For administration purposes, convicts were divided into three classes according to their sentences. There were men who had been transported for 'seven' years, for 'fourteen' years, or for 'life'. They were also classified as 'young', 'middle-aged', and 'old', and usually the crime for which they had been transported was specified, but such a description gave no indication of the character of the man. Finally they were divided into 'town thieves', 'rural labourers', and 'gentlemen'. This was a step in the right direction, but it was too vague to be of much use. The educated convicts were all classified as 'gentlemen' whether they came from the towns or the rural districts.[1] It is worth noting that the proportion of skilled tradesmen was very small. Very few men who had been apprenticed to a trade were among the convicts sent to Australia at any time.

The regulations as to hours of work were often flouted, and the severe taskmaster might work his assigned servants as many hours as he pleased. It was generally understood that Sunday was to be a holiday, or day of rest, but excuses were readily found for making the convicts work on this day, and this was a common source of discontent. Frequently men absconded on Saturday night, remained in the bush on Sunday, and returned on Monday to take the customary fifty lashes and resume work.

If flogging had any effect in preventing crime, it should have made the convict colonies the most virtuous places on earth, for the 'cat' was in almost continuous use in New South Wales and Van Diemen's Land. The 'cat' generally used was the ordinary military or naval one; but 'the cat used at Macquarie Harbour was a larger and heavier instrument than that used generally for the punishment of soldiers or sailors. It was called the thief's cat, or double cat-o-'nine-tails. It had only the usual number of tails, but each of these was a double twist of whipcord, and each tail had nine knots. It was a very formidable instrument indeed.'[2] Undoubtedly the influence of this barbarous instrument of torture tended to make the prisoners at Macquarie Harbour the most reckless and ferocious of the convicts of Australia. There can be no doubt that its influence was for evil and not for good. However frightful the tortures which were inflicted on the convicts in general, we have positive evidence that their lot was looked upon with envy by some of the

An 1848 engraving of a convict working in chains in the notorious 'iron gang'. Overwork, vicious punishment and degrading conditions, caused many convicts to escape in the bush. In the vernacular of the day they were called 'bolters'.

soldiers who guarded them. Several soldiers in New South Wales deliberately committed crimes so that they might be convicted, in the hope that, by good conduct, they might earn some of the indulgences open to convicts. The fact is that any prisoner who contrived to make friends with an official had his way made easy for him, while the independent were ruthlessly persecuted until, in many cases, they were finally forced to the gallows.

The prisoners of all classes in Government are fed with the coarsest food; governed with the most rigid discipline; subjected to the stern, and frequently capricious and tyrannical will of an overseer; for the slightest offence (sometimes for none at all — the victim of false accusation) brought before a magistrate, whom the Government has armed with the tremendous powers of a summary jurisdiction, and either flogged, or sentenced to solitary confinement, or retransported to an iron gang, where he must work in heavy irons, or to a penal settlement, where he will be ruled with a rod of iron. If assigned to a private individual he becomes a creature of chance. He may fall into the hands of a kind indulgent master, who will reward his fidelity with suitable acknowledgements; but, in ninety-nine cases out of a hundred, he will find his employer suspicious, or whimsical, or a blockhead, not knowing good conduct from bad, or a despot, who treats him like a slave, cursing and abusing, and getting him flogged for no reasonable cause. He may be harassed to the very death — he may be worked like a horse, and fed like a chameleon. The master, though not invested by law with uncontrolled power, has yet great authority, which may be abused in a thousand ways precluding redress. Even his legal power is sufficiently formidable. A single act of disobedience is a sufficient ground of complaint before the magistrate, and is always severely dealt with. But, besides the master's power, the prisoners are in some measure under a dominion to the free population at large; any man can give him in charge without ceremony. If seen drunk, if seen tippling in the public-house, if met after hours in the street, if unable to pay his trifling debt, if impertinent — the freeman has nothing more to do than to send him to the watch-house, and get him punished. The poor prisoner is at the mercy of all men.[3]

If this is a fair and unexaggerated statement of the conditions, it is no wonder the general tone of morality in the colony was low. J. T. Bigge wrote that 'every opportunity was seized for cheating. When the convicts attended at the store to draw their weekly rations, supplies were frequently drawn for men not at work there. False lists of men employed in the various gangs were made out'.[4]

In fact, the Government of the colony was a military despotism under which corruption was rampant, so that the authorities themselves set an example of immorality which the convicts were not slow to follow. 'The police made a considerable revenue by blackmailing convicts who were in business.'[5] Those who could pay were allowed to continue to enjoy a freedom to which they were not legally entitled, while those who would not, or could not, be blackmailed, to satisfy the exorbitant demands of the so-called custodians of the peace, soon 'got into trouble' and were prosecuted.

It was said that if a man could escape from a country district and go to Sydney he might, if he could

Interior of a convict ship. If anything, this early engraving makes the convict quarters appear cleaner and more spacious than they really were.

Convicts in a government jail gang in Sydney about 1830; the men worked in chains on government tasks during the day and were returned to the barracks at night.

afford to dress well, pass as a free man without attracting attention. A blacksmith named Brady, assigned to Major James Mudie, of Castle Forbes, eluded the police in this way for nearly two years. He was recognized by a fellow convict, some time before he was captured, but this man 'let him go for £5'. Such cases, however, were exceptions to the general rule. The majority of runaways went into the bush and not into the town, and the *Sydney* and *Hobart Town Gazettes* in early times contained numerous proclamations by the various governors calling upon all law-abiding people to assist the military in capturing runaways. Some of the issues of these *Gazettes* contain columns of the names and descriptions of persons styled 'absconders', 'absentees', 'bolters', or 'bushrangers'. In these the term 'bushranger' appears most frequently in New South Wales, while 'bolter' was the most popular in Van Diemen's Land. The first bushrangers, therefore, were men who 'took to the bush' to escape work, and it was quite possible for a man to be a bushranger without actually stealing.

But laziness was not the sole cause of bushranging in early times. A more powerful impulse perhaps was discontent, love of change. 'One of the most common indications of the misery of convicts under existing circumstances is a passionate desire for change of

place; and when serving considerate masters they are sometimes indulged in this by being transferred (though always as a sort of punishment) to their disadvantage. In other cases, however, the desire becomes so strong that they will steal, or commit some equal offence, expressly to be condemned to a road gang or penal settlement.'[6] In fact the monotony of their lives became insupportable, even in those cases where they were not cruelly treated. Captain Maconochie cited cases of men who committed crimes within a few months of their being entitled to a ticket-of-leave, thus forfeiting their chances of freedom. In some cases this was due to the 'inhuman treatment' of the master. In one case a valuable servant — a blacksmith — whose time had nearly expired, was goaded into running away so that he might be condemned to a further term of service before obtaining his ticket-of-leave. This was not an isolated case.

'Generally', said Dr J. D. Lang, 'the condition of the assigned servant in New South Wales is superior to that of the farm labourer of England. He is better clothed, better fed, and as comfortably lodged. He is under personal restraint, not being allowed to leave his

11

The old convict jail, Murray Street, Hobart Town, 1848

master's property without a pass, but he has many comforts and means of amusement which render his situation by no means irksome or severe.'[7] But it was just this restraint which these men found intolerable. They had not the patience, the long-suffering resignation of the English farm labourer. Many of them had been English farm labourers and had found the conditions in which they lived intolerable. When they realized that their lot was not improved by being sent to Australia, they rebelled again. 'The experience furnished by the penal settlements', said Judge Forbes, 'has proved that transportation is capable of being carried to an extreme of suffering such as to render death desirable, and to induce many prisoners to seek it under its most appalling aspects. . . . I have known cases in which it appeared that men had committed crimes at Norfolk Island, for the mere purpose of being sent to Sydney to be tried, and the cause of their desiring to be so sent was to avoid the state of endurance in which they were placed in Norfolk Island.'

Several cases occurred in which 'men at Norfolk Island cut the heads of their fellow-prisoners with the hoe while at work, with the certainty of being detected, and the certainty of being executed. They did this without malice, and when charged said it was better to be hung than to live in such a hell'.[8] Sir Richard Bourke said: 'Capital crimes have been committed in that penal settlement from a desperate determination to stake the chance of capital conviction and punishment in Sydney against the chances of escape which the passage might afford to the accused and to the witnesses summoned to attend the trial.'[9] The early bushrangers of Australia ranged therefore from the comparatively innocent wanderers in the bush, to such desperadoes as these. The crimes they committed varied from petty theft to burglary, bank robbery, robbery on the high road, and murder. The modern idea of a bushranger is a bold highwayman, and no doubt many of the bushrangers came up to this ideal, but the story of the bushrangers would not be complete if it took no note of the others.

The settlement on Norfolk Island was established with the view of sending all the reconvicted prisoners there. It was the penal settlement of a penal settlement. It was abandoned for a time, after the founding of a similar settlement on the banks of the Derwent River in Van Diemen's Land, but was later re-established as a place of punishment, and many of the most notorious of the bushrangers ended their days there. It was in the convict settlements on those islands that the greatest brutalities were perpetrated on the prisoners. Norfolk Island, Macquarie Harbour, and Port Arthur were each known as 'The Hell' among the 'old hands', as the convicts were called after transportation had been abolished. It was in these settlements that the more violent and refractory of the convicts were gradually collected, and the history of these places tends to prove that brutality cannot be cured by brutal means. Flogging which was an everyday occurrence had no reformatory effect. The early bushrangers thought nothing of it. It certainly did not deter them from absconding. When an escapee tired of wandering about the bush, he returned to the settlement to take his flogging 'like a man'. In the stories told by the old hands, an offender was represented as walking jauntily up to the triangles, throwing off his jumper, placing himself in position for tying, and then, when he had been secured, telling the flogger to do his 'd——est'. If the descriptions of the manner in which the floggers performed their task are true, the punishment was a terrible one.

It was said there were two floggers in Sydney who were regarded as artists in their profession. These men performed together, one being right-handed and the other left. They prided themselves on being able to flog a man without breaking the skin, and consequently there was no blood spilled. But the back of the flogged man puffed up like 'blown veal'. The swelling 'shook like jelly' and the effects were felt for a much longer period than when the back was cut and scored as it generally was. We are told that the ground in the Barrack Square in Sydney where the triangles stood, was saturated with human blood, and the flogging places elsewhere must have been in the same condition. When the man had received his dose and was untied, he would throw his jumper across his shoulders and walk away with a grin — or with some such remarks as 'Well, is that all you can do? —— you!' and afterwards boast that 'the —— couldn't get a whimper' out of him. I have heard of one case where the flagellator kept hitting a prisoner low down across the loins. The recipient turned his head round once and said fiercely: 'Hit higher, blast you!' The flogger took no notice, and the prisoner made no other sign until he was untied. Then he knocked the flogger down with his fist, and was immediately seized up for another 'dose'.

The convicts rather than be ashamed of floggings, boasted of them. But nothing pleased them more than

Flogging was the main form of punishment for convicts. The prisoner was chained to the 'triangle' and given from fifty to 1,000 lashes with the cat-o'-nine-tails, depending on his offence. In this early re-enactment, a doctor (left) observes and times the scourger's strokes.

stories about the flogging of 'freemen', as those settlers who had gone to the colonies neither as convicts nor officials were called. One story, which may or may not be true, has been told as having occurred in every convict district in Australia. It was to the effect that a master one day gave a letter to an assigned servant and told him to take it to the nearest jail. The servant, surmising that the letter was somewhat to the following effect:— 'Dear Sir, — Please give the bearer fifty for absconding (or what not), and oblige, yours truly, etc.,' told a plausible tale to the first freeman he met and induced him to deliver the letter. The point of the story generally lay in the ingenuity with which the convict induced the freeman to deliver the letter for him, but the astonishment of the freeman when he was seized up to the triangles in spite of his struggles and protestations, and given the 'fifty', was a perpetual source of joy and hilarity to the convicts who heard the story. It is quite probable that the incident may have occurred more than once. Although freemen were legally exempt from flogging, unless under sentence of a qualified Court, many authentic instances of freeman having been flogged have been told.

A storekeeper in Hobart Town had offended his neighbours, and one of them, in revenge, posted a written placard libelling the offender. The placard was affixed to a big gum stump at the corner of Collins and Elizabeth Streets. Just as the complainant

was putting this bill on the stump the man libelled in it passed and called the attention of the Military Commandant, who was near at hand at the time, to it. A sort of informal drum-head Court Martial was held on the spot, and the libeller was found guilty and sentenced to receive three hundred lashes, which were administered at once, in spite of the protests of the victim that he was a freeman and was therefore entitled to a judicial trial. When two hundred lashes had been administered, a cry of 'Ship ho' was raised, and the last hundred was got rid of as quickly as possible, the commandant, the flagellator, the spectators, and others all rushing away to the wharf to hear the news from Europe.[10]

If the law could be defied by a military official in the case of a free immigrant holding a good position, what chance of justice could there be for a convict? A story illustrating the reckless manner in which prisoners were flogged is told by the *Launceston Advertiser*. 'A prisoner was found guilty of absconding, and sentenced to receive fifty lashes, when some circumstances were disclosed which proved that the prisoner was innocent, but had lost his pass. "Never mind," said the Launceston magistrate, "the warrant is signed, let him be punished now; I will forgive him the next time he's brought up." '

The tyranny of the officials was boundless. One government rule was that all convicts should take off their hats to officers and officials whenever they passed. In January 1839, a party of convicts was building some steps at Woolloomooloo Bay, on Sir Maurice O'Connell's estate. Several of them were rolling a heavy stone down to be placed in position when an officer passed along and the convicts immediately rose up and took their hats off. The stone rolled quickly down the steep embankment, struck the overseer and knocked him down, almost breaking his leg. Captain O'Connell gave orders that the men should not salute anybody in future while at work. A few days later Colonel Wilson, Chief Police Magistrate of Sydney passed, accompanied by his daughter. The convicts continued at work without noticing him. 'Take off your hats', cried the Colonel. Several of the men did so, but Joseph Todd, who was carrying a heavy load, took no notice. 'Take off your hat, you scoundrel', said the Colonel. Todd said he had been ordered not to. The Colonel shouted 'I'll have your back skinned for you, you rascal', called the sergeant of police who acted as guard, and gave Todd in charge. Captain O'Connell appeared to defend his man and said Colonel Wilson was trespassing and had no right to interfere with assigned servants on their master's estate. Sergeant Goodwin deposed that the path was a common one and people frequented it to get to the bathing place. Sergeant Mather said that Todd had struggled when arrested. The Bench held that Todd being an assigned servant had been guilty of disorderly conduct in resisting the police. Had he been a freeman he would have been justified in resisting arrest without a warrant; being a prisoner, his conduct had been highly disorderly, and he was sentenced to receive fifty lashes. A week later Todd was again arrested for being out after hours, and was sentenced to receive thirty lashes. The paper charged Colonel Wilson with tyrannical conduct, and said that he went to see Todd flogged.[11]

I am not relating the worse cases in order to make a case for the bushrangers. I am simply offering facts to illustrate life in the colonies at the time, and thus account for the large number of men who 'took to the bush' and to indicate how the special Acts passed to prevent this breach of the law were as tyrannical as the acts of the officials or the masters which went so far to create it. The Bushranging Act (11 George IV., No. 10) authorized the military or civil police to arrest any person on the mere suspicion that he or she was illegally at large, and the onus of proof was thrown on the suspected party. This Act was a source of grievances. No-one was safe except well known officials, and it seems that the Act was extensively

Gallery of cells in the penitentiary, Port Arthur

*Right:*
Ruins of the convict prison at Norfolk Island. Some of the convict bushrangers were confined to the island after their capture.

*Right:*
The penal settlement at Port Arthur, Tasmania, showing the penitentiary (right)

used for purposes of extortion and blackmail. A young woman was arrested by an ex-constable and charged with being illegally at large. It was in vain that she protested that she was 'free' and did not require a pass. He insisted on taking her to the lock-up. Fortunately, while walking along the street she met someone who knew her and who threatened the ex-policeman with prosecution if he did not release her. The fellow did so and was not prosecuted. Probably had an inquiry been held it would have been found that he was acting in collusion with the police.

Even the officials were not always safe. Mr Jacques, the government auctioneer, had been to a dinner party. Being near the Custom House he decided to walk to the wharf and take the steamer which ran to Balmain. Not having walked to the wharf from that point before, he asked a constable which turning he should take. He was immediately arrested as a convict illegally at large. In spite of his protests he was conveyed to the nearest police station. The sergeant in charge refused to believe his story, and thought that the presence of a well-dressed man in that quarter was suspicious. Mr Jacques was consequently detained till morning, when he was recognized by the magistrate and discharged.

In 1834 a circular letter was addressed by the Governor to the various police magistrates in New South Wales, inquiring whether, in their opinion, the

MESS ROOM
REGULATIONS.

216. The Prisoners are cautioned against committing any of the undermentioned offences, for which they will be liable to punishment, viz :

217. Not observing the strictest silence and decorum. Not suspending their caps upon the racks provided for that purpose. Not standing up during Grace before and after Meals.

218. Not arranging their Mess Utensils according to the prescribed method after Meals. Making any slop on the tables. Not observing the utmost cleanliness, or throwing any of the refuse upon the floor. Scratching or defacing any part of the Dining Hall, or Furniture thereof. The Mess-men not remaining at their respective Tables until they have delivered over the Mess Utensils to the Officers on duty.

(Extracts from Port Arthur Approved Regulations.)

Mess Room regulations at Port Arthur

Act should be reaffirmed or not. The replies were by a large majority in favour of its being continued, while others merely suggested that it might be amended in various ways to prevent the abuses which had grown up under its operation. Judge Burton was almost alone in his condemnation of the Bushranging Act, which he said was repugnant to the laws of England. 'England and the United States of America', he said, 'are the only two countries in the world where passports are not compulsory,' and he deprecated the introduction of the passport system into Australia. It was held that the conditions existing in the colony made such an act necessary; it was therefore re-enacted without amendment.[12] It is worth noting to illustrate Colonial Office procedure of that day, that it was the paid officials, and not the public, who were consulted in this matter.

Considering the facts, the wonder is not that large numbers of prisoners took to the bush, but that all did not do so and the more we study the early history of the convict settlements the less we feel inclined to blame the early bushrangers, however savage or atrocious their actions. The story I have to tell shows a lamentable waste of life, and many even of the more notorious bushrangers exhibited qualities which might under happier conditions have fitted them for useful work. This is specially true of the earlier bushrangers who were generally the victims of unjust laws. Of the later ones, the native-born bushrangers, it is impossible to speak in the same terms. They were not driven to crime by want or oppression, but they were the vicious products of a vicious past; their crimes were due to vicious environment and education. They are gone now, but if we can draw some useful lessons from their lives, they may not have been altogether wasted.

From the evidence, it seems that the early bushrangers were very numerous. 'In one case it became known', said James Macarthur, 'that a gang of about sixty convicts, employed in the Government gangs in Liverpool, intended to break out on a certain night and take to the bush. It was considered advisable to allow them to break out, proper precautions having been made to capture them. It was the intention to attack our farming stations at Camden. We armed twelve of the best-conducted of our convict servants, but the absconders found that their design had been discovered and did not attempt to put it in force.'[13] Thus the bushrangers did not always go out singly, or in twos or threes. J. T. Bigge wrote:

At Windsor, and in the adjoining districts, the offence termed bushranging, or absconding in the woods, and living upon plunder and the robbing of orchards, are most prevalent . . . At Emu Plains, or the district of Evan, gambling, absence from work, insolence to overseers, neglect of work, and stealing, are the most common offences . . . As the population of New South Wales has, until lately, been virtually limited to the occupation of a small tract of land that lies between the Blue Mountains and the sea, and as few temptations to plunder existed in the tracts contiguous to these boundaries, excepting those that are afforded by the wild cattle in the cow-pastures, the offence of bushranging, or continued absence in the woods, has not of late been common. Instances have occurred of the departure of convicts for the purpose of traversing the country with a view to escape, of the escape of some from Newcastle, sent thither for punishment, and their wandering and temporary existence in the vicinity of Windsor; and latterly, a few instances of escape from the road parties in the districts of Liverpool and Bathurst; but there has been no systematic or continued efforts of desperate convicts to defy the attempts of the local Government in New South Wales, or to subsist by plunder, such as have existed until a very late period in Van Diemen's Land.[14]

It is in Van Diemen's Land, therefore, that the story of the more serious phases of bushranging first begins.

# 2 Island warfare

**Bushranging in Van Diemen's Land; Mike Howe, the King of the Ranges; the war against the aboriginals; Musquito, leader of the natives; a war of reprisals; brutal treatment of the aboriginals by bushrangers.**

The first settlement in Van Diemen's Land was founded in 1803, when a penal establishment was founded on the banks of the River Derwent to deal with the worst cases from Sydney. Although other penal stations were opened, the island continued to be the chief penal establishment of New South Wales until 1825, when it became an independent colony. The first shipment of convicts, direct from England to Van Diemen's Land, took place in 1823, and from that date, until transportation to the island finally ceased in 1853, 64,306 convicts were sent from the British Isles. The number sent previously from New South Wales was not large; nevertheless it included the majority of the most turbulent of the convicts and relieved the former colony of their charge and control. The island was in fact 'nothing but a jail on a large scale'.[1]

The early conditions in the colony appear to have been favourable to bushranging. In 1805 there was such a shortage of food stuffs, owing to the non-arrival of store ships from Sydney, that a famine appeared to be imminent. To relieve the store, the Lieutenant-Governor ordered the liberation of the convicts and sent them into the woods to catch kangaroos and other wild animals for food. When the stores arrived and food became plentiful, the attempts to recall the convicts were only partially successful. Many had learned how to subsist in the bush and disregarded the proclamations issued by the Lieutenant-Governor ordering them to return to work.

At first the bushrangers or bolters were similar to those of New South Wales and contented themselves with petty thefts. The first proclamation in which reference is made to 'a gang of bushrangers' was published in the *Hobart Town Gazette* by Lieutenant-Governor Davey and dated 10 September 1810. It offered rewards and indulgences to convicts for the capture of any members of a gang which, under the leadership of a convict named Whitehead, had been robbing settlers and farmers in the vicinity of Hobart Town.

Whitehead was the first to organize a gang which combined highway robbery with burglary and petty

Governor Davey invited the bushranger Mike Howe to surrender.

larceny. Bushrangers were not at that time specialists. From time to time other proclamations were issued in which this gang was mentioned, but it was not until 14 May 1813, that a special proclamation was published, calling upon the 'bolters' to surrender. Those who neglected to obey this order were to be proclaimed 'outlaws' on 1 December.

Very few particulars are published about this gang in the newspapers, and the proclamations rarely specify the facts in connection with the robberies committed. The newspapers of the time seldom mention the names of the bushrangers, and appear to have been quite averse to mentioning their Christian names. Thus Whitehead is referred to as 'the convict Whitehead', or the 'notorious bushranger Whitehead', and so on. He is debited, however, with one horrible crime. The gang captured a half-crazy fellow named John Hopkins, and accused him of trying to betray them. As a punishment for this offence a pair of moccasins, roughly made of bullock hide, was fitted on to his feet, and in these were placed a number of the great red ants, commonly known as 'bull-dog' or 'soldier' ants. The horrible barbarity of such a punishment can only be appreciated by those who have inadvertently stood on a 'soldier's' nest. The victim is said to have died in agony.

Whitehead was shot by a party of soldiers in October 1814, and Michael Howe, commonly called the 'First of the Australian bushrangers', was elected captain of the gang in his stead. Mike Howe, as he was usually called, was transported from England for highway robbery, and soon after his arrival in Sydney 'got into trouble'. He was again transported to Van Diemen's Land, where his violence caused him to be repeatedly flogged and otherwise punished. He made his escape and joined Whitehead's gang, and soon, by his superior education, gained an ascendency over his comrades. His previous experiences as a footpad in England no doubt tended to fit him for the leadership of the gang, and he is still regarded as one of the most notable of the revolters against law and order in the colonies. One of his earlier achievements was to organize a raid on a tribe of blacks for the purpose of providing himself and his comrades with wives. This is said to have been the first act in the tragedy which closed with the complete annihilation of the Tasmanian aboriginals. The natives, of course, resisted, and many of them were shot, and the women were forced away to the bushrangers' camp. In revenge, the natives attacked, not the bushrangers' camp, but the houses of settlers who had no connection with the bushrangers, and fights between the settlers and the aboriginals became frequent. some of the black women seem to have become reconciled to the change, and Howe's 'wife', Black Mary, is associated with him in most of the stories told of him. It is said that it was her knowledge of the bush which enabled him to escape so frequently from the military parties sent out to capture him.

Howe addressed a letter 'From the Bushrangers to the Hon. T. Davey, Lieutenant-Governor of Van Diemen's Land', in which he protested against the charge made against himself and his mates in the proclamations, of having been guilty of 'horrid and detestable crimes'. He asserted that he had never committed murder and had only used violence when it was necessary to avoid capture. The letter was conveyed to Hobart Town by an American whaler named Richard Westlick. He had an interview with his Excellency, and was sent back with a verbal message that the Governor 'did not wish to take the life of any man', but merely to preserve order. If Howe or any of his comrades would surrender, no charges should be made against them for their acts while 'in the bush'. No notice was taken of this generous offer, and the depredations continued.

Later Mike Howe addressed a letter 'From the

Lieutenant-Governor Sorell: he agreed to release Howe on parole.

Governor of the Ranges to the Governor of the Town', and sent it to Lieutenant-Governor Sorell, who had succeeded Colonel Davey. In this the bushranger offered to give himself up on condition that he received a free pardon. He demanded that some recognized official should be sent to meet him at an appointed spot, so that they might 'confer as gentleman to gentleman'. The fact that this insolent offer was accepted is evidence of the power of the bushrangers, and shows the anxiety of the Governor to put a stop to the robberies which harassed the industrious settlers and made the roads of the colony unsafe. Captain Nairne of the 46th Regiment, was sent out to meet the bushranger, and the result of their conference 'as gentlemen' was that Howe accompanied the captain back to Hobart Town.

On his arrival there he was informed that the Lieutenant-Governor had no power to grant pardons, but that he would write to Governor Macquarie in Sydney and urge him to grant a pardon without delay. Howe agreed to wait in Hobart Town. He was liberated on parole, and soon became very popular in the city. Then a rumour began to spread to the effect that Howe had committed no less than four murders, not reckoning the aboriginals he had killed, and that the Governor declined to grant him a pardon. As soon as Howe heard this unconfirmed rumour he broke his parole and returned to the bush. A proclamation was immediately issued declaring him an outlaw, and offering one hundred pounds reward for his capture,

The murders of aboriginals by Mike Howe and his followers led to the bloodthirsty 'war' between natives and whites.

dead or alive. Smaller rewards were offered for other members of his gang, whose names were known.

The estimates of the strength of his gang vary extremely from time to time. Sometimes he is said to have a hundred or more followers, while frequently he is represented as acting alone or in company with only one or two others.

It appears that many men, who 'bolted' into the bush as a relief to the monotony of their lives, became bushrangers, and when hard pressed, or when they tired of that pursuit, they returned to the town, gave themselves up, and were punished as ordinary bolters.

One day, not very long after his escape from Hobart Town, Howe was surprised while asleep by two ticket-of-leave men named Watts and Drew. They captured and tied him. Howe fought like a lion and managed to break loose. He snatched a knife and stabbed Watts. He then seized Watts' gun and shot Drew dead. Watts ran away, while Howe was employed in re-loading the gun, and hid in the scrub for a time. When the way was clear he crawled to a farm and gave information. He was cared for as well as circumstances permitted, but he died from loss of blood before a doctor could be brought to him. Howe was followed by the military, but escaped.

Several skirmishes took place between Howe's gang and the soldiers, and more than one of his accomplices were shot, but their chief always contrived to get away. At length a kangaroo hunter named Warburton led William Pugh, a soldier commonly known as 'Big

Bill' and a seaman named John Worrall, to where Howe was camped under a gumgree. A terrific fight took place and Howe's brains were beaten out before it was over.

For the time, bushranging in Van Diemen's Land was said to have been put down, but the 'Guerrilla War' between the whites and the natives inaugurated by the bushrangers, continued.

One of the black avengers was known as Musquito. In 1823 he was transported to Van Diemen's Land for the murder of a gin (presumably his wife, which is no crime according to native law) and having been employed on a cattle station in New South Wales, was appointed stock-keeper. Later he was employed as a tracker, and aided the soldiers in capturing some of the bushrangers. For this he was so persecuted by his fellow convicts that his life became a burden to him. He appealed to the authorities for protection; but, as this was not accorded to him, he became a bushranger himself.

Some of his attacks on settlers were so skilfully planned and carried out, that many people believed that the natives had been led by a white man. After about two years of bushranging, Musquito and Black Jack, the two leaders, were captured. Musquito was charged with the murder of William Holyoak, and Mr Gilbert Robertson appeared in his defence. In spite of the conciliator's efforts Musquito was convicted and sentenced to death. When the sentence had been pronounced Musquito said, 'Hanging no —— good for blackfellow.' Mr Bisdee asked him 'Why not as good for blackfellow as for whitefellow?' 'Oh,' exclaimed Musquito, 'Very good for whitefellow. He used to it.'

19

# 3 Cannibal convict

Pierce, the cannibal convict; escapes from Macquarie Harbour, the 'Western Hell'; the ruffian Jefferies; Matthew Brady the bushranger; Brady laughs at Governor Arthur's proclamation; his fight with Captain Balfour and betrayal by a comrade; John Batman captures Brady.

In a dispatch to the Colonial Secretary in 1822, Lieutenant-Governor Arthur said that bushranging had been 'totally suppressed in Van Diemen's Land during the past three years', or since the breaking up of Howe's gang. But the happy conditions suggested by this report were not destined to last as there was still a number of runaways or bolters in the bush. Bushranging had by this time come to mean the commission of more serious crimes than petty larceny, and it was in this sense that the Governor made use of the term. We have not yet arrived at the time when others besides highwaymen can be excluded. The next illustration is perhaps the most terrible of all the events connected with bushranging, although it concerns only the bushrangers themselves.

On 20 September 1822, Alexander Pierce, Bob Greenhill, Mathew Travers, Thomas Bodenham, Bill Cornelius or Kenelly, James Brown, John Mathers, and Alexander Dalton made their escape from the recently founded penal station at Macquarie Harbour. According to Pierce's confession, it appears that they 'made it up for to take a boat' and proceed to Hobart Town. Greenhill was at work at the mines, but they called for him, as he was a good navigator. Greenhill smashed up the miners' chests with an axe, and took all their provisions.

Pierce related that:

We then put out all the fires with buckets of water, so that the miners could not signal our escape; but, when we were a quarter of a mile out we saw fires all along the beach, so we could not have put them all out. We thought a boat would be dispatched after us, so we went a little further and then landed. We knew it was no use trying to go by water, so we broke up the boat. We then proceeded to the side of the mountain right opposite the settlement. We were afraid that Dr Spence or the Commandant would see us with the spy-glass, the settlement being so plain to us. So we agreed to lie down until the sun went round. When the sun was behind the hill we went to the top, kindled a fire, and camped all night. Next morning we started again, and walked all day. Little Brown, who came

back, and died in the hospital, was the worst walker of all. He was always behind, and kept cooeeing. So we said we would leave him behind if he did not keep up.

We kept off Gordon River for fear the soldiers might be after us. We travelled from daylight till dark night over very rough country for eight days. We were very weak for want of provisions. Our tinder got wet and we were very cold and hungry. Bill Cornelius said, 'I'm so hungry I could eat a piece of a man.' The next morning there were four of us for a feast. Bob Greenhill said he has 'seen the like done before and it eat much like pork'. Mathers spoke out and said it would be murder; and perhaps then we could not eat it. 'I'll warrant you', said Greenhill, 'I'll eat the first bit; but, you must all lend a hand, so that we'll all be equal in the crime.' We consulted about who should fall, and Greenhill said, 'Dalton, he volunteered to be a flogger. We will kill him.' We made a bit of a breakwind with boughs, and about three in the morning Dalton was asleep. Then Greenhill struck him on the head with an axe and he never spoke after. Greenhill called Travers, and he cut Dalton's throat to bleed him. Then we dragged him away a bit and cut him up. Travers and Greenhill put his heart and liver on the fire and ate them before they were right warm. The others refused to eat any that night, but the next morning it was cut up and divided and we all got our share.

We started a little after sunrise. One man was appointed each day to walk ahead and make a road. He carried nothing but a tomahawk. The others carried the things. This morning Cornelius and Brown said they would go ahead together and carry the pots. We had not gone far when the leaders were missing. We went back to look for them, but could see no signs of them. We said, 'They will go back and hang us all', but we thought they would not find the way, so we went on. We walked for four days through bad country, till we came to a big river. We thought it was the Gordon. We stopped a day and two nights looking for a place to cross. We felled trees, but the stream was too strong and carried them away. Travers and Bodenham couldn't swim, but at last we got over and cut a pole thirty or forty feet long and reached it across, where there was a rock jutting out into the river, and pulled them across. We got up the hill with great difficulty, it was so steep. The ground was very barren on the other side, and covered with scrub.

We were very weak and hungry. A consultation was held as to who should be the next victim. Bodenham did not know anything about it, and it was resolved to kill him. Me and Mathers went to gather wood, Travers saying, 'You'll hear it directly.' About two minutes after Mathers said, 'He's done; Greenhill hit him with the axe and Travers cut his throat.' Greenhill took Bodenham's shoes and put them on, for his own were very bad. We ate only the heart and liver that night.

Next day we camped and dried the meat. We travelled on for three days, and saw many emus and kangaroos, but could not catch them. Mathers and me went away together, and Mathers said, 'Let us go on by ourselves. You see what kind of a cove Greenhill is. He'd kill his own father before he'd fast for a day.' We travelled on for two days more. We boiled a piece of the meat, and it made Mathers so sick that he began to vomit. Greenhill started up and hit him on the forehead with the axe. Although he was cut, he was still stronger than Greenhill. He called out, 'Pierce, will you see me murdered?' and rushed at Greenhill. He took the axe from him and threw it to me. We walked on till night, and then Travers and Greenhill collared Mathers and got him down. They gave him half an hour to pray. When the half-hour was up Mathers handed the prayer-book to me and Greenhill killed him.

When crossing the second tier of mountains Travers got his foot stung by an insect and it swelled up. On the other side we got to a big river and camped for two nights. Me and Greenhill swam across and cut a long wattle, and pulled Travers over as he could not swim. Here the country got better and we travelled well for two days. Then Travers's foot got black, and he said he couldn't go any farther. He asked us to leave him to die in peace. When we were a little way away, Greenhill said: 'Pierce, it's no use for to be detained any longer; let's serve him like the rest.' I replied, 'I'll have no hand in it.' When we went back Travers was lying on his back asleep. It was about two o'clock in the day. Greenhill lifted the axe and hit him on the head, and then cut his throat.

We crossed the third tier of mountains and got into fine country, the grass being very long. Greenhill began to fret, and said he would never reach a post. I watched Greenhill for two nights and thought that he eyed me more than usual. He always carried the axe and kept it under his head when lying down. At length, just before day-break, Greenhill dozed off to sleep, and I snatched the axe and killed him with a blow. I took a thigh and one arm and travelled on four more days until the last was eaten. I then walked for two days with nothing to eat. I took off my belt meaning to hang myself, but took another turn and travelled on till I came to a fire with some pieces of kangaroo and opossum lying beside it. I ate as much as I could and carried the rest away.

George Arthur, Lieutenant-Governor of Van Diemen's Land from 1824 to 1837. He thought that bushranging had been 'totally suppressed' during his administration.

Some days later I came to a marsh. I saw a duck with ten young ones. I jumped into the water and the duck flew off, while the little ones dived. Two of them came up close to my legs and I caught one in each hand. Next day I saw a large mountain, and I thought it was Table Mountain. Then I came to a big river and travelled down it for two days. I came on a flock of sheep belonging to Tom Triffet, at the falls, and caught a lamb. While I was eating it the shepherd came up and said he would tell. I threatened to shoot him. Then he got friendly and took me to the hut, and fed me for three days. Then he told me that the master was coming up and I'd have to go. I went to another hut and stayed three weeks. Then I fell in with Davis and Cheetham and they said I could join them. They had 126 newly-marked sheep and said they were going to select some more. I shepherded the mob while they were away. They continued robbing the stations until the soldiers came. The soldiers captured the gang except Bill Davis, who snatched up his gun and ran away. Corporal Kelly followed and called on him to stop. As he kept on Kelly fired and missed, when Davis turned round and said, 'I've got you now.' Kelly cried out 'Murder', and the other soldiers ran forward and fired. Davis was wounded in the arm and gave in.

The confession may here be very much abridged, as the account Pierce gives of his acts is very rambling. About 250 sheep, a gold watch, two silver watches, and a number of other articles were found at the camp. Several of the gang were hanged and the others

sentenced to long terms of penal servitude. Pierce
denied having taken any active share in the robberies,
and as he was merely found in charge of the stolen, or
as he euphemistically called them 'the selected' sheep,
he was sent back to Macquarie Harbour to be dealt
with as a bolter.

On 16 November 1823, Pierce again absconded from
Macquarie Harbour in company with Thomas Cox. On
the 21st, as the schooner *Waterloo* was sailing down
the harbour, a man was observed standing on the
shore and signalling with smoke from a fire. These
signals had also been observed from the settlement,
and a boat was dispatched from there. The boat sent
by Mr Lucas from the schooner reached the place at
the same time that the boat from the settlement
arrived. On landing it was found that Alexander Pierce
had made the fire, and he was immediately arrested by
Lieutenant Cuthertson. Pierce said that he had killed
Cox and eaten part of the body. He volunteered to
show where the remainder was and it was found that
all the fleshy parts had been cut away, leaving the
bones and viscera.

It is impossible that Pierce could have committed
this murder through want of food. He had only been
away from the settlement for a few days, and some
flour, a piece of pork, some bread, and a few fish,
which Pierce and Cox had stolen from a party of
hunters, were found at the camp. Before his trial
Pierce said that he had been so horror-struck at the
crime he had committed that, when he signalled, he did
not know what he was about. After his conviction,
however, he said that man's flesh was delicious; far
better than fish or pork; and his craving for it had led
him to induce Cox to abscond so that he might kill and
eat him. He was wearing the clothes of the murdered
man when he was captured. Although he made no
secret of his cannibalism after his conviction, and in
fact boasted about it, he is believed to have very much
toned down his share in the murders during that
terrible journey across the Western Tiers. Possibly
Greenhill may have been the moving spirit in these
atrocities, but we have the fact that Pierce was the
sole survivor, and he gives but a very brief account of
the last struggle between himself and Greenhill.

22

Early view of Sarah (or Settlement) Island, the principal
station at Macquarie Harbour penal settlement

*Opposite:*
Alexander Pierce: a sketch made after he was hanged

The settlement at Macquarie Harbour, 'the Western
Hell' as the convicts called it, was opened as a penal
station on 3 January 1822. From that time until its
removal to Port Arthur in May 1827, one hundred and
twelve prisoners ran away. Of these, seventy-four are
reported to have perished in the woods.

Every precaution was taken at Macquarie Harbour
to prevent bolting. A line of posts was established
across the neck of land between Pirates' Bay and
Storm Bay and fierce dogs were chained at these
places to give notice when any one passed or
approached. This use of dogs gave rise to a report in
England that bloodhounds were used in Van Diemen's
Land to track runaway convicts or bushrangers.
However the dogs were used only as watch dogs and
not as hunting or tracking dogs.[1]

Three other men who ran away from Macquarie
Harbour were Jefferies, Hopkins, and Russell. Like
Pierce and his mates they started to cross the Western
Tiers. They lived fairly well for several days, as
Jefferies had a gun and ammunition which he had
stolen, supposedly from a soldier, but at length their
provisions failed and they could find no game. They
agreed to toss up to decide who should die to save the
others. Russell lost and was immediately shot by
Jefferies. The two men lived on the flesh for five days,
when they came to a sheep station. They immediately
threw away about five pounds weight of Russell's flesh
and killed two sheep. When the shepherd ran forward
at the sound of the shots, Jefferies told him that if he
interfered he would 'soon be settled'. They only
wanted 'a good feed'.

Jefferies and Hopkins appear to have adopted
bushranging as a profession. Of Hopkins we hear little,
but Jefferies established a character for brutality
which has been rivalled by few and surpassed by
none. When he bailed up Mr Tibbs' house he ordered

Mr and Mrs Tibbs and their stockman to go into the bushes with him. The stockman refused and was immediately shot. The other two then went across the cleared paddock towards the timbered country, Mrs Tibbs carrying her baby and Jefferies walking behind. When near the edge of the timber Jefferies ordered Mrs Tibbs to walk faster. The poor woman was weeping bitterly. She sobbed out that she was walking as fast as she could with the baby in her arms. Jefferies immediately snatched the baby from her and dashed its brains out against a sapling. Then he asked her 'Can you go faster now?' Mr Tibbs turned round and rushed at the bushranger, who shot him and then walked away, leaving Mrs Tibbs with her dead and dying.

At Georgetown Jefferies stuck up and robbed Mr

Baker and then compelled him to carry his knapsack. They had not walked far along the road when Jefferies, who was behind, shot Mr Baker without warning and for no apparent cause.

Jefferies was captured by John Batman, a native of Parramatta and afterwards one of the founders of the city of Melbourne. Batman had taken several aboriginals to Van Diemen's Land and was engaged by the Government to track and capture bushrangers. He caught Hopkins and several others.

It is quite a relief to turn from these cannibals to Matthew Brady, the central figure among the bushrangers of their epoch. Brady was a gentleman convict; an educated man. He was transported to Botany Bay for forgery, the capital sentence having been commuted. In Sydney he soon got into trouble for insubordination and was retransported to Van Diemen's Land. He was one of a gang of fourteen who escaped from Macquarie Harbour. His companions in this enterprise were James Bryant, John Burns, James Crawford, James McCabe, Patrick Connolly, John Griffiths, George Lacey, Charles Rider, Jeremiah Ryan, John thompson, Isaac Walker, and John Downes. They stole a whale boat on 7 June 1824, and pulled round the coast until they came to a favourable landing place, enabling them to walk to the settled districts. Here they were joined by James Tierney, and for some two years they defied the authorities.

In company with the 'notorious Dunne', Brady stuck up Mr Robert Bethune's house near Hobart Town when the males of the family were away. In the evening Mr Walter Bethune and Captain Bannister returned from the city on horseback, and Brady went out to meet them. He told the two gentlemen that they were prisoners and that resistance was useless. They were taken by surprise, and being unarmed, they surrendered at once. Brady called one of his men to 'take the gentlemen's horses to the stables and see that they were cared for'. He then conducted the gentlemen into the parlour as if he were the host and they merely visitors. The ladies of the family and the servants, except the cook, were already gathered there, and Brady ordered dinner and invited those present to take their seats at the table. He himself sat down, while his companions had food taken to them at their guard posts. When the meal was over Brady made a collection of watches, rings, money, and other valuables, and after profusely thanking Mr Bethune for his hospital treatment and the kind reception he had given them, Brady and his gang mounted and rode away.

On the following evening he rode into the little town of Sorell. The soldiers stationed there had been out kangarooing and were cleaning their muskets. Taken completely by surprise, they were easily overpowered, and were locked up in the jail after the prisoners were released. Mr Long, the jailer, contrived to make his escape, and ran to the residence of Dr Garrett. Here he found Lieutenant Green, who was in command of the military stationed at the town. The doctor and the lieutenant walked together to the jail, and the doctor was seized by Brady's orders and placed in a cell. Green refused to surrender, and was shot in the arm by one of the bushrangers and overpowered. The bushrangers made a good haul from the houses in the town and then left quietly. The only personal injury inflicted was the wound received by Lieutenant Green, who was forced to have his arm amputated.

On 27 August 1824, Governor Arthur issued a proclamation offering rewards for the capture of Brady, McCabe, Dunne, Murphy, and other bushrangers, and calling upon all Crown servants and respectable citizens to aid the soldiers in their capture.

Convicts at Macquarie Harbour lived miserably on two meals a day and laboured hard at felling forest trees and floating them across the harbour to the island settlement.

*Opposite:*
**William Brown, a bushranger in Brady's gang, was hanged in 1826.**

*Far Right:*
**Matthew Brady**

By way of reply, Brady and his gang paid a visit to Mr Young's house at Lake River. It was late at night, but the bushrangers soon roused the inmates. After having secured the men, Brady inquired whether there were any ladies inside, and on being told that there were he issued an order to them to get up and dress at once, and to go into any room they pleased, pledging his word that they should not be interfered with. While this was being done Brady sat on the verandah chatting with Mr Young. Among other things he spoke of the Governor's proclamation, and asked whether Mr Young had seen it. He laughed heartily at the idea of the soldiers capturing him. While the chief was thus employed the other members of the gang searched every room of the house, and collected everything they thought worth taking. The ladies had all gone into one room, and when the rest of the house had been searched they were requested to leave that room and go into another.

One day Brady walked alone into a house close to the town and 'made a swag' of all that was valuable. He called two of the convict servants and ordered them to take up the bundles and carry them into the bush. He was obeyed and the owner of the property made no effort to stop him, as it was thought that Brady's gang were not far off. On another occasion Brady ordered an assigned servant to leave his master's house and join the band. The man refused. Brady walked to the sideboard, filled a glass with rum, and asked the man whether he could drink that. The man said he never took strong liquor. 'Well, you will this time,' exclaimed Brady, pointing his pistol at the servant's head. 'Now choose.' The man took the glass and swallowed the rum. Brady laughed heartily as he staggered away. However, the next morning, the unfortunate man was found lying in the bush some distance from the house. His dog was lying beside him licking his face. He was still drunk. His employer found him and tried to rouse him. After he had shaken and called for some minutes the man opened his eyes, and called out 'Water, for God's sake water!' and rolled over dead. When Brady was informed some time after of the man's death, he said he was very sorry. He had made him drink the rum as a joke and without any thought or desire to injure him.

Brady stuck up the Duke of York Inn, and finding Captain Smith there, mistakenly knocked him down, thinking he was Colonel Balfour. On discovering his mistake the bushranger apologized. He then threatened to shoot Captain White, but Captain Smith said that White had a wife and family. Brady told the two officers to go away. He 'hated soldiers' and did not know what he might do if they stayed.

Colonel Balfour of the 49th regiment, with a strong party of soldiers, had been beating the bush for some time in hopes of capturing Brady and his gang. A report spread abroad that the gang intended to break open the Launceston jail and torture and shoot Mr Jefferies. The threat was treated with derision, but about 10 a.m. a man came into the town and said that the bushrangers had taken possession of Mr Dry's place, just outside the town. Colonel Balfour, with ten soldiers and some volunteers, started out and a fierce fight took place. Ultimately the bushrangers were driven off, but not before they had secured Mr Dry's horses. The soldiers followed and the bushrangers fired from behind the trees. Suddenly a report spread that the attack on Dry's place was a ruse to draw the soldiers from the town, and that a party of bushrangers under Bird and Dunne had gone to attack the jail. Colonel Balfour sent half his force back to protect the town. The report was found to be partly true. The bushrangers had entered the town and robbed Mr Wedge's house, but had not gone to the jail. At Dr Priest's house some shots were exchanged, and the doctor was wounded in the knee. The soldiers arrived at that time and the bushrangers made off.

The following day the gang made an attack on the farms of the Messrs Walker. They burned the wheatstacks and barns belonging to Mr Abraham Walker and also those of Mr Commissary Walker. They had Mr Dry's two carriage horses, stolen the day before. Brady was wearing Colonel Balfour's cap which had fallen off in the fight at Launceston. The next day they burned down the house of Mr Massey at South Esk, having sent him a letter a day or two before informing him of their intention.

Two of the gang called on Thomas Renton, and shouted for him to come out. When he did they charged him with having attempted to betray them. Renton denied the charge. A wrangle took place, during which one of the bushrangers shot Renton dead. It is highly improbable that Brady was aware of this outrage. He boasted loudly on every available occasion that he never killed a man intentionally, and he is known to have quarrelled with members of his

For years the early settlers in Van Diemen's Land were terrorized by bands of convict bushrangers who burned their haystacks, frightened their families and plundered their household goods and stock for revenge or for gain.

gang, who were too ready with their firearms. He drove McCabe out of the gang on account of his brutality, and McCabe was captured and hanged shortly afterwards.

The gang held amost complete control over the roads, and resistance was very rarely offered when they ordered a man to 'bail up'.[2] One of the customs established by the gang was to order their witnesses to remain where they were for half an hour, and the order was rarely disobeyed. Any person who declined was simply tied to a tree and left for any chance passer-by to unloose. On by-roads, or in cases where the prisoners were marched some distance off the high road into the bush before being plundered, being tied up was a very serious matter. Cases are known in which men have remained bound to a tree until they have died of starvation. Tying up the victims became a common practice with bushrangers, though some like Brady accepted the promise of the victims to remain

where they were left for a certain time to allow the bushrangers time to get away.

About the middle of 1825 a convict named Cowan or Cohen was permitted to escape from an iron gang with broken fetters on his legs. He was found by some of the gang and taken to a friendly blacksmith who knocked his irons off. He joined the gang and more than once led them into conflicts with soldiers from which they were only saved by the skill and bravery of Brady. Cowan was no doubt a clever man in his way; he completely hoodwinked Brady and his mates; he fought bravely in their skirmishes with the troops and was always eager to loot houses or other places attacked. He professed to rob 'on principle'. He is said

27

John Batman, the founder of Melbourne, first gained fame as a bounty hunter when he captured the bushranger Brady.

to have murdered the bushrangers Murphy and Williams while they slept, but there is no proof of this.

He betrayed the camp to Lieutenant Williams of the 40th Regiment, who was out with a party of soldiers in search of bushrangers. A terrific fight took place in which several were killed on each side; some of the bushrangers were captured while others escaped, but the gang was broken up. Cowan is said to have received a free pardon, several hundred pounds reward, and a free passage home for his services.[3]

Brady made his escape in the bush and was followed by John Batman and his black trackers. The bushranger had been wounded in the fight and could not travel fast. Batman came up to him in the mountains and called on him to surrender. 'Are you an officer?' asked Brady, coolly cocking his gun. 'I'm not a soldier,' replied Batman, 'I'm John Batman. If you raise that gun I'll shoot. There's no chance for you.' 'You're right,' replied Brady, 'my time's come. You're a brave man and I yield; but, I'd never give in to a soldier.' Brady was taken to the nearest lock-up, where as it happened, Jefferies the cannibal had been lodged some days before. Much to Brady's disgust the two men

were conveyed to Hobart Town in the same cart. Brady refused to sit on the same side of the cart as Jefferies, and kept as far from him as possible during the journey.[4]

The trial of Matthew Brady excited great interest. He and his gang had kept the country in a ferment for twenty-two months. Many of his companions had been shot or captured, but the leader had always escaped. Numerous stories were told to illustrate his reckless bravery and his skill in strategy. On the day of his trial a number of ladies were in the court and when the judge put on the black cap and the verdict of guilty was returned, they showed their sympathy by weeping so loudly that the judge had to pause until order was restored. Sentence of death was pronounced amidst signs of sorrow by all present.[5]

At the same session Jefferies, Hopkins, Bryant, Tilly, McKenny, Brown, Gregory, Hodgetts, and Perry were sentenced to death for bushranging, cattle, horse and sheep stealing, and for murder. Some of these had been in the bush with Brady. The prisoners were hanged two or three at a time at intervals of a few days, the last of the batch on 29 April 1826.

Remnants of the gang under the command of Dunne continued for a time to commit depredations. In one of their journeys they saw a tribe of aboriginals camped on the other side of the river. Dunne swam across and attacked them. He fought them for some time driving them back until he seized one of the women. He turned back, forcing her to accompany him across the river. He had this girl with him when an attack was made on Mr Thomson's house, but she escaped. On the following day two men were quietly driving in a cart along the road when the natives attacked and speared them, killing one and wounding the other. The blacks went on and burned the hut of Mr Nicholas. They attacked Mr Thomson's place and speared a man named Scott. The woman who had been stolen by Dunne was urging the natives on when Scott was killed. When the troops were sent out to drive the blacks back, when they came across the bushrangers and shot Dunne. One or two were captured and hanged.

The *Hobart Town Gazette* of 29 April 1826, said that for some months the roads had been safe, and with the executions to take place that day, the colony might be congratulated on having at length stamped out the crime of bushranging. In fact, it was only the close of the first epoch; the first act in the great bushranging tragedy which was to close so sensationally more than fifty years later.

# 4  The 'Terrible Hollow'

**Bushranging in New South Wales; the first bank robbery in Australia; bushrangers' hideout; murder of Dr Wardell; Will Underwood's gang; 'Jack the Rammer'; Hall, Mayne and others.**

Bushranging as we know it appears to have begun in New South Wales about 1822. In that year thirty-four bushrangers were hanged in Sydney. The crimes for which these men were executed were generally petty. Robberies from farms had become so prevalent that it seemed necessary to adopt severe measures. But beyond removing so many wrong-doers and preventing them from continuing their crimes, this severity of the judicial authorities does not appear to have had much effect. Bushranging not only continued, but the bushrangers became bolder and operated over a wider area.

On 16 March 1826, a desperate fight took place between a party of mounted troopers and seven bushrangers near Bathurst. The Blue Mountains had only been crossed thirteen years before, and the settlement was a very small one. The leader of the gang, Morris Connell, was shot dead by Corporal Brown and the other bushrangers ran away into the bush.

In the Windsor Court on 10 February 1827, Mr McCarthy was fined £14.10s., including costs, for having employed a returned bushranger instead of handing him over to the police for punishment. About the same time a bushranger was charged in Sydney with having bailed up a settler's house and compelling him to hand over some money and a bottle of wine. Taking the wine was more than the worthy magistrate could stand. 'What right', he demanded of the delinquent, 'have you to drink wine? Do you not know, you rascal, that when you were convicted you forfeited all rights?' 'Yes, your honour,' replied the culprit. 'But, I didn't forfeit my appetite.'

John Poole, James Ryan, and James Riley, assigned servants of Mr John Larnack, of Castle Forbes estate in the Hunter River district, took to the bush on 4 November 1833. Three other assigned servants, Anthony Hitchcock, alias Hath, Samuel Parrott or Powell, and David Jones, were sent away to Maitland the following morning, in charge of constable Samuel Cook. For insubordination they were placed under sentence of twelve months in a chain gang. About half-

a-mile from Castle Forbes, Poole, Ryan, and Riley, and another man named John Perry, who had been in the bush for some time, met the constable and called on him to stand or they would shoot him. Cook only had a

**A convict in the chain gang about 1843**

pistol with him and he snapped it at the robbers and then surrendered. The robbers took the pistol from him, led him some distance off the road and tied him to a tree. Parrott refused to go with the bushrangers and was tied to a tree near Cook.

The robbers went back to Mr Larnack's house which they reached about noon. They called upon Mrs Larnack to stand, but she and one of the female servants jumped through a window and ran. Perry followed them and brought them back, threatening to blow Mrs Larnack's brains out if she refused to do as she was told. The robbers took a double-barrelled gun which was always kept loaded in Mr Larnack's room, and some guns and fowling pieces from the dining-room. Hitchcock brought the shearers from the shed, walking behind them and threatening to shoot any man who resisted. The robbers broke open the door of the store and put the shearers inside. They emptied a chest of tea into a bag, took bags of flour, sugar, and other provisions from the store, and fastened up the door leaving Perry on guard. They took a quantity of pork from the kitchen, a bucket of milk from the dairy, and the silver-plate and other valuables from the house. Then, having made the shearers secure in the store and locked Mrs Larnack and the female servants in the kitchen, they went away after telling Mrs Larnack that they were sorry 'the old ——', the Major, was not at home, as they wanted to settle him. One of them added that when they could catch him they would 'stick his head on the chimney for an ornament'.

As soon as the news of the robbery became known, a party was organized to follow the bushrangers. Mr Robert Scott, mounted trooper Daniel Craddige, and a party of five caught up with the robbers at Mr Reid's station, Lamb's Valley. Some shots were exchanged before Jones and Perry ran away. Constable Craddige followed them and called on them to stand, which they did. He took them back, and by that time Mr Scott and the rest of the pursuing party had captured Hitchcock, Poole and Riley. The boy Ryan got away in the scrub but was discovered and caught next day. Alexander Flood, overseer to Messrs Robert and Helenes Scott, with two constables, took charge of the prisoners, and conducted them safely to Maitland for trial.

Mr John Larnack then said that on the morning of 5 November before the attack was made on the house, he was at the sheep-wash. The prisoners came up and said to the washers, 'Come out of the water, every —— one of you, or we'll blow your —— brains out.' Larnack jumped into the water among the washers. Hitchcock fired at him shouting, 'You'll never take me to court again, you ——.' He called on the washers to get out of the way and let him shoot the ——. Poole also said, 'I'll take care you never get another man flogged.'

Larnack scrambled out of the wash-pool on the opposite side to where the robbers were, and ran to the timber. He went on to Mr Danger's farm, and remained there till next day. He was only ten yards distant when Hitchcock fired at him. Shots from the

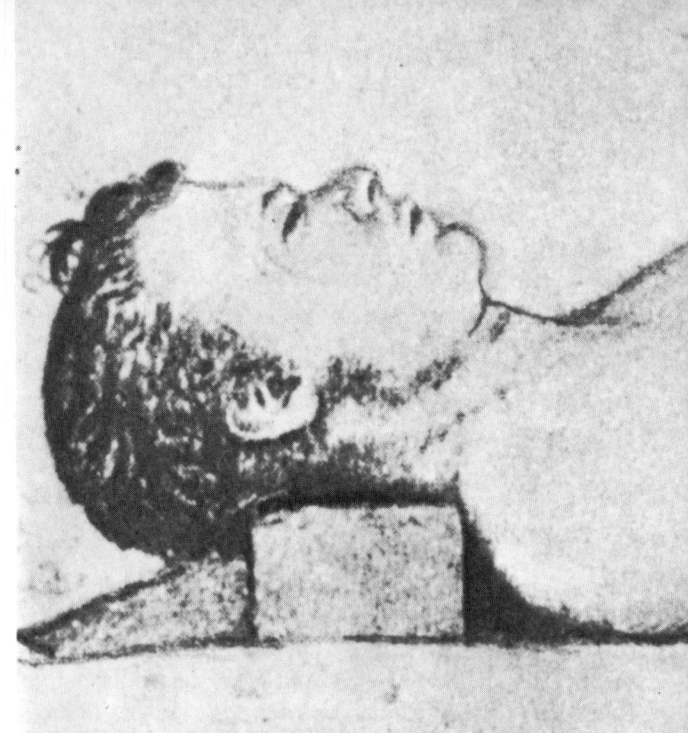

other bushrangers struck the water within twelve and eighteen inches of him, but none of them hit him. When they were captured the robbers had four double-barrelled guns, two single-barrelled fowling pieces, a musket, and two pistols.

When asked what they had to say in defence, Hitchcock called Ensign Zouch and other gentlemen to speak as to his character. It appears that until he was assigned to Major Mudie and Mr Larnack, he had always been well behaved. The prisoners complained that they were given short rations, that the flour was mouldy and the meat bad, and that they were repeatedly flogged. Some of them had been flogged for refusing to work on Sunday. Hitchcock had been sentenced to work in an iron gang, for an offence about which he knew nothing. Whatever the punishment threatened by the master, it was sure to be inflicted by the Bench. Jones was acquitted of the capital offence, but was sent to Norfolk Island for life. The other five prisoners were sentenced to death; Hitchcock and Poole were hanged at Maitland, and Ryan, Perry and Riley at Sydney. An inquiry was held as to the alleged ill-usage of assigned servants by Major Mudie and Mr Larnack. They were acquitted by Governor Bourke of the charges of tyranny and ill-treatment, but Major Mudie's name was removed from the Commission of the Peace. On returning to the station after the result of the inquiry had become known, he was greeted with cries of 'No more fifties now, you bloody old tyrant'.[1]

The beautiful valley of Burragorang is enclosed on all sides by precipitous mountains. There is only one practicable entrance, which in early times, before a government road was cut into it for the convenience of the farmers, was easily blocked with a few saplings, so that sheep, cattle, or horses turned into the valley

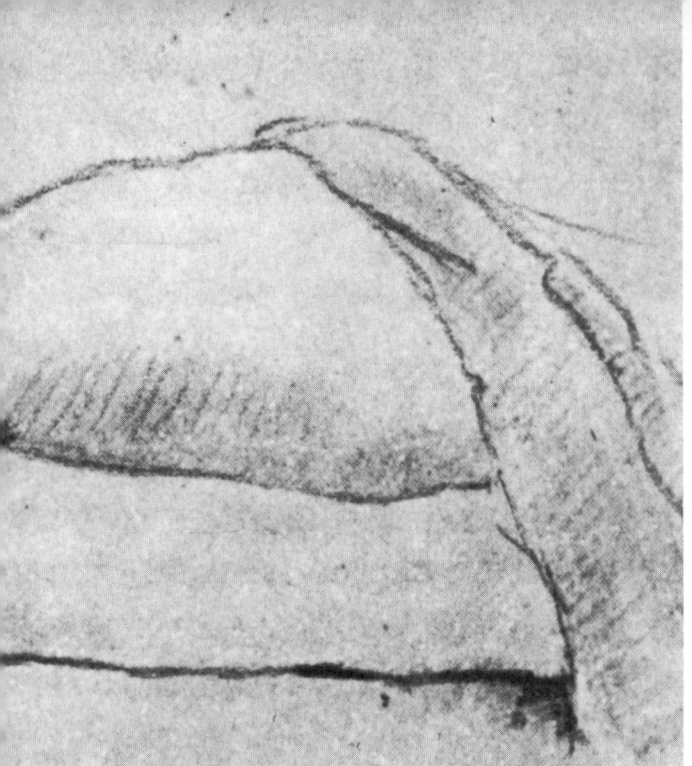

Sketch of Johnny Donohoe made after his death by Sir Thomas Mitchell. The bushranger, also known as 'Bold Jack Donahoe', was the original 'Wild Colonial Boy' of the popular folk song, and a member of Underwood's gang.

could not escape. Precisely how the entrance to this extensive enclosure was first found is not known. It is believed to have been discovered by a party of bushrangers who endeavoured to discover a road over the Blue Mountains. They wanted to reach a settlement of white men, which was supposed to lie somewhere in that direction. Whether this supposed settlement was a Dutch or an English settlement is not known, but there was a wide-spread belief that some of these settlements were not far from Sydney, and could be reached overland.

The valley is situated only about fifty-four miles from Sydney, and for many years was an absolutely secure hiding-place for bushrangers and their plunder. Later the valley came to be known from the horrible tales told of the convicts who made use of it as 'Terrible Hollow' and under this name it is introduced by Rolf Boldrewood in his *Robbery under Arms*. Among the old hands themselves it was known as 'The Camp', 'The Shelter', or 'The Pound'. Bark huts were erected in this valley by the bushrangers, and they retired there when hard pressed or wounded. When the secret of the entrance was betrayed to soldiers out in search of a party of bushrangers, it was evident that the valley had been long in use by the bushrangers. Cattle and sheep were running wild there, numbers of broken shackles, handcuffs, and other relics, were found, and evidence that several murders had been committed there. There are no records of these events however, and only the recollections of the legends which have been handed down among the old hands

remain to explain why this beautiful valley should have been called 'Terrible Hollow'.

One of these legends goes something like this: A settler was reported to have received a large sum of money. This became known to the bushrangers and they decided to rob him of it. They bailed up his place, tied his assigned servants, and searched everywhere for the money without success. The settler declared that he had not received the money, but was not believed. He was threatened with death if he refused to disclose its hiding place. He persisted in his assertion that he had no money, and a consultation was held by the bushrangers to decide what should be done with him. Some were for shooting him there and then; but as this obviously was not the way to extort money if he had any, it was resolved to take him to 'the camp', and there force him to say where the money was hidden. When they got him there they tied him to a sapling, built a circle of bushwood round him at some distance away, set fire to it, and slowly roasted him to death. His screams are said to have been fearful. No-one heard them in that solitude except the fiends who were torturing him and they had become too callous by the slightly less fiendish treatment of the authorities to heed his agonized cries. It is impossible to say whether this story is literally true or not, but certainly charred remains of human bones were discovered in the valley when it was searched, though whether the bodies had

The Reverend Samuel Marsden, Principal Chaplain of New South Wales, was stuck up by Donohoe and Underwood and relieved of £4.

One Sunday in September 1834, Dr Robert Wardell, a practising barrister in Sydney and editor of the *Australian*, was riding across his park which stretched from the Parramatta Road to Cook's River, to look after his herd of fallow deer, of which he was very proud. After jumping his horse over a log he found himself confronted by three armed men. Thinking they were poachers after his deer, he reined his horse in and cried, 'What are you doing here, you rascals?' The reply was a shot from one of the guns and the doctor fell.

His horse galloped to the house and alarmed the family. Men were dispatched in all directions to seek for the doctor, who was believed to have been thrown and injured. The search was continued all day and night, but with no result. The next day his body was found covered over with boughs, apparently to prevent the dingoes from tearing it rather than to hide it. John Jenkins, Thomas Tattersdale and Emanuel Brace were arrested on suspicion and charged with the murder. Evidence was produced that they had been seen in the neighbourhood, and they were committed for trial. Brace was a lad who had only recently been sent to the colony, and before the day of trial he consented to turn King's evidence. Although from his testimony it appeared that Jenkins was the man who had fired the gun, both he and Tattersdale were hanged for the crime. It was said that they had been guilty of various acts of bushranging.

The story of Jack the Rammer illustrates the relationship which sometimes existed between the bushrangers and the assigned servants, and indicates the difficulties with which law-abiding citizens had to cope. Jack had been living by robbery in the Monaro district for some time. One day Mr Charles Fisher Shepherd, the overseer of the Michelago sheep station, said something about all bushrangers being cowards. One of the assigned servants on the station, named Bull, replied, 'They'll be here next.' 'If they come here,' exclaimed Shepherd, 'I'll give them a benefit.' A few nights afterwards Shepherd was asleep in his hut. He was awakened by someone calling on him to come out. After a time he did so, and saw Jack the Rammer and a man named Boyd standing at the door. Jack cried out to him, 'Keep your hands down.' They stood for a second or two regarding him, and then Jack said, 'What a benefit you're giving us.' The two bushrangers then walked away.

Although he felt convinced that Bull was in league with the bushrangers and had reported his speech to them and that he probably could not expect any asisstance from the other assigned servants on the station, Shepherd loaded his gun with No. 4 shot, the largest he had, and started off after the bushrangers. It was about daybreak on a beautiful December morning in 1834, probably between three and four o'clock, and the air was soft and balmy as he made his way through the bush in the direction in which the bushrangers had

been burned before or after death could not be determined.

It was to this valley that Will Underwood and his gang were said to retire when hard pressed or when they needed rest. Underwood operated on the roads about Campbelltown, Liverpool, Penrith, and Windsor, sometimes sticking-up people, and robbing farms on Liberty Plains and other places between Parramatta and Sydney. The gang was a large one and continued to operate in the more populous districts for some two years. Among the members of this gang were Johnny Donohoe (also known as 'Bold Jack' Donahoe), Webber, and Walmsley. Donohoe was shot by a trooper named Maggleton, near Raby, in September 1830. Webber was shot a month later, and Walmsley was captured in another skirmish between troopers and bushrangers. Walmsley was sentenced to death, but was reprieved for disclosing the names of 'fences', or receivers of stolen property. His revelations caused quite a sensation as a number of hitherto highly respected persons were implicated. Underwood was shot in 1832, and shortly afterwards a 'traitor' is said to have led a party of soldiers into Terrible Hollow. There was a fight between the troops and the bushrangers found there at the time. Several of the bushrangers were captured and the gang broken up.

*Left:*
**Bushranging was a favourite subject of Australia's early film-makers.** *The Story of the Kelly Gang*, **made in 1907, was the first of several versions.**

*Above:*
**The latter-day 'bushranger' Johnny (or Jimmy) Governor was a red-headed half-caste aboriginal who, with his brother Joe and mate Jackie Underwood, was responsible for nine deaths and the terrorization of the New South Wales countryside in 1900. After a massive police hunt he was captured, and despite the fifty bullets taken from his body, walked to the Darlinghurst gallows in January, 1901.**

gone. After travelling some distance he came on a sort of camp and saw Boyd through the trees. He knelt down and fired, but missed. He was about to fire the other barrel when Bull stepped from behind a tree close by, and said 'Don't shoot him, sir.' 'By G——, I will,' exclaimed Shepherd, 'If you fire, by G——, I'll shoot you,' returned Bull. Before Shepherd could reply another bushranger named Keys fired at him from behind a tree and wounded him. Shepherd rushed forward, and was about to close with Keys when Boyd ran up and fired, wounding Shepherd in the head.

Keys seized him, but Shepherd shook himself free, and ran back to the station. He went to the house, roused the owner, and said to him, 'Good God, Catterall, I'm shot all to pieces, and you never help me.' 'What's the good?' returned Catterall. 'What can I do?' Just then the bushrangers came up, and Catterall went in and shut the door. Shepherd rushed across to his own hut, and tried to shut himself in, but Boyd thrust in the barrel of his gun in time to prevent him. Shepherd seized the gun and tried to wrench it out of Boyd's hands, but Keys pushed the door open and struck Shepherd on the head. Shepherd fell, and Boyd put the muzzle of his gun close against his chest and pulled the trigger. The bushrangers, including Bull, then went away.

It was some hours later when Shepherd regained consciousness, and yelled out as loud as he could. He continued calling for some minutes and at last Catterall came out of the house and went to the hut. 'Why,' he said, as he looked at Shepherd, 'I thought you were dead.' He went away, but soon returned with several of the station hands and had Shepherd carried into the house and put to bed. He sent for a doctor and the police. When the doctor arrived he took fourteen slugs and bullets out of various parts of Shepherd's body. He recovered, and lived for many years afterwards. In the meantime the police followed the bushrangers and shot

33

## GALLANT CAPTURE OF THE NEW SOUTH WALES POLICE.

*To prevent any historical mistake, a sketch of the Latest Bushranging Achievement is here placed on imperishable record.*

Boyd as he was trying to escape by swimming across the Snowy River. Keys and Bull were captured, and were subsequently hanged. Jack the Rammer escaped for a time, but was shot a few months later.

On 24 September 1838, the bushrangers Hall and Mayne stuck up Mr Joseph Roger's station at Currawang, near Yass. As they approached the kitchen door the men inside rushed out and the bushrangers fired among them. A lad named Patrick Fitzpatrick was struck in the mouth, the bullet coming out at the crown of his head. Three of the men were wounded.

The bushrangers appear to have regretted their act as soon as it was done. They made no attempt to get away, but assisted to carry the wounded men into the kitchen. Hall had been captured previously, but had succeeded in escaping from the Goulburn Jail shortly before this attack on Mr Roger's station. When sentenced to death, he said, 'I've been all over the

The press capitalised on the ineffectual attempts of the police to combat the bushranging scourge. This drawing was published by *Melbourne Punch* in 1863.

country in my time without taking the life of any one. I've been baited like a bull dog and I'm only sorry now that I didn't shoot every —— tyrant in New South Wales.' When taken from the court-house to the jail, he said to the crowd assembled there, 'I've never had anything to say against the prisoners, but I've a grudge against every —— swell in the country. I'll go to the gallows and die as comfortably as a biddy and be glad of the chance.' The trial took place on 15 May 1839, and between then and the date fixed for the execution, Hall made a desperate attempt to escape from Darlinghurst Jail. He failed and was hanged on 7 June, with Michael Welsh, Donald Maynard and his mate, Mayne.

34

# 5 The murderer Lynch

**The story of John Lynch; murder of Landregan; Lynch's trial and sentence, and his terrible confession; the murder of the Frazers, father and son; murder and cremation of the Mulligans.**

John Lynch is usually regarded as the most callous and brutal of the bushrangers of New South Wales. He was transported from Cavan, Ireland, in October 1831. For some months after his arrival in the colony he worked in a road gang in the neighbourhood of Sydney and was then assigned to Mr Barton as a farm servant. Soon after his arrival at the farm near Berrima, he appears to have exercised his ingenuity in stealing any articles which he could find and selling them to any person who would buy them. In 1835 he was arrested and tried at Berrima on a charge of having stolen a saddle from his employer but was acquitted. He 'bolted' into the bush and a few days afterwards a man named Thomas Smith, who had been witness in a case of highway robbery, was found dead in the scrub. Several bushrangers were arrested, Lynch among them, on suspicion of having decoyed Smith from his hut and beaten his brains out with clubs as 'a warning to traitors'. Lynch was again acquitted, but two others were hanged for the murder. During the following two or three years he was sentenced to twelve months' imprisonment for harbouring bushrangers, and on 21 February 1841 he was arrested at Mulligan's farm and charged with the murder of Kearns Landregan.

On the 19th, Mr Hugh Tinney was travelling to Sydney with his bullock dray and camped for the night at Ironstone Bridge. The next morning his driver was walking along the creek bank looking for the bullocks when he noticed some freshly cut scrub piled up. Being curious to know why it had been placed there, he pulled some branches away and discovered the newly-murdered body of a man. On examining further, he found that the head had been fearfully cut and battered. Round the neck was a piece of string and to this was attached an Agnus Dei and a temperance medal. Mr Tinney sent Sturges, the bullock-driver, to Berrima and he returned with Chief Constable Noel, Mr James Harper, the police magistrate, and Dr McDonald.

Signs of a camp were found not far away. A small fire had been lit as if to boil a quart pot of tea, and some remains of hay were found, showing that a horse

had been fed there. It was noticed that grey hairs were scattered about where the horse had rolled, and it was assumed that the horse was of that colour. During the day investigations were made by the police, and the following morning Chief Constable Chapman, Sergeant Freer, and Mr John Chalker, landlord of the Woolpack Inn, Nattai, went to Mulligan's farm, Wombat Brush, and identified John Dunleavy as John Lynch, a prisoner illegally at large. When arrested on the charge of having murdered Kearns Landregan, Lynch exclaimed: 'I am innocent, I leave it to God and man. I don't blame you, Chapman, but Chalker is interfering too much in what doesn't concern him.'

A grey horse was found at the farm, and Chalker identified this as the horse which Lynch had been driving when he stopped at the Woolpack for dinner. Lynch had 'shouted' for Landregan and the landlord before leaving, and Chalker gave him a bundle of hay for the horse. The hay was rye grass, similar to that found at the camp.

Lynch was tried at Berrima on 21 March 1842 before the Chief Justice, Sir James Dowling. Mary Landregan said that the body found was that of her husband. The temperance medal had been given to him by Father Mathew before they left Ireland. They were both teetotallers and had come to Australia as free immigrants. Her husband had about £40 when he left his last place and started to look for another job. She had not seen him since, but he had sent word by Susan Beale, servant at Mr Chalker's hotel, that he had contracted to put up fencing and do other work for Mr Dunleavy for £15.

A leather belt on which the words 'Jewish Harp' had been scratched, apparently with the point of a knife, was found at the farm, and was identified as the property of Kearns Landregan by his brother. He said that Kearns had promised to meet him at a public-house of that name in the neighbourhood, and had scratched the name on his belt so that he would remember it.

Further evidence showed that Lynch had purchased, at the Post Office Stores, Berrima, on 20 February, a merino dress, some women's caps, a pair of child's shoes, and some tobacco. He was served by Mrs Mary Higgins and gave her a £5 note in payment. From the store he went to Michael Doyle's White Horse Hotel, and bought two gallons of rum, four gallons of wine, half a chest of tea, and a bag of sugar. He gave his name as John Dunleavy, Wombat, and said he had taken Mulligan's farm. He gave six £1 notes and a note of hand for £5.2s. in payment. The goods were placed in a cart drawn by a grey horse. Some of the bank notes were identified as having been among those carried by Landregan.

There were a number of witnesses, and the case against the prisoner with regard to the murder of Landregan was very clear. It was also stated that Mr and Mrs Mulligan and their two children had disappeared suddenly, and that there was a suspicion that they had been murdered. Lynch produced a letter dated from Wollongong supposed to have been signed by Mulligan, but the writing was said to be unlike Mulligan's. Several other mysterious disappearances were mentioned.

When asked what he had to say, Lynch replied that he had met Landregan on the road and Landregan asked him to carry his swag for him. Landregan said he had been gambling at McMahon's public-house and must have left his money there. Lynch told him to get up and ride as far as he was going his way. When they reached Bolland's, Lynch asked Landregan to have a drink, but Landregan refused, saying his wife was there and that he did not want her to see him. When they got a little further along the road Landregan got down, took his swag, and walked away into the bush; he had not seen him since. Lynch complained that he had been treated very unfairly. He had, he said, been sent out for seven years but had been treated as a 'lifer'. He had served his time fairly, but he could not get his rights. When his father died in Ireland he had left him between £600 and £700. That was how he bought Mulligan's farm.

Lynch was found guilty and, in passing sentence, his Honour said:

John Lynch, the trade in blood which has so long marked your career is at last terminated, not by any sense of remorse, or the sating of any appetite for slaughter on your part, but by the energy of a few zealous spirits, roused into activity by the frightful picture of atrocity which the last tragic passage of your worthless life exhibits. It is now credibly believed, if not actually ascertained, that no less than nine other individuals have fallen by your hands. How many more have been violently ushered into another world remains undiscovered, save in the dark pages of your own memory. By your own confession it is admitted that as late as 1835 justice was invoked on your head for a frightful murder committed in this immediate neighbourhood. Your unlucky escape on that occasion has, it would seem, whetted your tigrine relish for human gore — but at

length you have fallen into toils from which you cannot escape.

For some days after his sentence John Lynch continued to assert that he was innocent, but apparently finding that there was no hope of a reprieve, he asked to see the Rev. Mr Sumner on the day before that fixed for his execution. In the presence of the police magistrates and the minister he made a very extraordinary confession, of which the following is a brief summary:

He arrived in the colony in 1832 in the *Dunvegan Castle*. The entry on his indent was: 'False pretences; sentence, life'. This was wrong. He had only been sentenced to seven years' penal servitude. He had applied to the authorities at the Hyde Park Barracks for his free papers, but had been kept waiting a fortnight without getting any satisfaction. So he returned to the Berrima district where he had been assigned. He went to John Mulligan for advice and assistance. Mulligan had a lot of goods and valuables which Lynch is supposed to have stolen and left at the farm. He wanted to sell them but Mulligan refused to give a fair price for them. Because Lynch had made up his mind to live honestly, this treatment disgusted him. He complained bitterly of the dishonesty of men who were in a good position and who 'ought to have known better'. He left Mulligan's and went to T. B. Humphrey's farm at Oldbury and stole eight bullocks, which he had himself broken in, and started with them for Sydney, with the intention of selling them, so that he might 'start honest'.

At Mount Razorback he fell in with a man named Ireland who was in charge of a loaded team belonging to Mr Thomas Cowper. The load was a valuable one, consisting of wheat, bacon, and other farm produce. Lynch thought it would pay him better to kill Ireland and take possession of the dray and its load than to sell Mr Humphrey's bullocks. He therefore camped with Ireland that night, and 'they were very friendly'. In the morning an aboriginal boy who accompanied Ireland went to look for the bullocks and Lynch followed and killed him. He returned to the camp without his absence having been noticed by Ireland, and watched for a chance. Ireland had no suspicion of foul play, and Lynch soon got near enough to him to strike him with his tomahawk. Lynch hid the bodies in a cleft between two rocks and piled stones over them. He remained at the camp two days.

On the second day two other teams arrived at the camp in charge of men named Lee and Lagge, and they all agreed to travel together for company. Near Liverpool Mr Cowper rode up and was surprised to find a stranger in charge of his dray. Lynch told him a plausible story to the effect that Ireland had been taken suddenly ill and had asked him to take the team on. The native boy had stayed behind to nurse Ireland and they were to follow as soon as Ireland got well enough. Mr Cowper believed him and before riding

The courthouse and barracks at Berrima where John Lynch was hanged in 1842

away arranged with Lynch where they should meet in Sydney. Lee and Lagge were bound for Parramatta, so when they reached the junction of the Dog Trap and Liverpool roads, they parted company with Lynch.

Left by himself, Lynch drove on night and day, reaching Sydney two days before the time appointed for him to meet Mr Cowper. He hired a man who was half drunk to sell the load, and as soon as he had received the money he started away with the team on the Illawarra road. Near George's River he met Chief Constable McAlister of Campbelltown, and fearing that he might have been recognized, he turned off the road on to a cross track leading towards the Berrima road. He knew there would soon be a hue and cry after him and thought that McAlister would probably report having met him on the Illawarra road. He travelled on until he returned to Razorback, near where the murder had been committed.

Here he met the Frazers, father and son, driving a horse team owned by Mr Bawten. He kept company with them and they camped together at Bargo Brush. Another horse team with two men and their wives also camped there. After supper Lynch was lying under his dray when a mounted trooper rode up and asked Frazer some questions about a stolen dray which belonged to Mr Cowper. The Frazers were unable to give him any information and the trooper rode away without noticing Lynch, who was lying under the very dray he was inquiring about.

This narrow escape gave Lynch a terrible shock. He lay awake all night thinking of the danger he was running by keeping this dray. He 'prayed to Almighty God to assist and enlighten' him in this emergency, and

feeling strengthened he decided to kill the Frazers and take their dray. Having arrived at this decision he became calmer and thought out the details of his plan carefully.

In the morning Lynch left the camp under the pretence that he was going to look for his bullocks, but in reality to drive them away. On his return he reported that he could not find them and spoke of the trouble bullocks gave by their wandering habits. He asked the Frazers to help him to pull his dray into the bush where he could leave it safely until he could return with another team of bullocks and take it home. There was nothing surprising in this, as bullocks frequently strayed away home as soon as they were unyoked and would travel astonishing distances, even when hobbled. The Frazers helped Lynch to drag the dray away from the road to where there was a clump of trees, and then yoked up their horses. Lynch put the few things he had in the dray into Frazer's cart and they all started together. That night they camped at Cordeaux Flat.

In the morning young Frazer started to find the horses with Lynch accompanying him. Lynch wore a coat because, he said, it was rather cold. In fact, it was to hide his tomahawk. When they were in the bush out of sight of the camp, Lynch found 'no difficulty in settling him'. He struck one blow, and 'the young fellow fell like a log of wood'. Lynch returned to the camp leading one horse, and said the lad was looking for the other. This made Frazer very uneasy,

37

not on account of his son, but because he had never known the horses to separate before, and thought that someone must have stolen the other horse. He 'fidgeted about' until Lynch, who had been watching for an opportunity, got behind him and 'struck him one blow and killed him dead'. Lynch buried the two bodies a little way off the road and remained at the camp all day.

The next morning he drove through Berrima to Mulligan's farm. He told Mrs Mulligan that the dray and horses belonged to a gentleman in Sydney. He asked her for the £30 which he said her husband owed him for the articles he had left at the farm, and which he had obtained by burglary and highway robbery. Mrs Mulligan assured him on oath that all she had in the house was £9. Lynch felt sure she was only 'putting him off', and felt very discouraged. He walked to Mr Gray's Black Horse Inn, about three miles down the road, and bought two bottles of rum. On his return he gave some to Mr and Mrs Mulligan, but 'took very little' himself.

He sat down on a log near the fence and thought, 'This man passed me by as if he didn't know me when I was in the iron gang in Berrima. He never offered me a shilling though he has made pounds out of me, and I risked my life to obtain it. It would be a judgment on him to take all he's got for the way he's treated a poor prisoner. Oh, Almighty God, assist me and direct me what to do.' After praying he felt strengthened and returned to the hut. Mrs Mulligan told him that she had dreamed that she had a baby and that he had taken it away and killed it. 'It was all covered with blood and looked horrible.' Lynch joked with her about this dream, but at the same time he 'felt very frightened'. He believed that 'she could foretell things', and he knew that 'she could toss balls and turn cups'. He went away again and prayed to God to enlighten

him, and at last made up his mind to 'kill the lot'.

He returned to the hut and 'talked pleasantly'. Then he asked young Mulligan who was about sixteen years of age, to 'come and cut some wood' for the fire. The boy went with him and as they walked along Lynch spoke to the lad of the fine property he would have 'when the old man died', adding, 'Ah, Johnny, you don't know what's in store for you'. They chopped up several sticks and when the boy was stooping, Lynch swung the axe round and 'hit him on the head'. He threw a few branches over the body, and picking up an armful of the wood they had cut, walked back to the house.

Mrs Mulligan asked him where her boy was, and Lynch replied that he'd 'gone to the paddock with the horses'. Mrs Mulligan was very uneasy and asked Lynch to fire his gun off, as a signal to the boy to return. Lynch said this might bring the police round and he didn't want them 'to see that dray'. Mulligan also objected to the gun being fired. Both Mulligan and his wife were very upset. The old man paced up and down in front of the house, while the old woman, after asking Lynch several times what he had done with her boy, started up the path to look for him. Then said Lynch, 'I knew it was time for something to be done'. He got his tomahawk without being seen, walked up to the old man and cried 'Look!' As Mulligan turned round and looked up the road where Lynch pointed, Lynch struck him 'one tap' and he 'fell like a log'. Lynch then followed Mrs Mulligan, tripped her up and killed her.

He walked back to the hut and saw the daughter, a girl of fourteen, standing behind the table with a large butcher's knife in her hand. She was trembling violently. He said to her 'Put down that knife'. She hesitated and he cried louder, 'Put down that knife'. Then she put it down. He walked round the table and took her hand. He said he did not wish to hurt her, but if he let her live she would 'only put him away'. He told her to 'pray for her soul', as she had 'only ten minutes to live'. She sobbed bitterly and he tried to comfort her, talking very seriously, and telling her that life was full of trouble, and that she would be better dead. Then he took her into the inner room, and after having raped her, brought her out again and killed her with the tomahawk. He dragged the four bodies together, heaped firewood over them and set fire to the heap. 'I never seen nothing like it,' he said. 'They burned as if they was bags of fat.' He threw the greater part of their clothing on to the fire and burned it.

He stayed at the farm all next day, and when he had 'made things right', went to Sydney. Here he placed an advertisement in the *Sydney Gazette* to the effect that as Mrs Mulligan had left her home without his consent he would not be responsible for any debts she might contract. This was signed 'John Mulligan'. He returned to the farm and wrote letters informing those people to whom he knew Mulligan owed money that he had sold the farm to John Dunleavy, who would pay their accounts. These letters he also signed 'John Mulligan'.

Lynch then engaged Terence Barnett and his wife to work on the farm, and stayed there quietly for six months. The stories he told in the neighbourhood induced the belief that Mulligan had taken him in with regard to the farm, and that he had paid more for it than it was worth.

At the end of six months Lynch paid another visit to Sydney, and on his return journey met Kearns Landregan, who said he was looking for work. Lynch engaged him to put up some fencing. Landregan agreed and got into the cart. Lynch drove on until they were passing Crisp's Inn. Here Landregan crouched down as if to hide himself. Lynch asked him what he did that for. Landregan replied that he had summoned Crisp for stealing a bundle of clothes from him and didn't want a row about it then. Lynch felt sorry that he had engaged Landregan and decided to get rid of him. He camped at Ironstone Bridge and when Landregan was sitting on a log near the camp fire, Lynch crept up behind him and struck him with the tomahawk. In his confession Lynch was very particular in pointing out that in all his previous murders he had not struck any one of his victims more than one blow with the tomahawk or axe. Landregan, however, was a big powerful man, who boasted that he had never met his match in wrestling, and Lynch felt afraid of him. So he departed from his rule and struck Landregan twice. He attributed his 'ill-luck' in being caught and convicted to this breach of the rule he had laid down for himself.

Lynch seems to have persuaded himself that he was acting under Divine inspiration in committing his murders. He was very emphatic in hs assertions that he never committed a murder without having first prayed to Almighty God to assist and direct him, until

Native troopers were valued for their ability to track fugitives.

*Left:*
John Lynch killed to take possession of a bullock team like this.

he felt sufficiently strengthened to carry out his intentions. He appeared to believe that he was justified in taking life.

Whatever may be thought of his confessions, there can be no doubt that the main facts were correct. After his death a search was made at the places where he said he had hidden or buried his victims, and in all cases the remains were found as he had stated they would be. With regard to the Mulligans, a large heap of ashes was searched and found to contain human remains. The confession only included his more serious crimes. He said nothing about the numerous robberies he had committed at various times, nor of his relations with other bushrangers.

Lynch was hanged at Berrima on 22 April 1842. At that time he was only twenty-nine years of age. He was about five feet three and a half inches in height, of fair complexion with brown hair and hazel eyes. There was nothing ferocious in his appearance.

# 6 A gentleman bushranger

**Jackey Jackey, the Gentleman Bushranger; dispute with Paddy Curran; capture at Bungendore; escape at Bargo Brush; Jackey Jackey visits Sydney; captured and sent to Norfolk Island for life; Curran tried for murder and rape, and hanged.**

William Westwood, better known as Jackey Jackey, was the darling of the old hands. He was only an errand boy in England, and was transported for some trifling offence when he was sixteen years of age. He landed in Sydney in 1837, and was assigned to Mr Phillip Gidley King, at Gidley in the Goulburn district. He stayed at the station for nearly three years, and then, with a notorious scoundrel named Paddy Curran, stuck up and robbed his employer's house. The partnership between Jackey Jackey and Curran, however, did not last very long. Curran disgusted Jackey Jackey by his brutality to women. In one of their mutual enterprises Curran criminally assaulted a woman, the wife of the farmer whose place they had stuck up. Jackey Jackey was furious. He declared that even if a man was a bushranger he might be a gentleman, and added that he would never see a woman insulted. He threatened to shoot Curran unless he left at once, and stripped him of his horse, arms and ammunition.

This story is the key-note to Jackey Jackey's character. To the old hands he was always the gentleman bushranger. The stories told by them about the Jewboy and other bushrangers, and even about Matthew Brady, were generally coarse and sometimes brutal, but Jackey Jackey was always polite and well-behaved. Numerous legends have collected round the name of Jackey Jackey and many of them are obviously variants of the stories told of the historical highwaymen of England. For instance, Jackey Jackey is said to have bailed up the carriage of the Commissary. When he discovered that the Commissary's wife was inside he dismounted, opened the door, and sweeping the ground with his cabbage tree hat as he bowed low before her, he invited her to favour him with a step on the green.

He rode incredible distances in incredibly short periods of time. He is represented as bailing up a man near Goulburn and telling him to note the time by his watch and then racing away and bailing up another man at Braidwood or some other place a hundred or a hundred and fifty miles away in a few hours and

asking that person to note the time. Many of the popular stories told about him are so evidently apocryphal that little notice can be taken of them. But one thing is certain and that is that he was always well mounted. He scorned to steal an inferior horse and would travel miles to secure a racer. He stole racehorses from Mr Murray, Mr Julian, and many other gentlemen in the districts over which he ranged.

Although he appears to have been of humble origin he is credited with having been highly educated. This point was especially insisted upon by his eulogists among the old hands. By them he was always represented as being 'able to hold his own', in conversation, with 'the best of 'em'. I remember one old fellow telling me that Jackey Jackey met Governor Gipps. According to him the governor and the bushranger had a long conversation and parted mutually pleased with each other. 'You and me', said the old chap, 'couldn't have understood what they said

Sir George Gipps

though it was all English; but, they talked grammar.' What his precise meaning was I had no idea, but I have always thought that he meant that their conversation was all carried on it what he might have called 'dictionary words', that is, words not used by the uneducated.

Everything said of Jackey Jackey contributes to his credit from the old hand point of view. He was emphatically 'a good man'. The meaning attached to words is purely conventional, and is therefore liable to vary with the conventionalities. The point of view of the convict being entirely different from that of the law-abiding citizen, the terms 'good' and 'bad' changed places in their vocabulary. Thus the clergy, the magistrates, the freemen, were generally 'bad men', while those who resisted authority, who fought against law and order, were 'good men'. Even the cannibal Pierce was a good man from their point of view, however strongly they might condemn his methods. But Jackey Jackey, although he continued the fight to the bitter end and ended his life on the gallows when he was only twenty-six, never did anything mean or brutal or unworthy of a gentleman bushranger until he was almost goaded to madness by the cruel discipline of Norfolk Island.

Paddy Curran was 'out in the bush' several months before Jackey Jackey joined him, and he was not the only bushranger at work in the district. On 31 December 1839, the station of the Rev. Mr Cartwright was struck up and robbed. On the same day a skirmish between the police and seven mounted bushrangers took place near Yass. One of the police horses was killed, and the police were compelled to retreat. On the same day Mr Heffernan's house, not far from Goulburn, was stuck up and robbed of £21 in money, a case of duelling pistols, a valuable mare, and other property. Mr Israel Shepherd also lost a valuable horse, besides some money, and Mr Charles Campbell was reported to have been shot dead. This is a heavy record for one day, and as the robberies took place so far distant from each other, there must have been at least three separate parties concerned in them. About the same time it was reported that Scotchy and Whitton were plundering the stations on the Lachlan River in all directions, and that Mr Arthur Rankin had left his station and retired to Sydney because of the trouble in the country districts. The robberies continued all through the year 1840, and a great part of 1841.

On 13 January 1841 a man ran into the township of Bungendore, and said that Jackey Jackey had followed and fired at him. A few minutes later Jackey Jackey himself hove in sight on the plains mounted on a splendid mare, which he had stolen from the Messrs Macarthur. He was dressed in a fine suit of clothes which he had obtained when he stuck up and robbed the store at Boro a few days before. He stopped to speak to a man near Eccleton's. In the meantime Mr

Death mask of Jackey Jackey Westwood

Powell, the resident magistrate, and his brother, Mr Frank Powell, promptly mounted and went towards the bushranger. They were joined by Richard Rutledge who was unarmed.

As they approached Jackey Jackey wheeled round and fired at them, but failed to hit any one. Mr Balcombe and the Rev. Mr McGrath drove up in a gig, and Mr McGrath jumped down and presented his gun. Seeing himself surrounded, Jackey Jackey surrendered. He explained that his mare had come a long journey and was unfit to travel, and that his musket was out of order and would not go off. He was conducted to the inn and placed in a room, two ticket-of-leave men being placed there to guard him. Jackey Jackey sat very quietly for some time. Then he jumped up suddenly, knocked down one of his guards, snatched his musket, jumped through the window, and ran across the plain. Frank Powell, who was close at hand, followed him, and with the assistance of Dr Wilson's postman, recaptured him.

Among other exploits prior to this capture Jackey Jackey had robbed the Queanbeyan, Tarago, and other mails; he stuck up Mr Julian, Mr Edinburgh, and a number of other people on the roads at various times and places; stole horses from all the principal owners and breeders in the district; fired at the driver of the Bungendore mail, who escaped; and robbed the Boro Creek store of clothing, money, provisions, and other articles, on the Tuesday before his capture.

For several months Lieutenant Christie and the whole of the mounted police of the district had been trying to capture him, and he had more than once escaped only by the superior fleetness of his horses. As soon as possible after his capture he was handed over to Lieutenant Christie, who conducted him to Goulburn where he was placed in the lock-up. The following day he was being taken to Bargo Brush, on the road to Sydney, when he made a desperate attempt to escape on foot, running for a mile before he was recaptured. He was then tied on the horse and the journey was resumed. That night he broke out of the Bargo lock-up, taking with him the watch-house keeper's arms and ammunition. He soon stole a horse, and on the following day stuck up Mr Francis Macarthur on the Goulburn Plains. He robbed Mr Macarthur of his watch, money, and other valuables, and took one of his carriage horses because it was better than the animal he was riding.

On Tuesday, 18 May 1841, a gentleman mounted on a spirited horse pulled up at the tollbar on the Parramatta Road, Sydney, and asked the tollkeeper if he could oblige him with a pipe of tobacco. The tollkeeper gave him a piece, and the gentleman dismounted and filled his pipe. As he stood at the door of the tollhouse he remarked on a firelock hanging over the mantlepiece, and asked what it was for. 'For bushrangers,' replied the toll man. 'But there are none now. I've never seen it taken down since I've been here.' 'Did you ever hear of Jackey Jackey?' inquired the gentleman. 'Oh, yes,' replied the toll man, 'but he's a long way away. He never comes to Sydney. If he did he'd soon be caught.' 'Not at all,' replied the gentleman laughing. 'They don't know how to catch him, nor to keep him when they do catch him. I'm Jackey Jackey.' He raised the lapels of his coat as he spoke and showed a brace of pistols stuck in his belt on each side. The tollman looked very much alarmed, but the bushranger said to him, 'Don't be frightened, I am not going to hurt you. I've been in Sydney for three days and I'm going back to Monaro.' He informed the tollman that he had taken a horse in Sydney, but that he was too old and stiff, so he had taken the liberty of exchanging him for the one he had with him at Grose's Farm. 'Ain't you afraid of being took?' asked the tollman. Jackey laughed. 'I'd like to see who'll stop me while I've these little bull-dogs about me,' he said, tapping his pistols. He stood chatting while he smoked, regardless of the fact that Grose's Farm, now the grounds of the Sydney University, was within a stone's-throw of the toll-bar. He offered the tollman some money and asked him to go to the public-house for some rum. The tollman replied, 'I can't leave the bar.' 'All right,' returned Jackey, 'then I'll get it myself.' He went away to Toogood's Inn and returned in a few minutes with a half-pint of rum. He gave some to the tollkeeper and took a stiff glass himself. Then he shook hands with the tollman, mounted his horse, and rode on.

Escape attempt by convicts at Darlinghurst jail, Sydney, where Jackey Jackey was confined in 1841.

On 8 July a great commotion was caused in George Street, Sydney, by a soldier arresting a well-dressed man and asserting that he recognized him as Jackey Jackey. A large number of people assembled and there were plenty of them quite ready to assist in the capture of the noted bushranger. When the prisoner was taken to the police court, it was soon proved that he was a freeman. He was discharged and the soldier censured for being too officious. Since the visit of the bushranger in May had become known a constant look-out had been kept in case he should repeat his visit.

Jackey Jackey did not stay free for long however. One day he went into Gray's Black Horse Inn on the Berrima road, called for some refreshments, went into a sitting room, and threw himself on the sofa. He was served by Miss Gray, and while he was drinking she pounced on him and screamed. Her father and mother came to her assistance, but Jackey Jackey fought with so much determination that he would no doubt have got away. A carpenter named Waters was working near, however, and hearing the noise he rushed in and

Tollgates were a target for robbers because of the money collected by the toll-keeper for the upkeep of the road.

struck Jackey Jackey on the head with his shingling hammer. Knocked senseless, the noted bushranger was easily secured. (Black Horse Inn was about three miles from Mulligan's farm, and was the place where Lynch had bought the rum to treat Mr and Mrs Mulligan just before he murdered them.)

Jackey Jackey was captured only for the £30 reward offered for him dead or alive. He was tried for the robbery of the Boro store, and was sentenced to penal servitude for life. He was at first confined in Darlinghurst Jail, Sydney, but after being discovered attempting to escape, he was transferred to Cockatoo Island at the mouth of the Parramatta River. While here he organized a band of twenty-five prisoners, and made a desperate attempt to escape. The gang tied up a warder, and then jumped into the harbour with the intention of swimming to Balmain. The water police however, were informed of the mutiny and captured the whole gang.

The gang was tried for this attempt at escape and sentenced to be sent to Port Arthur, Van Diemen's Land. Being such a desperate lot they were chained down in the hold of the brig. In spite of this precaution, they got loose and were only prevented from capturing the brig by the hatches being put on and battened down. They reached Port Arthur in an almost suffocated condition and were nearly starved, as they had had no food for several days; the captain of the brig not daring to remove the hatches, either to let in air, or to pass food to the prisoners.

Jackey Jackey succeeded in escaping from Port Arthur and immediately resumed his bushranging career. He was captured after a very short run and was sent to Glenorchy Probation Station for milder treatment. Probably this attempt at reformation came too late, as it had little beneficial effect. Jackey Jackey made his escape and again began bushranging. He was captured in a house in Hobart Town and sentenced to death. The sentence was commuted to penal servitude for life and he was sent to Norfolk Island.

In the meantime Jackey Jackey's old mate, Paddy Curran, continued to rob as before. In 1840 he went to Major Lockyer's station and entered the men's hut while they were having their Christmas dinner. He had a pair of handcuffs hanging at his belt, and was thought to be a constable out on the spree. He helped himself freely to the good things on the table, and behaved generally as if he had been drinking. One of the men, however, said he did not believe that the visitor was 'a drunken trap', and Curran immediately knocked him down with the butt of his gun. The man jumped up at once and rushed at Curran. There was a struggle for a time, and the man got Curran down. But he was too exhausted to hold him, and Curran got up. The other men, who were all assigned servants on the estate, looked on and applauded the wrestlers, but not one of them made any motion to assist his mate, otherwise Curran might easily have been captured. After his wrestling match Curran walked out of the hut, mounted his horse, and rode away.

43

On the following day Curran again went to the station, and found Mr North, son-in-law to Major Lockyer, and another man in the store. He called on them to bail up, and both men held their hands up. Curran was about to enter the store-door when he was pinioned from behind. Mr North and his store-keeper rushed forward, and after a severe struggle, during which the bushranger tried hard to get his gun free, he was captured and tied. The man who had pinioned him was the man with whom he had had the wrestling match the day before. Curran was taken to Goulburn for examination, and was remanded to Berrima to take his trial, 'where', said the *Port Phillip Herald*, 'it is to be hoped he will be more securely confined, and not allowed to escape, as he did before'.

Paddy Curran and James Berry, another bushranger, were sent to Berrima for trial in charge of Constables McGuire and Wilsmore. They stopped at a hut on the road for rest and food. After they had finished their meal Constable Wilsmore left the hut, and stayed away for some time. At length Constable McGuire went to the door of the hut to call him, and Berry and Curran, taking advantage of his action, immediately rushed upon him. They were handcuffed together, and this no doubt hampered their movements. McGuire fought hard. The bushrangers had seized the guns, and each held one. McGuire endeavoured to wrest the gun from Curran with one hand, while he held Berry's gun off with the other hand. He yelled for Wilsmore, but Wilsmore did not come. At length Berry got his gun loose and shot McGuire in the back of the head and in the shoulder.

At this moment Constable Wilsmore returned, and seeing his mate apparently dead and the prisoners in possession of the guns, ran away. Curran and Berry beat McGuire about the head until he was dead, and a 'fearful spectacle to look upon'. Then they searched his body, and finding the key of the handcuffs, released themselves and made off.

The two bushrangers continued their depredations for a few months, before they were tracked down by the police and captured. Curran was tried on 15 September 1841, for the murder of Mr Fuller. He afterwards confessed to this murder. He said he was in company with two other bushrangers on the road near Bungendore when he heard two men quarrelling. Curran and his mates went towards the road and hid behind trees. Presently two men riding on one horse came in sight and appeared to be having a dispute about something. They were talking loudly and swearing at each other. Curran stepped out behind the tree and called on them to stop. Instead of doing so they wheeled the horse and began to gallop away. Curran fired and both men fell, while the horse bolted along the road and soon got out of sight. One of the men jumped up as soon as he fell and ran into the bush and they did not see him again. The other man was Mr Fuller, and he was either dead or at the point of death.

Jackey Jackey was one of several well-known bushrangers who were transported to Norfolk Island. Above: the old commissariat store. Top right: the harbour. Centre right: the settlement as it was in Westwood's time. Below right: ruins of the military barracks.

'I turned him over and took about £11 in money and a pocket-knife out of his pockets,' said the bushranger.

Curran was also tried for having raped Mary Wilsmore. He went to the hut occupied by Wilsmore on 8 February. It was near Bungendore. He ordered Mrs Wilsmore to get him some tea. A bushranger named White was with him. Mrs Wilsmore went outside to get some wood to make up the fire, and Curran followed her, knocked her down, and dragged her away to some scrub where he committed the offence. He was found guilty of both crimes and was sentenced to be hanged. There was another case of rape, several cases of murder, and numbers of robberies and burglaries charged against him, but none of these was heard.

James Berry was tried for the murder of Constable McGuire, and was sentenced to death.

# 7 The Jewboy gang

**Robberies around Maitland; the story of Budge, the bullock driver; Mr E. D. Day captures the Jewboy gang and is publicly acclaimed; assigned servants' attempt at bushranging; some other gangs.**

One of the most notorious of the early Australian bushrangers was Edward Davis, commonly known as the Jewboy. Next to Jackey Jackey, and perhaps Matthew Brady, more yarns have been told about this hero of the roads than of any other bushranger in the pre-gold era. The Jewboy gang varied in numbers from time to time, no doubt from the cause already noted in the cases of Mike Howe and Matthew Brady. Numbers of runaways joined the gang for a time and then returned to what was called civilization. They gave themselves up as ordinary runaways and 'took their fifties like men'. Others were shot or captured, and either hanged or sent to a penal settlement to continue their careers there.

The Jewboy appears to have commenced his depredations in 1839 in what were then the northern districts of the colony of New South Wales. His range extended from about Maitland to the New England ranges, and he took possession of the Great Northern Road. But he was not particular and either he, or members of his gang, or perhaps independent bushrangers who were only supposed to belong to the Jewboy gang, travelled considerable distances from the road.

Major Sutton was stopped on the road by armed men, and robbed on his return from attending the Maitland police sessions, and a hut belonging to Mr Windeyer, near Stroud, was broken into and robbed. Robberies were very frequent about Maitland, and in the Upper Hunter and Patterson River districts. These were all credited to the Jewboy gang, which was just coming into notoriety.

During the year 1840, the Jewboy gang committed numerous crimes. They robbed Mr Deake's house at Wollombi and stole his horses; they took horses from several other stations; they held the roads at various places for a day at a time, and robbed every one who passed along. The headquarters of the gang were at Doughboy Hollow in the Liverpool Ranges, and it was said that any man riding along the road near Murrurundi or Quirindi, or between these places and Tamworth, was 'almost certain to lose his horse and

whatever property he might have about him, and be compelled to walk to the next stage and perhaps farther, while the bushrangers were riding his horse to death harrying other honest people'.

One of the stories told of the Jewboy was that he 'rounded up' the chief constable of the district with a party of constables and volunteers who had gone out to seek for him. After having 'yarded them like a mob of cattle', he took their horses, arms, and whatever money they had, and rode away laughing. However sometimes the tables were turned on the bushranger. A bullock-driver named Budge was bailed up by two of the gang. Budge had a little boy with him, and one of the bushrangers stood over Budge and the child while the other was ransacking the dray. Budge kept his eye on the sentry and, noticing him look round to see how his mate was getting on, sprang on him, snatched the pistol from his hand, and knocked him down. Then he ordered the other bushranger to get off his dray, and made the two stand side by side. He kept them standing thus for about two hours in hopes that some travellers would pass along and assist him to take them to the nearest lock-up. Unfortunately no one came, and he was forced at length to let them go. He kept their arms and saddles, and these he delivered to the Commissary on arriving at his destination. There were two guns and four pistols, all loaded.

On Sunday, 26 September, some of the gang bailed up the mail-man between Muswellbrook and Patrick's Plains, and are supposed to have taken some £250 from the letters. After this robbery one of the bushrangers bolted from his mates, taking the greater part of the proceeds of their industry with him. He made his way to Sydney, where he passed himself off for a time as a free immigrant. He was arrested under the Bushrangers' Act and charged with being illegally at large. Then news of the mail robbery reached Sydney, and the fellow was sent to Muswellbrook, where he

The bush track to Murrurundi was a favourite haunt of the Jewboy and his companions.

was identified by the mail-man and sentenced to penal servitude.

The gang afterwards went to Scone and stuck up Mr Danger's store and Mr Chiver's Inn. The storeman in charge, named Graham, fired at the bushrangers and then ran for the soldiers, but one of the bushrangers followed him and before he reached the watchhouse shot him dead. They hastily made a bundle of the articles that took their fancy, and left the town. They went to Captain Pike's station and seized the overseer, taking him with them. When they were far enough in the bush they formed themselves into 'a court', and tried him 'for want of feeling'. He was found guilty and sentenced to receive three dozen lashes, 'which he got in good style'.

On Sunday, 21 December 1840, Captain Horsley, of Woodbury, Hexham, on the Hunter River, about five miles from Maitland, was awakened and alarmed by the violent barking of his dogs. He rose twice during the night and went out on to the veranda of the house, but could see nothing. As the noise continued he went out for the third time, when three men rushed at him. They threatened him with their guns and compelled him to surrender. They then took him back to his bedroom, made him get into bed, lie down, and cover his face with a pillow. The captain and Mrs Horsley were told that if either of them moved, they would both be shot instantly. The robbers demanded the keys, and after being told where to find them they opened the drawers, cabinets, and cupboards, and

A party of police, about 1880. In 1811 Governor Macquarie introduced a system of district constables, but it was not until 1862 that a New South Wales Police Force was established.

made bundles of the clothes, jewellery, plate, and money. They collected all the guns and pistols in the house, using the most violent and profane language during their search for plunder. Apparently they were disturbed in their work, as they left very suddenly and in their flight dropped two gold rings and two silver candlesticks which were picked up the following day outside the house.

On hearing of this outrage, Mr Edward Denny Day headed the soldiers and followed the bushrangers. They received news of them at several points on the Great Northern Road as the robbers bailed up people as they went along. They crossed the Page River at Murrurundi and came up to the bushrangers near Doughboy Hollow. Here the Jewboy made a stand. The fight was a desperate one, but ultimately the bushrangers were beaten and Edward Davis (the Jewboy), John Everett, John Shea, Robert Chitty, James Bryant, and John Marshall were captured. Richard Glanvill, the remaining member of the gang, made his escape, but was so closely pursued that he was captured in the scrub on the following day, 24 December. They were tried and convicted and were hanged on 16 March 1841.

# 8 Cashan captured

**Bushranging in South Australia; highway robbery in the Port Phillip District; a bloody battle between bushrangers and civilians; Cashan and McIntyre; capture of Cashan; McIntyre continues bushranging but is also captured and hanged.**

Three bushrangers named Wilson, Green, and another, robbed the settlers in the vicinity of Lyndoch Valley, South Australia, and extorted heavy contributions from their victims in the latter part of the year 1839 and the beginning of 1840. These robberies had been going on for some months before news reached Adelaide. The colony had only been founded a little more than three years before, and communication was difficult and very irregular. There were no roads and the undeveloped state of the police force prevented the authorities from coping effectually with such an outbreak as this.

The robbers called at Mr Read's station and knocked at the door of the house. A woman opened the door and was immediately knocked down by one of the robbers. Another robber fired his musket at her at such close range that the wadding of the gun bruised her cheek without the slugs injuring her. When he heard of this outrage, Mr Inman, Superintendent of Police, immediately left Adelaide with a party of mounted troopers. As he proceeded on his way, news of other robberies were spread about. The movements of the police appear to have been known to the bushrangers, as they were fired at when passing through some scrub. Not knowing how many men there might be in the gang, Mr Inman intrenched himself, and sent to Adelaide for more men. In a few days parties of mounted police arrived from Gawler and Mount Barker. The district was thoroughly searched, without success.

About the middle of February, three men on horseback arrived in Melbourne. Their headquarters was the Royal Highlander Inn, in Queen Street, where they spent money freely and drank heavily. One of the men was recognized by the police as a convict from Van Diemen's Land, free by service. He was arrested on suspicion of having stolen the horse he rode from Mr Cox, but as Mr Cox's superintendent could not swear to the animal, although he bore the station brand, the man was discharged and immediately left Melbourne. On Sunday, 23 February, Wilson was arrested for drunkenness and rowydism, and was

These aboriginal troopers called Corunguiam and Munight were members of one of the seven separate forces operating in Victoria before the formation of the Victoria Police Force in 1852.

fined 5s. next morning at the police court. While there he was seen and recognized by two South Australian policemen who had been to Sydney with some prisoners, and were on their way home. Wilson and Green were both arrested that evening and charged with the robbery at Mr Read's station, South Australia. They were detained until warrants could be obtained from Adelaide, where they were sent and convicted. The robbers had travelled from South Australia to Melbourne, via Portland Bay, and had probably stolen the horses and perhaps some other property on the road. The third man, whose name is not given, was searched for, but was not found. It was supposed he had crossed the Murray into New South Wales.

What is generally said to be the first highway robbery in the Port Phillip district took place in April 1842. A gang, composed of John Ellis, alias Yanky Jack, Jack Williams, Young Fogarty, and a 'Van Diemonian' named Jepps, bailed up Mr Darling and a friend as they were riding to an out-station on the Dandenong run to brand cattle. The robbers took £2 and a silver watch from Mr Darling, and one shilling and sixpence from his friend. Mr Darling was riding a thoroughbred horse, and Jack Williams remarked that he was a fine beast, and ordered Mr Darling to show off his paces. This was a blunder on the part of the bushranger and Mr Darling was not slow in taking advantage of it. He did not wish to lose his horse, and therefore jerked the bit, rolled about in the saddle, and pretended that he had as much as he could do to keep his seat while the horse was cantering.

Williams watched as the horse went past him a couple of times, and then said, 'That'll do. He seems to be a —— rough 'un.' He contented himself with the horse the friend was riding, giving him his knocked-up horse in exchange. Williams then produced a bottle of rum, and after having taken a swig himself passed it to Mr Darling and his friend with the remark that 'a drop of grog was good on a cold day'. He took five shillings from his pocket, gave this to Darling to 'drink their healths with at the next public-house', said 'good day' and rode on after his mates.

The gang went along the main road up the Plenty River robbing the stations on either side of the road as they came to them. They stuck up Messrs Serjeantson, Peet, Bond, Langor, Marsh, Fleming, Rider, Bear, and Captain Harrison, collecting a goodly assortment of watches and chains, mostly silver, and some money. It was after dark when they finished at Mr Bear's house, and they camped by the creek within sight of the house for the night.

Early next morning the gang took to the road again and robbed Messrs Sherwin, Roland, and Wills. At about nine o'clock they reached Mr Campbell Hunter's station as the family was sitting down to a breakfast of roast duck, kippered herrings, and coffee. Williams walked into the room pistol in hand and cried, 'Put up your hands'. He was immediately obeyed. Looking round he said 'Gentlemen, you must make room for your betters'. Those present were Messrs Campbell Hunter, Alexander Hunter, Streatham, Rumbold, Boswell, and Dr Grimes. They were made to stand up against the wall while the roast ducks and other good things were removed to a slab hut used as a store room. The bushrangers had only just begun their breakfast when a large party of armed men galloped up.

News of the robberies of the previous day had reached Melbourne in the evening, and Messrs P. Snodgrass and H. Fowler of the Melbourne Club, had decided to 'go out for a hunt'. They got their arms and horses and were joined by several other gentlemen, among whom were Mr Sergeantson, and others who had been robbed; there were about thirty altogether. The bushrangers hastily made their prisoners promise not to take part in the comming fight, ahd then took up

positions behind the fence. Underterred by this show of resistance, Mr Gourlay jumped his horse over the fence, landing close to Jack Williams, so close, in fact, that the flash from the bushranger's pistol singed his whiskers and burned his cheek. The bushranger dashed his pistol down on the ground with an oath, and drew another, but Mr Snodgrass, leaning over the fence, shot him in the head before he could make use of it. Thinking he had killed his man, Snodgrass turned to Yanky Bill. Then Williams jumped up and fired point blank at Gourlay, who shouted, 'Tell my friends I died game', and fell. Mr Chamberlain shot Williams through the head and killed him. Much to the surprise of those near, Mr Gourlay jumped up again almost as quickly as he had fallen, and it was soon discovered that the pistol bullet had smashed his powder flask and glanced off, inflicting only a severe bruise.

After the death of their leader the bushrangers rushed to the hut and took shelter there, pointing their pistols through the openings between the slabs. A fierce fusilade took place, during which Mr Fowler was severely wounded. Then there was a pause. It seemed that the robbers ammunition was spent. A horse dealer residing in the neighbourhood, named John Ewart, but usually known as Hoppy Jack, volunteered to go in and speak to the bushrangers. At first this was objected to as being too dangerous, but Hoppy Jack insisted, and said it would be 'all right'. He advanced towards the hut waving a white handkerchief, and after a few words at the door was admitted. The result of this embassy was that the bushrangers agreed to surrender provided that their captors would sign a petition to the judge to deal leniently with them. This was readily agreed to, and the men came out and gave themselves up just as a party of mounted police appeared on the scene, and the prisoners were handed over to them.

This raid was principally remarkable for the

The act of bushranging was such an everyday occurrence that it inspired many artists. This portrayal of bushrangers on the St Kilda Road (near Melbourne) was painted by William Strutt in about 1887.

This satirical lithograph of the 1850s was captioned: 'The way Her Majesty's Mails and the public protectors are served in New South Wales' and reflected public disquiet at the failure of the authorities to stamp out bushranging.

boldness and rapidity with which it was executed. The bushrangers travelled directly from one station to the next, taking the shortest route, which was generally along the main road. The robberies were effected in very short time at each station, the bushrangers contenting themselves with money, watches, rings, and other property carried on the person. There was no time wasted in breaking open boxes or drawers, and there was no necessity to spare their horses, as a knocked-up horse could be exchanged for a fresh one almost whenever the robbers pleased.

Mr Gourlay was little the worse for his bruises and burns, although the powder marks on his face remained, but Mr Fowler died a few days after the fight. The prisoners were tried and convicted, and in spite of the recommendation to mercy duly signed by their captors and forwarded to the judge, were sentenced to death for the murder of Fowler. Jepps confessed that it was he who fired the fatal shot, but he also said that he had refused to join in an attempt to murder Judge Willis, the resident judge in Port Phillip. The convicted men were all hanged in Melbourne, in May 1842.

During the following two years there was little bushranging in any part of New South Wales. In 1844 McIntyre and Cashan, alias Nowlan, held the roads between Hartley, Bathurst, and Mudgee for several days, robbing all who passed. On 2 December 1845, they stopped the mail at Bowenfels, on the main Sydney road at the foot of the Blue Mountains, on the western side. They called on the passengers to hand over their money and valuables, but two of them resisted and drew their pistols. A fight took place and Cashan was captured, while McIntyre ran away into the bush. Cashan was taken to Bathurst, tried, convicted, and sentenced to be transported for life. He was being taken to Sydney in April, to be sent to Cockatoo Island, when the escort stopped at Weatherboard Hut for the night. Cashan was lodged in the lock-up. He broke out during the night, and could not be found. He travelled to Gundagai, where he stuck up Mr Nicholson's station, taking clothes, provisions, horse, saddle, and bridle.

Mr Andrews, who was in charge of the station, and who was absent when Cashan called, heard of the robbery and followed the bushranger. He rode to Charles Simpson's station, but was told by Edwin and Alfred Tompson, who resided there, that no bushranger had been seen. While they were talking a man on horseback came in sight. Andrews recognized him as the robber from the description that had been given of him and the horse he was riding. Andrews retreated into the house out of sight, and Cashan rode up, dismounted, and asked for refreshments. He was immediately seized by the Tompsons and told that he was a prisoner. He struggled hard to escape, but finding that this was no use, he became quiet and said he was ready to go wherever they wished him to. They took him towards the house, which was only a few steps distant, when suddenly he broke away with a laugh, ran down the bank, and plunged into the Murrumbidgee River.

The river was in flood at the time, and was therefore twice its ordinary width, and running strongly. Cashan, encumbered with a greatcoat and perhaps with other stolen property, could make no headway against the current. He sank at once, rose some distance lower down, and succeeded in grasping the branches of a swamp oak hanging over the water. After a struggle he contrived to haul himself out of the water, and took a seat in the fork of the tree. He was still on the same side of the river as Simpson's station, and not far from the bank, although the flood waters prevented Alfred and Edwin Tompson from getting close to him. Edwin Tompson covered him with his pistol, and threatened to shoot him if he moved. They talked for some time, and the bushranger, seeing no chance of escape, agreed to give himself up. He dropped into the water, swam to the bank, and walked quietly to the house, where he was tied and made secure for the night.

The next day he was taken to Yass by the Tompsons and Andrews, and in spite of his frequent attempts to break the handcuffs and make his escape, he was safely lodged in the lock-up. He was identified as one of the men who had burned Dr Bell's house at

Braidwood, and robbed the Braidwood mail. When robbing the Braidwood mail in company with McIntyre, he nearly committed murder, one of the passengers having been dangerously wounded. He was convicted and sentenced to be hanged.

In the meantime, his former partner had not been idle. On 21 April 1846, the two brothers Cutts were travelling towards Sydney with a number of horses, when they were stopped at Meadow Flat, less than a quarter of a mile from Howard's Inn. They were compelled to dismount, place their money on the ground, and retire. They deposited £3 18s. in notes and silver and a watch on the ground, and then stepped back several paces as they had been ordered to. William Cutts begged that a seal attached to his watch might be returned to him, as it was a present from his dead wife. The bushranger, who was supposed to be McIntyre, told him that 'if there was any more palaver' he would get his brains blown out. The robber took up the money and watch, mounted his horse, and rode away. As soon as information of the robbery was received in Bathurst the mounted troopers started in pursuit of the bushranger.

On Monday 11 August, two men went to the Golden Fleece Inn, Gammon Plains, and remained there drinking till Friday. On that day the landlord, Mr Perfrement, received his copy of the *Maitland Mercury*, and saw in it a list of the numbers of the bank notes recently stolen from the Singleton mail. He compared the numbers with those of the notes he had received from his two guests, and finding that some of them corresponded, he went to the police station and gave information. The inn was not a large building, but there were several out-houses and the bushrangers were in some of these. Perfrement and the police went to one of these huts at the rear of the inn and found McIntyre there. Perfrement put his hand on the bushranger's shoulder and said 'You're a prisoner.' 'Am I,' exclaimed McIntyre jumping backwards, 'Come on.'

Constable Barker rushed in and a fierce wrestling match began and lasted for some minutes. Then McIntyre got on top and tried to get his pistol cut from his belt. Mr Perfrement, who had snatched the other pistol from him when the wrestling first began, now threatened to shoot him if he did not surrender, but as the bushranger took no notice Perfrement endeavoured to twist the other pistol out of his hand. When this struggle was going on Barker wriggled from under the bushranger, got up, and struck him heavily with his fist stunning him. McIntyre lay still for several minutes before he regained consciousness, and by that time his hands were tied. His companion was found asleep in another hut and was easily captured. They were tried in Maitland. McIntyre was subsequently hanged

At Pentridge Jail, Melbourne, difficult prisoners were punished by long bouts of solitary confinement.

# 9 The scourge of Cash & Co.

**More bushranging in Van Diemen's Land; some brutal attacks; an enterprising group; the art of politeness by bushrangers; a bushranger hunt in the streets of Hobart Town; the capture of Martin Cash and the break-up of the gang.**

For some years the roads in Van Diemen's Land had been comparatively safe, and very few highway robberies were recorded. The newspapers generally asserted that bushranging in its worst form had been stamped out. This assertion, however, is not altogether borne out by the evidence, and the most that can be said is that bushranging was not as prevalent as in former times. No bushranger had exercised his calling for a sufficiently long time to earn notoriety. However this comparatively happy condition did not last very long.

The bushrangers James Regan, William Davis, James Atterill, alias Thompson, and Anthony Bankes had committed a number of raids on the settlers and the Government resolved to make a decisive effort to capture them. Consequently, on 21 February 1838, Captain Mackenzie, with three privates of the 21st Fusiliers, two constables of the Field Police, and two prisoner volunteers, went to Jerusalem. He was informed by the Police Magistrate of Richmond that another house had been robbed by the bushrangers, who had retired to the Brown Mountain. A guide was found and the party started the following morning. They struck into the bush a short distance beyond Mr Tomley's. At two o'clock they came to a hut where the stockman, an intelligent lad, informed them that the bushrangers had robbed his master's house on the previous night at ten o'clock, taking a horse to carry the robber Bankes, who had been wounded. The lad was taken as a guide, and led them up a ravine, which soon became too steep for the horses. They reached the summit of the Brown Mountain about dusk, but without seeing any fire or other indication of a camp. They reached Mr Ree's house, on the Richmond side, about midnight, and returned to Jerusalem at six on Friday morning, having been marching for twenty-three hours over very rough country.

After six hours' rest Captain Mackenzie took Wesley, one of Mr Johnson's shepherds, as guide, and resumed the search. They reached Mr Stokell's house at dusk, and approached it with great caution. Finding no one there, Captain Mackenzie left two sentries, and

pushed on to Romney's, where they arrived at about half-past one. The moon was shining brightly. The hut was surrounded, and Captain Mackenzie called for three volunteers, telling the men that it was a forlorn hope, as the robbers would probably shoot two out of the three, the moonlight being so bright. The captain called on Regan by name to surrender, but received no answer. He then walked up to the window, and said to the occupant of the hut, 'Tucker, you old blockhead! why don't you open the door?' There was a rattle of musketry, and the captain stepped back into the shadow of the hut. Captain Mackenzie called out to his men not to fire unless the bushrangers did, or unless they rushed out and tried to escape. Then Constable Peacock advanced to the window and looked in. Captain Mackenzie said if the door was not opened he would fire, and after waiting a minute or so told Private Cockburn to shoot, but not too low. Cockburn fired into the window. The door was opened and a man came out. 'I'm Tucker', said the man, 'don't shoot', and threw himself on his face.

The captain went to the door and looked in, when Private Cockburn cried, 'Take care, captain, the fellow is going to fire. They are all armed'. This raised a cheer among the soldiers, who now knew that their men were there. Regan it appears had tried to bring his musket to bear on the captain, but could not do so without exposing himself. The captain gave the word to fire, and a volley was poured into the hut. Then the captain asked Regan to surrender, promising not to hurt him. Regan endeavoured to induce the captain to promise not to prosecute them, but he refused, saying it was more than he could do.

Finally they consented to surrender, and Atterill crawled out naked. He was tied. Regan was then called, and he refused to come out on his hands and knees, saying that he'd sooner be shot than be treated like a dog. The captain told him he might walk out if he

This lithograph by McGready, Thompson and Niven depicts a brutal attack on a gold escort by bushrangers.

came without arms and held his hands up. He did so, and the police then went in and brought out the other two. The prisoners were handcuffed and placed in a cart. About £14, found in their clothes, and their guns and pistols, were carried in another cart. Tucker was employed by Mr Romney and was considered the best guide in the district. The robbers had taken possession of his hut and intended to make him show them the way across the mountains on the following day.

The party reached Richmond on Saturday night, and early next day the bushrangers were lodged in the jail at Hobart Town. The prisoners were tried and convicted of several acts of bushranging, ranging from highway robbery to burglary. They were all sentenced to death, but only Regan was hanged.[1] The *Cornwall Chronicle* said 'His inquisitors were conscious that, had he been permitted to give his dying attestation to the treatment he had received from his master, it would have been so appalling and horrible as to leave the guilt of his crimes, in the estimation of an impartial public, not on his own head, but on theirs . . . The Government is afraid to hear the dying statements of the condemned.'

On 15 April 1841, James Broomfield and Jonas Hopkins bailed up and robbed Henry Atkins of Bonney, taking seven five pound notes from him. In company with James McCallum the same two bushrangers went about midnight to the house of Thomas Bates, at Norfolk Plains. They woke him up, demanding something to drink. Bates told them that there was plenty of water in the cask. This did not satisfy them and they broke into the kitchen. They took some flour and grain from the cask and made a damper. While this was baking they took a watch, some money, and a quantity of clothes out of the bedroom. When they had had a meal, they left with their plunder, but were followed and captured. They were convicted of robbery with firearms and were sentenced to death; their sentences were, however, commuted to imprisonment for life.

On 9 January 1841, Hogan the bushranger walked into a public-house kept by Mrs Bonny at Deloraine, and asked for two case bottles of rum. After these were given to him, he took a ham and a pudding and walked away, saying that he wanted them for his mate who was ill. Although there were five or six men in the bar at the time, no attempt was made to detain him.

On 10 July 1841, Hogan and his mate Armytage visited the Travellers' Rest Inn, within four miles of Launceston. There were eight men in the bar and they took all the money they could get, some grog, and provisions. Hogan said he was tired of the bush, and wished 'it was all over'. Armytage looked ill and miserable. As soon as news of the robbery was conveyed to Launceston the police followed them but without success as the bushrangers were too well acquainted with the country. Nothing further is known about Armytage, who is supposed to have died in the

bush; but Hogan was captured and sentenced to penal servitude on Norfolk Island.

John Gunn, George Griffths, William Lambeth, Samuel Harrison, and Thomas Hurn stuck up and robbed Daniel Downie on 5 September 1842, of clothing and money. They were followed by Constables Patrick Flynn and George Marsden, and a volunteer named Joseph Masson. The bushrangers were armed with a fowling-piece and a musket. They went next morning to the hut of James Thompson, and told him not to be frightened as they did not intend to hurt him. They took his money and were walking away, when the constables came up and called on them to stand. They surrendered and were taken to jail. When they were convicted, sentence of death was recorded against each of them, but they were not hanged.

On 4 May 1843, Mr Thomas Massey, of Ellerslie, South Esk River, was sitting on his verandah when John Conway came up, presented a gun at his head, and cried 'Stand.' 'No, thank you,' replied Mr Massey,

Convict labourers at work on the slopes of Hobart Town, 1828; a watercolour by G. W. Evans.

'I'm very comfortable sitting down. What do you want?' Conway then asked where the hired help was. Mr Massey replied, 'Out in the kitchen.' A man named Riley Jeffs was standing a short distance away with Henry Blunt and a man named Pockett, both of whom had their hands tied behind them. Jeffs left the two tied men and went round to the kitchen, while Conway demanded money and firearms. Jeffs returned with the manservant and tied his hands. The robbers then took two double-barrelled guns, a single-barrelled fowling-piece, with a shot belt and powder flask, some tea, sugar, flour, and a gallon of rum.

After they had gone Constable Thomas Connell, of Campbelltown, with Joseph Masson, Matthew Perry, Edward Quin, Aaron Dunn, and Stephen Wright followed the bushrangers to Blunt's hut, where two men ran away. One of them was lame and was soon caught. It was Jeffs, who said he had accidentally wounded himself the day before, after he left Mr Massey's. The other man, Conway, was captured after a chase. At their trial, Mary Bryan, servant at Mr

Massey's, said she recognized Conway by his big nose. 'How many inches? Did you measure it?' asked Jeffs, but the question was ruled out of order by Judge Montagu. The prisoners were then tried for the murder of Constable William Ward.

They went to Mr James Gilligan's house, Clifton Lodge, Break-o-day Road, and asked Sarah Vasco, the servant, whether anyone was at home. She replied, 'Only master and mistress and a gentleman.' They had four men with their hands tied behind them. Jeffs stopped with these at the kitchen door, while Conway walked into the passage. When he reached the parlour door he presented his gun and cried, 'Stand, or I'll blow the contents of this through you.' Ward, who was sitting near the door, jumped up and grappled with the bushranger. They struggled together into the passage. Mrs Gilligan pushed her husband to prevent him from going out, and slammed the parlour door. Mr. Gilligan heard the struggle along the passage, and then a gun went off. He got the door open at last and went out. He saw Ward lying on the floor of the kitchen. Jeffs and Conway and the four men whose hands were tied were looking at him. Conway said to Gilligan, 'You go back into your room, old man, or I'll mark you.'

In the fight in the passage both of the men had endeavoured to obtain possession of the gun, but between them they let it fall and it exploded without injuring any one. Conway then broke away and ran into the kitchen. Ward followed him and was grappled by Jeffs. While they were wrestling Conway drew a pistol and watched for a chance, and when Ward was on top holding Jeffs down Conway deliberately put the pistol to his shoulder and fired. Ward rolled over dead, and Jeffs got up. The robbers then demanded money, and Mrs Gilligan went to the bedroom upstairs to fetch some. Conway accompanied her. Mrs Gilligan said, 'It's a great pity, Mr Ward had a large family.' 'Well,' replied Conway, 'why didn't he keep out of our road? We tried to shoot him before.'

Jeffs and Conway were hanged at Launceston in July. The *Launceston Advertiser* said that there were more than a thousand men, women, and boys present to see Jeffs and Conway hanged. (An earlier census of the town had shown that the population was 4,458.) Numbers of people took their blankets with them and slept in the square all night. They were singing songs and making a great noise. The paper said the scene was a disgraceful one, and doubted whether such exhibitions could have any beneficial effect.

John Fletcher and Henry Lee stuck up and robbed Daniel Griffin at Cocked Hat Hill, on 6 November 1844. In passing sentence of death, Judge Montagu said that he was determined to put down robbery on the high road between Hobart Town and Launceston, and especially about Cocked Hat Hill. It was a horrid place. No man was safe there. The residents were fortunate in having so active and energetic an officer stationed there as Constable Harvey. He would sentence the prisoners to transportation for life. When they were being removed from court, Lee said as he was passing Constable Harvey: 'I'll rip your —— guts out, you ——, if ever I get out.'

Among the more notorious of the Van Diemen's Land convict bushrangers of later days was Martin Cash, who, first singly, and then in association with Lawrence Kavanagh and Thomas (George) Jones, committed many crimes among the small settlers during 1843.

Cash was transported in 1827 when he was eighteen years old, despite the influence of wealthy and well-connected friends and relations. Through good conduct he gained a ticket-of-leave and eventually his freedom, whereupon he settled down to work as a farm hand in the Hunter River district of New South Wales. But after nine years of quiet, his troubles began.

Martin Cash in his bushranging days

*Right:*
Martin Cash: a photograph taken when he was sixty — and respectable. The most successful of the Van Diemen's Land bushrangers ended his eventful life at the age of sixty-seven on his apple-orchard at Glenorchy, near Hobart, 'in the calm and tranquil enjoyment of rural retirement'.

One morning he was innocently branding cattle for an acquaintance when two strangers rode up, watched the operation, and again rode away. After this the friend told him the cattle were stolen beasts and the men who had ridden away would certainly report what they had seen. Cash was considerably alarmed. 'Norfolk Island for life' was the punishment for illegally branding, and he made up his mind to leave the colony as quickly as possible, taking with him a woman called Bessie Clifford, whom he had induced to leave her husband some time before.

Leaving her at Mudgee, Cash set off to collect for sale some cattle of his own from a distant Namoi station only to find that his treacherous friend of the branding episode had sold them behind his back. Cash accordingly recouped himself from his friend's herd,

sold the animals on his way back to Mudgee, picked up Bessie there and struck southwards to Bathurst.

After narrowly escaping arrest, he and Bessie Clifford took a ship to Hobart Town in 1837, but within twelve months of setting foot in Van Diemen's Land Cash's troubles resumed. On two occasions he was wrongfully charged with theft; and, although the first case against him broke down, he had beaten the arresting constables so badly that he became a 'marked man'. When brought up on the second occasion he was convicted and sentenced to seven years' transportation to one of the penal settlements, some distance from Hobart Town. He had not been there more than a day when he made his escape, having been sent out with a road-making party to draw stones in a handcart. Choosing a suitable spot and a favourable opportunity, he slipped away from his companions and hid in the bush until darkness had set in, when he started on his way back to Campbell Town, where he had left the disconsolate Bessie.

During the night he stealthily entered the kitchen of a settler, appropriated a quantity of provisions, and pursued his journey until daylight, when, having turned off into the bush, he was in the act of cooking at a fire, when he was pounced upon by three soldiers and retaken. For escaping he was subsequently brought before the Police Magistrate at Oatlands, and received an additional sentence of nine months' hard labour in a chain gang, and nine months in a road party.

However, while in goal awaiting transit, he again managed to escape and made his way to Bessie at Campbelltown. The two decided to leave Tasmania for Melbourne as soon as possible and, with a view to raising the necessary cash, went to the Huon.

In this district Cash and his escapades were unknown, and after a year's steady work the money was saved. But justice was not to be baulked; while detained a day or two in Hobart, Cash was recognised, seized by six constables, and again lodged in prison. Tried on the charge of absconding, his twelve month's honest work was put down to 'cleverness'. 'But,' said the presiding magistrate, the well-known John Price, 'you will not best me, Martin' and Cash got two years added to his original sentence, and four years at Port Arthur besides.

Here he met two men, Kavanagh and Jones, who had been transported for robbery under arms, committed near Sydney, and the three plotted a scheme for simultaneous escape. Cash's new comrades relied greatly upon the man who had already proved his ability as an absconder, and said they would trust his guidance.

On the afternoon of Boxing Day Cash, who was one of a gang that drew the stone carts, walked across the quarry and looked steadily at his two mates. At once they dropped their picks and sprang into the scrub, followed by Cash himself. Almost as soon as they

started, their absence was discovered by the sentries; a hue and cry was raised, and the rest of the gang placed under strict guard, while as many soldiers as could be spared set about searching for the runaways. The semaphore signals were also kept in full play, so as to put all the sentries on their guard.

Having picked up some provisions, which had been placed conveniently for them by one of the cooks on the settlement who had been let into the secret, the trio made their way through the scrub to the foot of Mount Arthur. Here they hid for three days, hoping that by that time the sentries at the Neck would have relaxed their vigilance. On the third night they left their hiding place, and worked their way northwards through the scrub, often on hands and knees for a mile at a time, till their clothes were torn to shreds.

At dusk next day they came in sight of Eagle Hawk Neck, and saw that the line was literally swarming with constables and prisoners. They lay concealed for three hours waiting for the coast to become clear, and then, with some trouble, swam the inlet. When they reached the further side each one was stark naked, the clothes having been washed from their heads by the waves which had buffeted them in crossing.

Travelling without boots over rugged ironstone ridges and forging through prickly scrub without clothing to protect the body, were not pleasant exercises. Cash, therefore, led his mates to a roadside hut which he had noted on his last escape, and fortunately reached it when the soldiers and prisoners were absent, except for one man, who acted as cook. The convicts made a simultaneous rush, Kavanagh arming himself with an axe which was standing at the door. The cook, seeing three naked men enter, completely lost his head, and before he could recover his senses was seized and securely lashed to one of the centre posts of the hut. The escapees then helped themselves to clothes, of which there were plenty, belonging to the prisoners who were away at work, as well as to flour, beef, tea, sugar, and a flint and tinder box, and departed.

Next day, when Kavanagh put the question what was to be done, Jones answered, 'Take up arms and stand no repairs,' and to this they all agreed, though the decision meant certain death if they were ever caught. Their next move, therefore, was towards the more settled districts in the valley of the Derwent. At

**Eagle Hawk Neck, a contemporary sketch showing the guard positions. The narrow isthmus joins the Tasman Peninsula to the Forestier Peninsula of the mainland. The penitentiary was on the Tasman Peninsula, and on Eagle Hawk Neck, the only land exit, a row of dogs and guards (right) effectively prevented the escape of convicts. Cash by-passed the barrier by swimming around the southern flank.**

*Below:*
**Sir John and Lady Franklin inspect the line of guard dogs across Eagle Hawk Neck, 1840.**

Pittwater they obtained provisions from a hut, and proceeded towards Jerusalem, securing on their way a couple of guns, with ammunition, and some decent clothes. At Jerusalem a third gun and more provisions were obtained, and a complete outfit of clothes for each of them at the Bagdad public house. Still making westward, they stuck up a farmer's house at Broadmarsh, and then camped for a few days to prepare for more serious business.

They now decided to attack the Woolpack Inn, about ten miles from New Norfolk, but before reaching the place they fell in with a convict shepherd who told them that they would encounter an armed party at the inn, as a party of constables were stationed there. To this Cash replied that an encounter would suit them very well, as it would give them an opportunity of proving their arms.

Having planted their swag about a quarter of a mile away, they took the nearest road to the inn, and immediately 'bailed up' the landlady, her two sons, and three men who were drinking there. While dealing with them people were seen moving outside; these proved to be an advancing party of constables, who had been made aware of the presence of the three desperadoes.

The latter at once marched outside the house, Cash taking the lead. The leader of the constables challenged Cash to stand. He stood, but only to take surer aim, and the challenger fell. There was an exchange of shots, but the darkness prevented any proper aim, and no damage was done on either side. Kavanagh and Jones now retired without acquainting their leader of the fact, and when he turned to speak to them he found that he was alone. He then retreated to the house, the constables apparently not caring to follow, and having secured a keg of brandy got out into the darkness and started for the spot where the swag had been left. Here he found his two companions; and after holding a 'council of war', and testing the quality of the brandy, the gang went into hiding at the Dromedary, a rocky outcrop nearby. Three days later, after pillaging a farmhouse for provisions, they reached the house of an old acquaintance of Cash's, who entertained them on the best and promised to take a message to the town for Bessie Clifford, who was residing there. On the way they learned that two of the constables had been seriously wounded by their fire, but not fatally. Next morning the promise was fulfilled and Bessie joined the party, who had in the meantime made a kind of fortress of logs for themselves on the top of the Dromedary.

After the party had remained at the fortress for three days, they learned that a detachment of H.M. 51st King's Own Light Infantry under Major Ainsworth were scouring the bush in search of them. They decided to remain in hiding for a few days longer, and in order that Bessie might not be exposed to danger in case of an attack they escorted her part of

the way into the town and then left her. But the police were on the watch, and she had not been long in town before she was arrested.

A few days afterwards Cash and his colleagues attacked the residence of Mr Charles Kerr, in the Hamilton district. On the morning of their arrival they secured two of Mr Kerr's shepherds, who gave them the necessary information concerning their master's premises and the number of hands in his employ, together with similar information concerning other neighbouring settlers. Going up to the house with these two men about dusk they were met by a young lady, who immediately ran back crying 'Here are the bushrangers', and then fainted.

Leaving Kavanagh in charge of the men in the kitchen, Cash repaired to the drawing-room where he found Mrs Kerr and the young lady, whom he urged not to be alarmed, as they should not be subjected to any insult. At Cash's request Mrs Kerr pointed out the men's hut, and Cash and Kavanagh went there to find Mr Kerr and three working hands. When the whole of the occupants had been placed in one room, the robbers released Mr Kerr and permitted him to sit down in the room, after which Jones, having produced

**Hobart Town about 1830. The settlement had changed little when Martin Cash and Bessie Clifford arrived there from New South Wales seven years later.**

*Right:*
**The entrance hall of the Port Arthur penitentiary**

*Below:*
**The prisoners' mess room at Port Arthur, where Martin Cash was, for a time, an inmate**

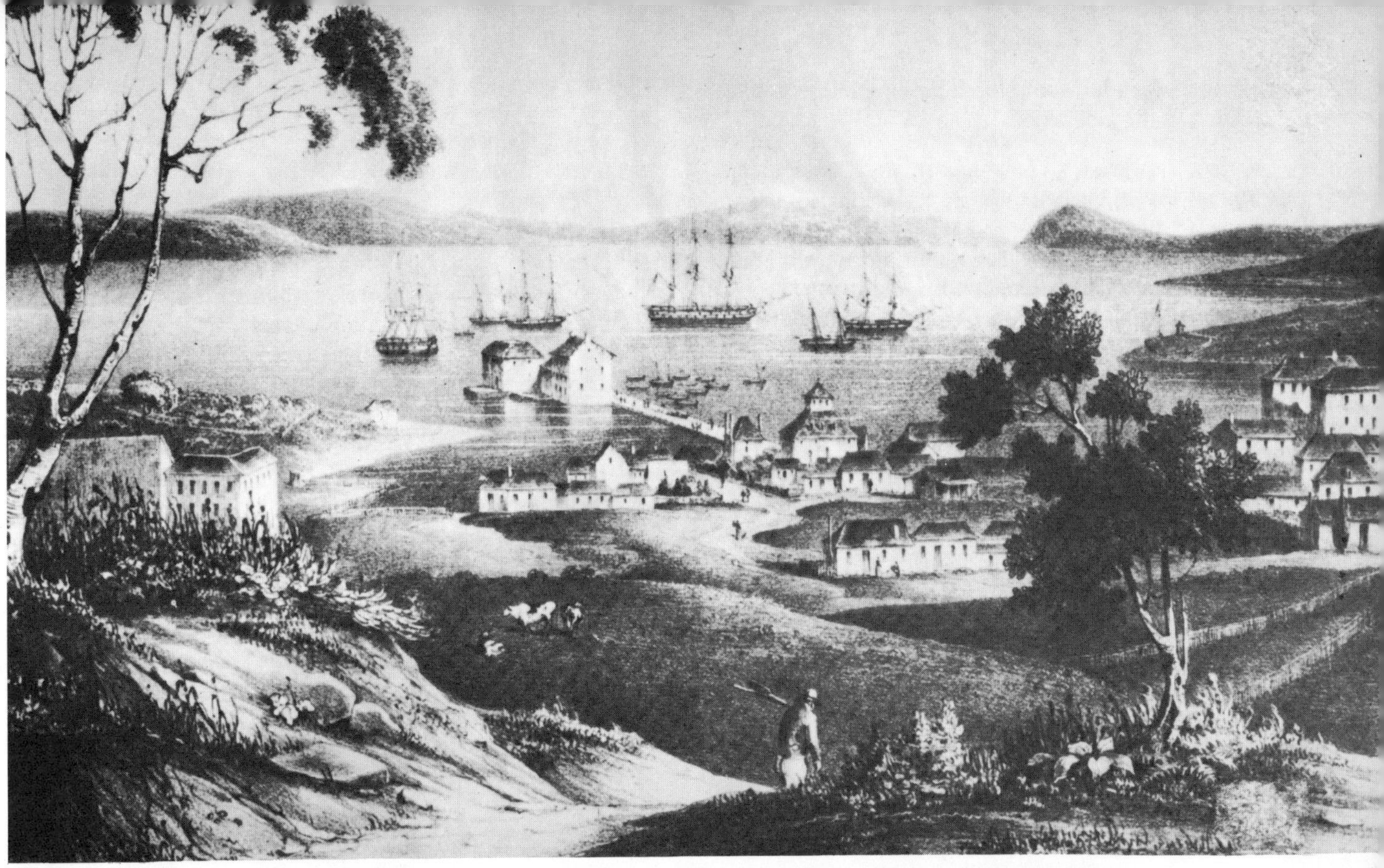

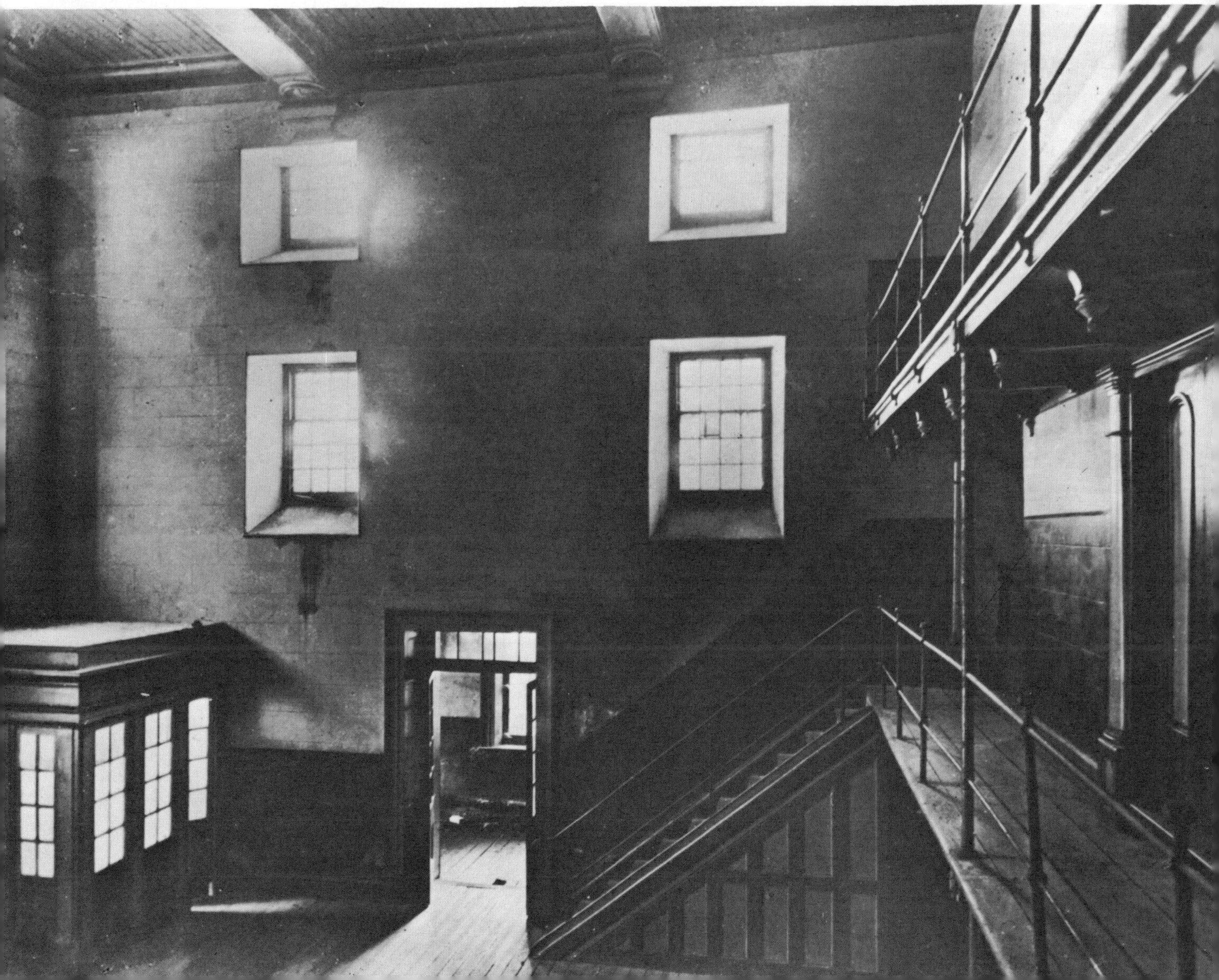

writing materials, wrote the following letter to his Excellency the Governor:

'Messrs. Cash and Co. beg to notify his Excellency Sir John Franklin and his satellites that a very respectable person named Mrs. Cash is now falsely imprisoned in Hobart Town, and if the said Mrs. Cash is not released forthwith, and properly remunerated, we will, in the first instance, visit government House, and beginning with Sir John, administer a wholesome lesson in the shape of a sound flogging; after which we will pay the same currency to all his followers.

'Given under our hands, this day, at the residence of Mr. Kerr, of Dunrobin.

CASH<br>
KAVANAGH<br>
JONES

Two more attacks on stations in the Hamilton district brought the gang so much spoil that they determined to rest awhile at their friend's house under the Dromedary, where they had an old Irish fiddler to play to them.

On 2 April 1842, it was reported that Martin Cash had been captured in a house in Harrington Street, Hobart Town, by Constables Kirby and Williams. He was lodged in the lock-up, but during the night succeeded in making his escape.

On 25 March 1843, Cash, Kavanagh and Jones, armed 'to the teeth', bailed up Mr Panton at Broad Marsh, and fired at Dr Macdonald. The police started in pursuit. On 18 April, the gang visited Mr Hay, who was in his barn overlooking five shearers who were at work. They were ordered to stand up and put down their shears. Then the men were forced to tie each other. While the bushrangers were plundering the house, Mr Ward came up. He was ordered to stand, but instead of obeying he ran away. Cash followed and fired his pistol, the shot grazing Ward's ear. Ward, however, kept on and hid behind a tree. The bushrangers decamped, taking very little plunder with them.

On the 19th they captured Mr John Clark and his overseer, Mr Denholme, and compelled them to accompany the bushrangers to the late Mr Allardyce's house on the Clyde River. They went into the parlour, and after arranging the chairs, invited the gentlemen to sit down. Then they called for brandy and glasses. The servant brought in a bottle of brandy and a tin pannikin. Cash was in a great rage. He swore at the servant, and asked him in an indignant tone, 'Is that a proper thing for gentlemen to drink out of? Take it away and bring glasses.'

When they had had some refreshments, Cash sat talking to Messrs Clarke and Denholme, while Kavanagh and Jones collected the plunder. The bushrangers were said to be very haggard in appearance and not well dressed.

On 18 May they invited themselves to visit Captain McKay, on the Dee River, and dined with him in the

REW
FIFTY SOVEREIGNS,

WHEREAS the three Convicts (Runawa JONES, and LAWRENCE KAVENAGH having committed divers Capital Felonies, and I am authorised by His Excellency the Lieuter to any person or persons who shall apprehend either of the said Felons; and should this servi pecuniary Reward, a CONDITIONAL PAI

19th January, 1843.

DESCRIPTION OF TH

Martin Cash, per Francis Freeling, tried at Launceston Q. S., 24th Mar head small and round, hair curly and carroty, whiskers red small, forehead remarkably long feet, a very swift runner.

Lawrence Kavenagh, per Marian Watson, tried at Sydney, 12th April 184 grey, whiskers brown, visage long, forehead high, eyebrows brown, eyes lig Remarks A. D. above elbow joint left arm, 2 scars on palm of left hand, l

George Jones, per Marian Watson, tried at Sydney, 14th April 1842, life, whiskers brown, visage long, forehead perpendicular, eyebrows brown, eyes H. W. anchor on right arm, breast hairy.

most amicable manner. After dinner they loaded two horses with clothing, provisions, and other articles from the store. Then, taking Captain McKay with them, they went to Mr Gellibrand's, where they loaded a third horse. With this the bushrangers appear to have been satisfied, as they went away.

'Messrs Cash & Co.', as some of the Van Diemen's Land papers called the gang, visited Mr Christopher Gatenby, of the Isis, on 1 July, and politely apologised for their intrusion. Just as politely they asked for a supply of provisions, which they said were necessary owing to the police having recently captured their camp and taken away all that they could find there. Mr Gatenby opened the store and gave what they required, and then Cash said he should feel extremely obliged if Mr Gatenby and four of his servants would carry the provisions to their new camp. He explained that this was necessary, as the police had taken their horses.

The invitation was so pressing that Mr Gatenby could not refuse. He took up a portion of the swag, while his servants shouldered the rest, and escorted by the three bushrangers they started into the bush. After walking for about two miles Cash said he would not trouble Mr Gatenby to go any farther, as he

**ARD!**

**l a Conditional Pardon.**

Port Arthur) MARTIN CASH, GEORGE
descriptions are as under, stand charged with
w illegally at large: This is to give Notice, that
vernor to offer a Reward of Fifty Sovereigns
to be apprehended and lodged in safe custody
rformed by a Convict, then, in addition to such

**M. FORSTER,**
Chief Police Magistrate.

**E-NAMED CONVICTS.**

ars, labourer, 6 feet, age 33, native place Wexford, complexion very ruddy,
s red, eyes blue small, nose small, mouth large, chin small. Remarks

mason, 5 feet 10½, age 30, complexion pale, head long large, hair brown to
e long and sharp, mouth and chin medium size, native place Wicklow
r on right hand.

feet 7, age 27, complexion ruddy fair, freckled, head long, hair brown,
nedium, mouth medium, chin pointed, native place Westminster. Remarks

JAMES BARNARD, GOVERNMENT PRINTER, HOBART TOWN

**An 1843 police poster offering rewards for the capture of
Cash, Kavanagh and Jones**

thought that they could manage without him. The load
he was carrying was distributed among the
bushrangers, and Mr Gatenby returned home, after
having been profusely thanked for his generosity in
giving them the provisions and his kindness in carrying
them so far. The servants were taken two or three
miles farther into the bush, and were then allowed to
deposit their loads under a gum tree and return home.
Cash denied that the gang had had an encounter with
the Campbelltown constables. He said that the
constables found their hiding place when he and his
mates were absent.

From his old camp under the Dromedary, Cash
learned from the papers that Bessie had been released
by the Governor, and he flattered himself that this was
the result of the threatening letter he had sent to his
Excellency shortly after the arrest of that lady; but the
truth of the matter was that she had been liberated in
the hope that some clue to Cash's movements might be
obtained through her, and that he might be even
induced to visit Hobart Town if he learned that she
was living there in freedom.

At last, on 22 August 1843, Cash made up his mind to
visit Hobart and look for Bessie as it was rumoured
that she had deserted him for another. Disguised as
sailors, he and Kavanagh arrived safely in town,
looked up their friend the old fiddler, and started with
him to find Bessie's house. Unfortunately they were
compelled to ask directions of a man in the street. The
man at once pointed out the house, but at the same
time called out to another man standing near, 'This is
the party we are looking for', at which Cash made off,
the two men following him, and firing at him as he ran.
The ensuing events were reported by the Hobart
Town *Review*:

By this time a number of persons had joined in the
pursuit, and the alarm increasing, a man named
Cunliffe, a carpenter, came from his house as he
passed, and lifting his hand Cash discharged his
pistol, which wounded Cunliffe in the fingers. Cash
then crossed Elizabeth-street and ran along
Brisbane-street, making for the paddock, and as he
passed the public-house called the Commodore,
opposite Trinity Church, one of the Penitentiary
constables, named Winstanley, seized him. A
struggle ensued, when Cash drew a pistol and shot
him through the body: he died the next day. A
person named Oldfield coming up, Cash fired at him,
wounding him in the face. At this moment another
man tripped him up, and a number of persons
arriving, he was handcuffed, but not until he had
made much resistance, in the course of which he
was much beaten. He was then taken to the
Penitentiary to be identified, but he was so
disfigured in the struggle to capture him that Mr.
Gunn could not then recognise him. He was,
however, conveyed to the gaol, no doubt existing of
his identity.

Kavanagh was wounded in a gun battle soon after,
and surrendered to a magistrate. Then a week after
Cash's capture the *Review* contained the following:

Cash and Kavanagh. — We have already
furnished our readers with full particulars of the
capture of these unfortunate men. They were both
tried separately yesterday — Cash, for the murder
of the constable (Winstanley); Kavanagh, for the
robbing of the Launceston coach. Cash was
defended by the late Attorney-General, Mr. Edward
Macdowell, who, although evidently labouring (we
sincerely regret to say) under severe indisposition,
yet defended the unhappy man with his usual
zealous judgment. The jury found both prisoners
guilty, but a point of law, as to whether Winstanley
knew Cash to be a proscribed absentee when he met
his death — whether the melancholy event,
deplorable as it was, could be wilful murder, a chief
element of which is malice prepense, and on some
other subjects, is reserved for the decision of both
judges.

Cash had walked into the dock in the most
unconcerned manner, and stood during the trial with
his arms folded. He was dressed in blue jacket and
trousers, and blue striped shirt, a black handkerchief

65

round his neck, and a green one round his head to cover up the wounds he had received at the time of his capture. He said he had been standing quietly in the street when a constable came up and cried out, 'It's Cash, blow his brains out'. He had then fired and run. The constables were all cowards. They thronged round him when he was down, but they would never have caught him if it had not been for Cunliffe. Judge Montagu said in reply that he could see no proof of cowardice in the action of the police. They were not such fast runners as the prisoner. Charles Cunliffe was the more active, and consequently he had caught the prisoner first. For this he deserved credit, but the police had arrived at the spot without delay and were also to be complimented for their share in the capture of so dangerous a character as the prisoner. He then sentenced the prisoner to be hanged on Monday, the 18th instant.

The indictment against him was drawn up in the usual elaborate manner, charging him 'for that he did, on the 29th August, with a certain pistol of the value of five shillings, being then and there loaded with gunpowder, which gunpowder exploded and discharged a leaden bullet, which did strike, prostrate and wound the left breast of the said Peter Winstanley, of which wound he died on the 31st August.'

On conviction Cash and Kavanagh were removed to the cells to await execution, but two days before the time arrived they were informed that the sentence of death had been commuted to transportation to Norfolk Island for life.

Here Kavanagh was hanged within a year for joining in a mutiny; Cash, however, after many ups and downs, and (if we can believe his own story at all) a great deal of petty persecution from the Commandant, John Price, managed to escape the utmost penalty. Through the instrumentality of the commandant who succeeded Price, a petition for a remission of his sentence was favourably received. He served for a time as constable at the Cascade, and having married a convict servant of the resident surgeon on Norfolk Island, he went back to Van Diemen's Land when the establishment at the island was broken up. Here for a time he served as caretaker at the Government Gardens, and subsequently went to New Zealand, where he managed to accumulate a little property. After residing there for four years he returned to Tasmania, and purchased a farm at Glenorchy, near Hobart, where he passed the remainder of his days 'in the calm and tranquil enjoyment of rural retirement'.

After the capture of Cash and Kavanagh, Jones, the remaining member of the infamous 'Cash & Co.', endeavoured to form a new gang. On 6 December 1843 in company with John Liddell and James Dalton he stuck up Catherine Smith's house at Effingham Banks. They tied the servants and went into Mrs Smith's bedroom. The lady requested them to go out while she

66

dressed, and they complied. When Mrs Smith got up the bushrangers ordered the servants to get them some supper, telling them that they need not be afraid, as nobody would hurt them. They made the servants sit down while they ate. After their meal they opened the drawers and took out clothes and other articles which suited them, and went away.

On 11 December they stuck up a hawker named John McCall. They drove his cart half a mile into the bush off the road, and tied McCall to a tree. Then they made a bundle of the articles they wanted in the cart, and went away.

On 30 December, Thomas Jones, 'late with Messrs Cash & Co.', with another man named Moore, dressed as sporting gentlemen, went to Mr William Field's and inquired if he was in. When they were told he was not, they went to the men's hut and bailed up the two men there. As the others came in they were compelled to stand in a row against the wall. When Mr Shanklin, the overseer, came in, Moore told him to kneel down and say his prayers as he intended to shoot him. The men interceded for the overseer, saying that he always had treated them well. Moore asserted that Shanklin had 'got him an extension of time', and he meant to have revenge. He was very violent in his language.

Jones had been looking on very quietly, but he now said, 'Oh, let the —— go, and let him beware how he behaves in the future'. Moore at first objected, but gave way, and Shanklin was made to stand up with the

The headstone on Martin Cash's grave salutes the memory of 'that brave but unfortunate *Irishman*'.

*Left:*

The penal settlement at Port Arthur in 1859, during occupation. Notorious for bad conditions and difficulty of escape, the prison was abandoned in 1877.

assigned servants. The robbers broke open Mr Field's desk and took £50 out of it. They also took tea, sugar, flour, and other things from the store.

In the meantime the police had not been idle. They had had several brushes with the bushrangers, and had captured Liddell and Dalton. After this last robbery secret information was given to the authorities, who set a watch and trapped the whole party of bushrangers in the hut of the man who had been harbouring them on the Dromedary. Moore, one of the gang, crept outside the hut on his hands and knees, and was immediately shot by one of the constables. Jones came out next, and received a heavy charge of shot in the face, which blinded him, rendering his capture an easy matter. The other bushranger, Platt, was taken without being injured.

Jones and all his associates, including Liddell and Dalton were eventually tried and sentenced to death, but were told that probably their sentences would be commuted to penal servitude. On hearing this Liddell exclaimed, 'I don't want mercy from you or any one else. I've been eleven years at Port Arthur and I don't want to go there again. I'd rather die than live.'

Judge Montagu said that this statement showed a deplorable frame of mind and exhorted Liddell to think of the future. Dalton complained that he had been knocked down by Thompson, the jailer. Mr Thompson said that the prisoner was a very desperate man. 'But you'd no right to put irons on my neck,' cried Dalton.

The judge said it was the duty of the jailer to prevent escape. If he deemed it necessary he had a perfect right to put irons on the neck of a prisoner as well as on his hands and feet. He should report the behaviour of the prisoners in the proper quarter and he could not recommend either Liddell or Dalton to mercy. 'I don't care a —— what you do,' exclaimed Dalton.

George Cumsden, who had also been associated with Jones in some of his robberies since the capture of Cash and Kavanagh, was also sentenced to death, 'without the hope of mercy'. He had threatened to 'blow a hole through' any witness who appeared against him.

There was again a lull in bushranging in Van Diemen's Land, and again the papers asserted that the crime had been stamped out. The majority of those convicted had been sent to Norfolk Island, and this, it was said, would act as a deterrent to other trouble makers. Norfolk Island was feared more than death.

# 10 Gold mania

**The gold-digging era; influx of convicts from Van Diemen's Land; passing of the Criminals' Influx Prevention Act; attitude of the diggers to bushrangers and other thieves; the Nelson gold robbery; insecurity of the Melbourne streets.**

Before entering upon the next stage in the story of the bushrangers, it may be advisable to say something of the vast change which suddenly took place in the conditions in Australia about this time. In 1842-3 the colony of New South Wales was plunged into a financial crisis, about which it is unnecessary to say much here, but from which the colony was only beginning to recover in 1851. Wages were still very low, and numbers of men were out of work.

In April 1851, the news that gold had been discovered at Summerhill Creek, in the Bathurst district, roused something like a ferment in the colony. Men employed in Sydney threw down their tools to 'go to the diggings'. There was a general exodus from the coast cities and towns to the ranges, then considered far away in the interior. Wages jumped from about one shilling per day for labour to ten or more, meat rose from one penny per pound for the best cuts, to sixpence. The roads leading to Orange, the Turon, and other early goldfields in New South Wales, were thronged by men, either going to the diggings to seek their fortune, or returning disappointed. In July 1851, the Port Phillip district of New South Wales became the independent colony of Victoria, and in August the news that gold had been struck in the Ballarat district of the newly-established colony turned the tide of gold-seekers in that direction. The original police establishment could not cope with a huge sparsely-populated colony, and was wholly inadequate to the requirements.

There were two jails in the colony; one at Melbourne the other at Geelong; neither of them very large. The Geelong jail, in fact, was little more than a lockdup, and had only recently been enclosed within a high wall. The Melbourne jail stood on what was then the boundary of the city of Melbourne. It was a larger and more imposing building than the Geelong jail, but still wholly inadequate for the requirements, and therefore one of the first duties of the Legislative Council of the new colony was to provide accommodation for evil doers, who could no longer be sent to the jails of Sydney to serve out their terms of punishment. This was done by the establishment of 'stockades' at Collingwood and Pentridge, both near Melbourne, and the purchase of two old trading vessels, the *President* and the *Success*, in September 1852, to be converted into convict hulks for the safe keeping of the more desperate of the malefactors. Subsequently three other hulks were added to the list, and these were in use for many years after large prisons had been erected at Melbourne, Geelong, Ballarat, Bendigo, and other centres.

Looking back, it appears that the Colonial Office was guilty of a serious tactical blunder in appointing Mr Charles Joseph Latrobe as the first Governor of Victoria. He had been appointed Resident Magistrate, or superintendent, of the Port Phillip District in 1839, and during the agitation for the separation of that district Mr Latrobe, very naturally perhaps, did all that he could to prevent the inhabitants from gaining their end. Consequently he was perhaps the most hated man that has ever lived in Australia. He was usually called 'the Governor's poodle', and was vehemently denounced by the advocates of separation. When that was carried, and Mr Latrobe became Lieutenant Governor, his harsh treatment of the diggers nearly drove them into rebellion.

This is not the place to give the history of the Ballarat riot, but some reference to it is necessary. A most exhorbitant licence fee was imposed on all residents on proclaimed goldfields, and this tax was collected in a most arbitrary and brutal manner. There were no jails nor lockups on the diggings at the time, and men arrested for all sorts of offences — murder, bushranging, stealing, or the non-payment of licence fees — were simply fastened with handcuffs to a bullock chain attached to a tree stump by a huge

The increasing numbers of convicts flowing into Victoria during the 1850s prompted the authorities to acquire five prison hulks, and in six years over 5,000 convicts passed through these floating cells of despair. The best-known of these vessels, the *Success* (pictured), later became a touring sideshow of the convict days.

**C. J. Latrobe**

staple. Later, some boxes made of corrugated iron were put up as cells and these were known as 'the Dutch ovens', or 'the sardine boxes'. Prisoners confined in them on hot summer nights suffered tortures, and begged to be put 'on the chain' as a relief.

Mr Latrobe soon came to be as hated by the new-comers as he had been by the older inhabitants of the district. But whatever may be said as to the harshness of his treatment of the gold diggers, the efforts he made to check the lawlessness rampant in the colony cannot be too highly commended. He and the Legislative Council organized a fine body of police in a very short time. The horse police were as well-disciplined and mounted as any similar body in any part of the world, but allowing for their efficiency, it would have been impossible for them to repress lawlessness as rapidly and completely as they did, had they not been assisted by the attitude of the general public.

The antagonism between the free and the convict elements in the population, of which I have already spoken, was continued long after the abolition of the convict system, and even passed on to those who landed in the country during the rush to the diggings. There was a general tendency at the time to credit all sorts of misdeeds to the convicts; it was the custom to assume that all crimes were committed by the 'old hands', and that any man arrested for any criminal offence had been 'sent out'. Thus, when Mr Lachlan McLachlan was appointed police magistrate of

Bendigo, he merely expressed openly the opinion held by other magistrates, and the public generally, when he declared that nearly all thefts were perpetrated by 'old hands'. He asserted that he could distinguish a convict from a freeman at a glance. He would order the police to make the prisoner walk down the court, and would exclaim: 'Turn him round again, sergeant. Ah! I thought so! I can see the marks of the irons on his legs.'[1]

By this he meant that the man had acquired a sort of limp through wearing irons, and that he could detect it. All such men were sent to jail for six or twelve months, not so much for the crime or offence with which they stood charged, as because they were ex-convicts. Generally the public endorsed this apparent injustice. 'It's a pity we ain't got more magistrates like Bendigo Mac' was an expression frequently heard in all parts of the colony.

It is possible that the fashion of crediting all crimes and offences to convicts, however unjust it may have been, tended to prevent others from committing crimes. Whether this was so or not, it is certain that the diggers steadily set their faces, as a class, against crime. They never hesitated, even during the height of their dispute with the authorities, to hand over to the police any person detected stealing. Probably they were forced into this attitude in self-defence. The diggings were merely huge camps, everybody living in tents or 'houses' made of wooden rafters and uprights, covered with calico or canvas. Even the big hotels and theatres were calico structures. It was so easy for a person to rip open a tent and thrust his hand under the pillow or into any other place where he thought gold might be concealed.

But such thefts, although numerous, constituted only a minority of the crimes committed on the goldfields. All round were holes twenty or thirty feet deep, and the paths from one part of the field to another wound in and out between these holes so that it was dangerous for a stranger to travel about after dark. It was so easy to stab a man and throw his body down a hole that the very facilities offered operated as a temptation to murder. Scarcely a day passed without a body being found murdered and rifled. Thus a peculiar sort of morality was developed on the diggings and the diggers, while resisting the police, jeering at them and showing their hatred of them in every possible way, still assisted them in capturing thieves and other criminals.

Beyond the limits of the goldfields the roads were infested by footpads and bushrangers who hated the diggers for their antagonism to their class. To them the digger was fair game. It was popularly supposed that these bushrangers were all convicts from Van Diemen's Land, hence they were known as 'Van Demonians', 'Derwenters' from the River Derwent and 'Tother siders'. The newspapers were full of references to their doings. The *Geelong Advertiser* of

The Mount Alexander gold escort *en route* to Melbourne, 1853. The provision of armed, mounted troopers did not, however, render gold coaches safe from bushrangers.

2 June 1851, warned the public that 'large numbers of men — half bushranger, half goldseeker — are travelling along the roads, especially the Sydney road, robbing all who are unprotected'. These were said to be Van Demonians who had landed in Geelong or Melbourne, and who were making their way to the goldfields of New South Wales. In the same month the Melbourne *Herald* published several articles calling the attention of the authorities to the large 'influx of Van Diemen's Land expirees who are thronging into Port Phillip'. These 'villains', it was said, were travelling along all the roads which led to the diggings on the Sydney side, and lived by plundering honest travellers.

On 23 June the mail coach was bailed up at Bruce's Creek, between Portland and Geelong. The coach, with three passengers on board, was going down the hill to the crossing-place, when two men stepped from behind gum trees, presented their pistols, and cried 'Bail up'. The driver, William Freere, instead of complying began to flog his horses, but before they could respond their heads were seized by one of the bushrangers, while the other put his pistol to Freere's head, and threatened to blow his brains out. The coach was taken some distance off the road, and its occupants were tied to trees.

The robbers went very leisurely through the letters, and when all that was of value had been extracted one of the bushrangers took a saddle and bridle belonging

to one of the passengers, Thomas Gibson, and set it aside with the remark, 'Ah, this is just what I wanted'. This bushranger was dressed 'in a black suit of fashionable cut, and wore black kid gloves'. He was afterwards identified as Owen Suffolk, while his companion was Christopher Farrell.

Suffolk took one of the coach-horses, put the saddle and bridle on, and mounted. Farrell jumped on the other horse barebacked. The tied men begged hard to be let loose, offering to swear that they would not give information to the police, or move from the spot until their captors were away, but their requests were only laughed at. The road was little used at that time and the next mail, which might possibly be the first vehicle to pass, would not come for a week. Moreover, they were out of sight of the road. The struggle to get free was therefore a struggle for life, and it was a severe one. Gibson was the first to get one hand loose. After this the rest was comparatively easy. In less than an hour they were all free, and they walked straight to the township at Bruce's Creek to tell the police. The robbers were caught in Geelong a day or two later. Suffolk was strolling along the beach near the wharf, and Farrell was found in a boarding-house not far away. They were sentenced to ten years' servitude.

71

**Geelong in the 1850s**

On 28 January 1852, the Melbourne *Herald* reported that 'a gang of Vandemonians have kept the road between Bendigo and Eaglehawk Gully for three days, robbing all who passed'. The police were sent out and the gang was broken up. One was shot and three others traced to Halliday's Inn at Kyneton, where they were captured. They had thirty-three pounds weight of gold in their possession, and were taken on to Melbourne for trial.

Such reports were so frequent that the Legislative Council was compelled to take action, and as a consequence the Act known as the Criminals' Influx Prevention Act (18 Vic., No. 3) was passed in November. This Act was specially designed to keep ex-convicts out of the colony. It was impossible to prevent those from New South Wales from crossing the Murray River, but it no doubt checked the influx of the more desperate criminals from Van Diemen's Land, where transportation was continued for many years after it had ceased to New South Wales. Although the Act prevented ex-convicts from landing at Victorian ports it could not prevent them landing at Sydney or Adelaide and walking overland to the Victorian diggings. In spite of this the Act was undoubtedly very effective in checking the landing of criminally-minded persons. There were, however, so many in the colony prior to the passing of the Act that the police had plenty of employment in hunting them down.

But to return to the knights of the road. A pitiful story was told of an old man and his son who had left their work in Melbourne, and gone to the diggings to 'make their pile'. They were unsuccessful, like a good many more, and started to walk back to Melbourne to return to their ordinary work. They were bailed up on the edge of the Black Forest. The bushrangers refused to believe that they had no gold. It was a stale trick they said, to throw a bag of gold behind a log and swear they hadn't got any, and then go back and pick it up when the bushrangers had gone away. It was in vain that the old man swore that he had no gold to throw away. One of the bushrangers compelled him to hold out his hand and fired a bullet through the palm. As he continued to declare that he had no gold the bushranger was about to shoot through the palm of the other hand, when the boy made a rush at him and was shot dead by the other bushranger. The old man was then allowed to go his sorrowful way.

Bushranging was the common subject of conversation. Little else was talked of, and even the children played bushranger. Two young lads thought it would be good fun to 'stick up' their father. He was a farmer living on the Barrabool Hills, about eight or nine miles from Geelong. He went into town with some produce and was returning at nightfall. When about half-a-mile from his own gateway, he was ordered to bail up by two persons on horseback. Without hesitation he snatched up a gun from the bottom of the dray and fired. One of the bushrangers fell and the other cried out, 'Oh, father, you've shot Johnny! We were only in fun'. It was too late. The father's aim had been too sure and the boy was taken home to his mother dead.

On 24 October 1852, Henry Johnston, John Finegan, John Donovan, Charles Bowe, and John Baylie, known as the Eureka gang, were tried for highway robbery in Melbourne. William Cook said he was riding from Melbourne to Bendigo, on 4 August, when he was bailed up by Finegan and Donovan near Aitken's Gap. Three other men sat on their horses some distance away along the road, but did not interfere. One of the bushrangers held a pistol to his head, while the other stripped him naked and searched his clothes. He also felt him all over, under the armpits and elsewhere. They took £2 14s. and a pistol from him. Finegan wanted to take everything, but Donovan would not agree to that and gave him back his clothes. Then he returned one of the £1 notes and the fourteen shillings in silver.

Welsley Anderson identified Baylie and Donovan as the two men who had robbed him on a Sunday in August, near Buninyong. The proceedings were very similar to those in the first case. All the other prisoners were identified by witnesses. The robberies had been committed over a wide range of country, and were all of a similar character. When asked what they had to say in defence, one of the prisoners asked the Judge whether he thought they were crows. 'Here's one man' ,he continued, 'says we stuck him up at Aitken's Gap, another at the Porcupine, another near Mount Egerton, and others at other places, and the police says they caught us in the Crown Hotel, Buninyong. Why, your Honour, horses couldn't get over the ground in the time'. The jury, however, seemed to have formed a better opinion of the power of the bushrangers' horses. Finegan and Donovan, who appeared to have been the leaders and to have taken part in the majority of the robberies, were sent to jail for twelve years, and the others for six years each.

# 11 Captain Melville's daring

**Captain Melville's exploits and sensational capture; condemned to the prison hulks; Melville associated with two riots and the murder of John Price whilst on the hulks; removed to the Melbourne goal.**

Of all the bushrangers of the 'roaring fifties' none was more talked of than Frank McCallum, alias Captain Melville. Every now and then, during the latter half of the year 1852, stories were told of daring robberies committed by Captain Melville, and rewards were offered for the capture of the captain, dead or alive, or any person who aided and abetted him. On 18 December 1852, he rode up to a sheep station near Wardy Yallock and asked Mr Wilson, the overseer, who was the owner. 'Mr Aitcheson,' was the reply. 'Is he at home?' asked Melville.

Mr Wilson having no suspicion as to who the civilly spoken visitor was, went into the house and returned with Mr Aitcheson. Melville drew out a pistol, pointed it towards them, and ordered them to 'put up' their hands. The two gentlemen complied at once and were marched to the wool-shed. Here they found the sixteen shearers and other workmen sitting in a row down the middle of the shearing floor and William Roberts, Melville's mate, standing sentry over them pistol in hand. Aitcheson and Wilson were conducted to the head of the row and ordered to seat themselves, which they did. Melville then searched about until he found a rope. This he cut into lengths and then mounted guard while Roberts called the prisoners out one by one and tied them to the fence. Mr Aitcheson asked Melville what he wanted, and the bushranger replied, 'Gold and horses, and we're going to get them.'

When all the men were securely tied the bushrangers cautioned them not to attempt to get loose until permission was given and then walked to the house. Melville told Mrs Aitcheson not to be afraid as he never interfered with ladies any more than was necessary. He told all the women and girls to go into one room. One of the women was told to get some food ready and part of this was taken, with two bottles of brandy, to the men at the shed. Melville and Roberts both ate heartily. They searched the house thoroughly, and took all the money and jewellery they could find. They picked out two fine horses with saddles and bridles, and when mounted they stopped at the wool-shed to bid good-bye to Mr Aitcheson and their 'other friends'. Melville informed them that Mrs Aitcheson

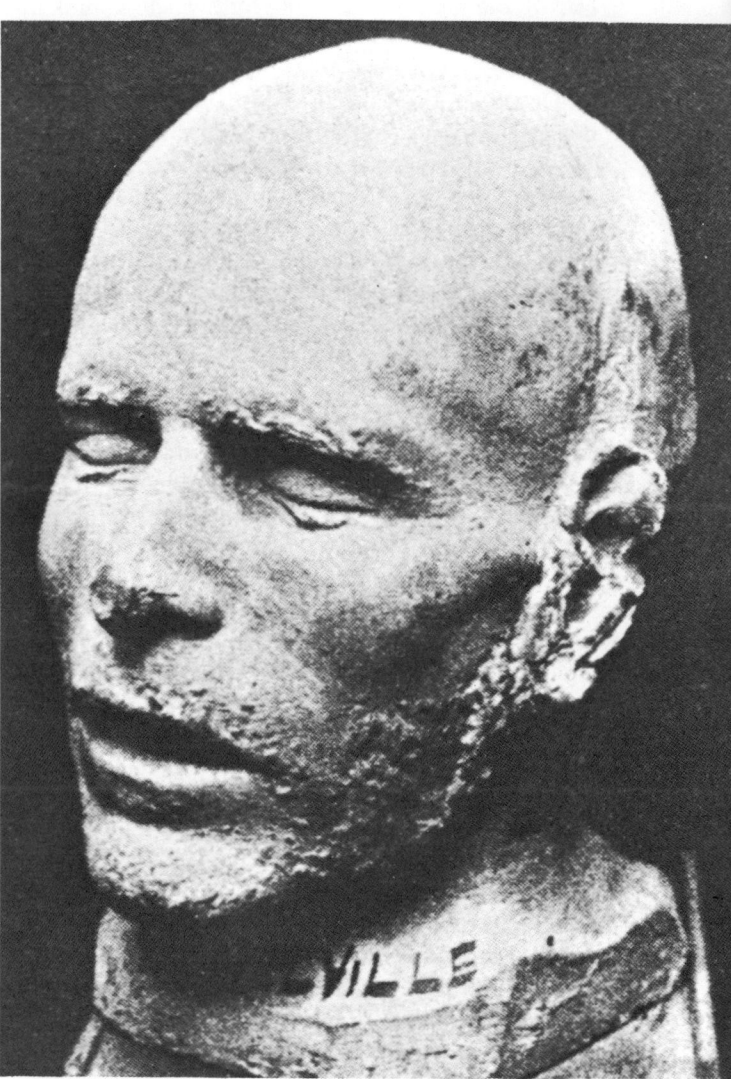

The death mask of Frank McCallum, *alias* 'Captain Melville'

would come and untie them as soon as he and his mate were out of sight along the road.

The boldness with which this robbery was conceived and carried out caused quite an excitement throughout the colony. The idea of eighteen men permitting two to tie and rob them without a struggle caused as much amusement perhaps as wonder. People

73

talked of little else for days, and everywhere the question was asked, 'What next?' This, however, was not all. After leaving the station the bushrangers only travelled a few miles and camped in the bush. The following morning they stuck up two diggers, Thomas Wearne and William Madden, on the Ballarat Road, and robbed them of £33. After taking the money, Melville asked them where they were going. 'To Geelong to see our friends, and spend Christmas. But now we shall have to go back to the diggings,' was the reply. Melville drew Roberts apart. After a brief conversation he came back, handed the diggers a £10 note, and hoped that would be sufficient to enable them to enjoy their holidays.

During the next few days the bushrangers stuck up and robbed a large number of travellers on the Ballarat Road, travelling themselves towards Geelong at the time. On the morning of the 24th, they stuck up and robbed a man near Fyan's Ford, about five miles from the town, and then rode straight into Geelong. They put up at an hotel in Corio Street, where they had dinner and saw that their horses were fed. Then they went to a house of ill-fame, a little off the street, and not far from the Corio Street lock-up. One of the women was sent to a public-house in Moorabool Street for some bottles of brandy, and the spree began.

The liquor loosened Melville's tongue, and he informed one of the women who he was, and boasted of his exploits. This woman told the others, and as there was a hundred pounds reward offered for 'such information as would lead to his apprehension', the chance of making money was too good to be missed. One of the women put her arms round his neck and talked to him, while another slipped out by the back door and went to the police station to inform the police as to the character of their visitors.

Somehow Melville became suspicious. He suddenly pushed the woman away, and called to Roberts to go and fetch the horses, swearing that he would leave the town at once. Roberts, however, was too drunk to heed him. He was asleep with his head resting on the table. Melville jumped up and shook him, but finding that he could not rouse him, resolved to go alone. He opened the front door and saw a woman with two policemen just entering the gate. Slamming the door hurriedly, he rushed across the room and seizing a chair, dashed it through the back window. Jumping clear, he raced down the yard to the back fence and climbed over in time to meet another constable who was hurrying up towards the back of the house. Without a moment's hesitation Melville knocked the policeman down and ran across a piece of vacant land. His first intention had been, of course, to go for his horse, but on reaching Corio Street after this enforced detour, he knew he would have to pass the lock-up to reach the stable where his horse was. This was too dangerous, and he took the opposite direction.

On its western side Geelong proper — that is, the

older part of the town — was separated from its western portion by a deep gulley, which in early times was closed up by a dam. In 1852 the dam was still there, and the wall formed the roadway which connected Geelong with Ashby, Kildare, and other suburbs. The dam wall was in a line with Malop Street, and Melville raced away across the vacant lots to that street, followed by several policemen.

It was near sundown, and as Melville came to the dam Mr Guy was returning from his afternoon ride. Mr Guy was a young gentleman who had not been long in the colony. He was lodging at the Black Bull Inn, Malop Street, where the most extensive stables in the district were. The Black Bull was a great sporting house and there were always some racehorses there, either in training or waiting for engagements. As Mr Guy was an excellent horseman, he frequently took one or other of these horses out for an airing. On this occasion he had been for a gallop across the plains to Cowey's Creek, and was walking his horse quietly back to allow him to get cool. When crossing the dam a man suddenly rushed up and seized him by the leg. He was lifted out of the saddle, and half fell, half jumped

Interior of the prison hulk *Success* where Melville was confined in 1853

to the ground. He landed on his feet and rushed round the horse in time to collar the man who was trying to mount.

The horse was a spirited animal and objected strongly to this summary change of riders, otherwise, perhaps, the bushranger would have got away. He reared and plunged and prevented the bushranger from mounting. Guy seized the bushranger, and received a heavy blow for his trouble, but he held on gamely, and in the struggle the horse broke away and galloped off to his stable. A moment later the police came up, and Melville was captured. Mr Guy was highly complimented for his plucky fight with so redoubtable an opponent, but he replied that he wasn't going 'to lose a horse in that manner if he could help it'. Of course, he was intensely surprised when he was informed that he had captured the notorious bushranger, Captain Melville.

Melville and Roberts were lodged in the old jail in South Geelong, and I remember going to see 'the bushrangers' conveyed across the flat and up the hill to the court-house to stand their trial. They were seated in a dray, heavily ironed — there was no 'black Maria' in Geelong in those days — and drawn by two horses. There were several armed policemen on the dray, and others marched before and behind. The court-house, of course, was crowded, and, as boys were not admitted, I was not present.

Melville was convicted on three charges of highway robbery and was sentenced to twelve years' penal servitude on one, and to ten years each on two other charges, making in all thirty-two years. A number of other charges were withdrawn. Similar sentences were passed on Roberts, but they were made concurrent. Melville was taken by boat from Geelong to the hulk *President* in Hobson's Bay, 'until the devilish spirit he had for so long a time exhibited appeared to be broken', to quote the Melbourne *Herald*. Rather more than a year later he was removed to the hulk *Success* 'for milder treatment', and was permitted to go ashore to work in the government stone quarry at Point Gellibrand. At that time Melville was engaged in translating the Bible into the language of the Australian aboriginals, 'in which he could converse fluently'. For more than two years the public heard nothing of Captain Melville.

On 22 October 1856, a launch with fifty or sixty convicts on board was being towed from the hulks *Success* and *Lysander* to the landing-place near the quarry, when Mr Jackson, the officer in charge, observed that the prisoners were crowding towards the bow of the launch. He shouted to them to go back and trim the launch. Some obeyed, but those nearest the bow seized the tow-rope and rapidly pulled the launch up to the stern of the boat which was towing it. Then the prisoners began jumping into the boat. Mr Jackson was hurled into the water. Corporal Owen Owens's head was smashed, and he and John Turner, one of the rowers, were thrown overboard. The other rowers jumped, some on to the wharf, the others into the water. The convicts seized the oars and pulled rapidly down the bay, Captain Melville standing up in the boat, waving the hammer with which it was said Owens had been killed, and shouting 'Adieu to Victoria!'

The desperadoes, however, were not to be allowed to escape as easily as they imagined. The guard on the hulk *Lysander* fired at them as they passed, and the water-police from Williamstown soon followed and overtook them. Being threatened with muskets at close range, and having no arms themselves, they surrendered and were towed back quietly to the *Success*.

Nine of the conspirators were tried for mutiny, Melville at his own request being placed first at the bar alone. In the charge sheet he was described as Thomas Smith, alias Frank McCallum, alias Captain Melville, and was said to have been transported to Van Diemen's Land in 1838. This contradicts the many rumours about him during his bushranging career. The one most often heard was that he had come to the colony in charge of an emigrant ship from England, and that he and his crew had deserted her and gone to the diggings. Being unlucky, he had taken to bushranging. This report was frequently denied, but still it was extensively believed, especially in the Geelong district.

After hearing the evidence, the jury was unable to agree on a verdict of murder in the first degree, as there was a doubt as to who struck the blow which killed Corporal Owens. the Judge ruled that if, in an attempt to escape from lawful custody any person is killed, all of those attempting to escape are guilty of murder; consequently Melville was found guilty and sentenced to death. The other prisoners were acquitted. The sentence was afterwards commuted to imprisonment for life, and when Melville was informed of the 'mercy' which had been extended to him, he remarked quietly, 'Well, you'll be sorry for it'.

On 26 March 1857, Mr John Price, Inspector-General of convicts in the Colony of Victoria, attended

at the quarry near Williamstown to hear any petitions or complaints which the convicts might have to present. Convict James Kelly was the first called and he asked for a ticket-of-leave. Mr Price replied that he was unable to agree to this request. As he walked away Kelly was heard by Captain Blatchford to mutter, 'Bloody tyrant, your race is nearly run'. He appeared to be in a furious passion, but very little notice was taken of him at the time. Several of the prisoners pressed forward and began to crowd round Mr Price, loudly complaining that they had not received the due amount of rations. Some exclaimed that they were being cheated. Mr Price stepped back and said in a loud voice, so as to be heard above the din, that these complaints must be given in proper form, when full inquiries should be made. If the charges were true the abuses should be rectified, but if they were false or unfounded, those making them would be punished.

Suddenly a rush was made. Kelly threw a heavy stone, shouting, 'Down with the bloody tyrant'. The stone struck Mr Price and he reeled. The convicts pressed forward shouting 'Give it him, give it him', and a volley of stones was sent flying through the air. Captain Blatchford was struck several times and rushed off to summon the guard, which was stationed on the other side of the quarry tramway, behind a

A labour gang from the hulk, *Success* (left), brutally attacked and killed John Price, Inspector-General of Convicts in the colony of Victoria in March, 1857. Melville was accused of planning the attack.

large heap of stones. A convict named Bryant was said to have struck Price with a heavy navvy's shovel. He then shouted, 'Come on. He's cooked. He wants no more'.

When Captain Blatchford returned with the guard the convicts had placed Price's body on a hand barrow, which they held up in their hands. The remainder stood round as if waiting for orders. The face of the murdered man was calm, even pleasant to look at, but the back of his head was terribly battered, and the heap of stones was covered with his blood and brains. The guards surrounded the convicts, who offered no resistance, and they were marched away to the wharf and taken on board the *Success*. Soon afterwards shouts of 'The bloody tyrant's done for, hooray', and much cheering were heard on board this vessel and on the *Lysander*.

Fearing that a general mutiny of convicts might take place, the harbour defence vessel *Victoria*, with her guns loaded and the crew at their quarters, was laid alongside the *Success* ready to sink her if necessary. The convicts, however, were very quiet and allowed themselves to be conducted to their cells without opposition. Fifteen convicts were placed on trial for this murder.

Melville had been removed from the hulks to the Melbourne jail a short time before the uprising,

because it was believed that he had been planning a general mutiny, and now it was said that the murder of Mr Price had been included in his scheme. During the first two or three months of his residence at 'Wintle's Hotel', as the Melbourne jail was facetiously called, Melville behaved very quietly, and was treated as an ordinary prisoner. On 28 July 1857, he made a savage attack on Mr Wintle, the Governor of the jail, and was afterwards confined to his cell. Later it was reported that for weeks he would behave in the most exemplary manner, but would suddenly and unexpectedly break out into a paroxysm of fury, during which he would destroy everything possible. At these times the warders and officers were ordered to keep away from his cell, and leave him to himself. He was placed under medical observation to decide whether he was sane or not, and great care was taken, it was said, not to excite him.

On 10 August he was locked up as usual, and appeared to be in his normal condition as regards health and spirits, but when his cell was opened next morning, he was found lying dead on the ground. A blue handkerchief with red spots, which he had brought with him from the hulks, was tied round his neck with a slip knot, and twisted up tightly. Dr McCrae was called in immediately, and said that death was due to strangulation. He had been dead some three or four hours. The doctor was of the opinion that the prisoner had tied the knot himself. A verdict of *felo de se* was returned by the coroner's jury which heard the case.

A variety of opinions were expressed as to this verdict. So far as is known, there is no evidence to prove that Melville came to his death in any other way than that stated at the inquest, but there were numbers of people who asserted their belief that the bushranger was strangled by the jailers. As a rule these people did not blame the jailers for this act. The opinion generally expressed was that Melville was little better than a wild beast, and was better dead than alive. They also asserted that it would have been more satisfactory if the bushranger had been hanged openly instead of murdered secretly, and they blamed the Governor and the Judge for having been so 'soft-hearted' as to commute his sentence when he was condemned to the gallows. There appears, however, to be no evidence in support of this view. The records of the inquest are brief, but they seem to prove clearly enough that the most noted bushranger of the gold-digging era took his own life in one of the paroxysms to which he was liable. Whether these paroxysms were due to his harsh treatment on the hulks is another matter.

# 12 Gold escort attacked

**More bushranging among the goldfields; sticking up in Melbourne streets; lack of police protection; murders and robberies at the diggings; robbery of the McIvor Gold escort; a bushranger intimidated by a bottle of brandy; prevalence of horse stealing.**

The arrest of Captain Melville, although it removed the central figure in this the third bushranging epoch in Australia, by no means put a stop to the crime. Melville had been a specialist, a true highwayman, while the others were merely general practitioners who were not very particular what crimes they committed so long as they secured booty.

On 24 January 1853, the driver of the mail coach from Colac to Geelong was ordered to bail up near Mr Dennie's station. The driver kept on. One of the bushrangers reached out to grasp the reins, while the other fired at the driver. The report frightened the horse of the man who was trying to seize the reins, and it bolted throwing the rider. The mail-man whipped his horses into a gallop and got safely away.

Richard Bryant and William Mack walked into Mr J. Jackson's store at Fryer's Creek, Mount Alexander, and ordered the storeman to bail up. They took all the money that was in the till, a quantity of gold dust, and a bundle of the most valuable articles they could find. They were arrested by Constable Bloomfield in a house in Melbourne and sentenced to twelve years' imprisonment.

The *Geelong Advertiser* of 5 March 1853 reported:

The shameful want of adequate protection along the main roads leading to the diggings has repeatedly been exemplified in the robberies, assaults, and murders committed by bushrangers upon a number of luckless wayfarers, with the grossest and most notorious impunity. These unavenged offences against society and the public peace have been excused by some, on account of the difficulty of keeping afoot such an extended line of patrol as would effectually intimidate marauders. . . . When we are in possession of the fact that the Sydney Executive could and did accomplish such protective arrangements over a hundred and fifty miles of country, we may be allowed to doubt the alleged inability of the Victorian Government to render equally efficient aid out of a revenue probably ten times as great as that derived by the sister colony from the same source; at least we might reasonably suppose that townships between Melbourne and

Mount Alexander, Geelong and Ballarat, would be supplied with police, mounted or otherwise, to act in a radius of ten miles or so when called upon. . . .

At that time the police were too busy harrying the diggers for the exorbitant licence to attend to the roads. Later in the year, when the Melbourne papers backed up the demand for better police protection, police stations were established at the larger camping places where townships had grown up. In the meantime numbers of murders were committed without the perpetrators of the crimes being discovered.

Mr and Mrs Skinner were travelling from Bendigo to the new rush at McIvor and camped for the night on the banks of Eve Creek. In the morning Skinner went to look for his horse while his wife prepared breakfast. She went to the lagoon to fill the billy to make the tea and saw the half-immersed body of a man. When her husband returned he drew the body out of the water and saw that the head had been fearfully battered. A pocket-knife, pipe, tobacco, and a silk handkerchief were found in the pockets, but no gold or money. An inquiry was held in this case, and a verdict of murder was pronounced against some person or persons unknown; and that was all. There were hundreds of such cases in which no inquiry was held at all.

John Shannon was travelling from Ballarat to Geelong, and stopped for the night at an inn at Batesford. He called on Mr White, a butcher, and had tea and was about to return to his inn, when three men stopped him at the door. One of these men asked, 'Is this the butcher's shop?' 'Yes', replied Shannon. 'Ah! you're just the bloke we want', exclaimed the man. The three men then hustled Shannon back into the shop and compelled him to stand with his back to the wall and his arms stretched out. White was placed in a similar position, and made to stand while the robbers emptied the till. They then searched Shannon's pockets, and

**Frederick Charles Standish was appointed Victorian Chief Commissioner of Police in 1858. Years later he supervised the pursuit of Ned Kelly.**

WALHALLA. GOLD. ESCORT 6.000. OUNCES £73.000

took out a parcel of gold and some money. When he objected, one of the men who had been standing on guard at the door drew a pistol, put the muzzle close to Shannon's breast, and pulled the trigger. Shannon fell. The man who had been searching him turned the body over, and then said, 'Barry, it's finished; we'll be off.' The three men then left, no attempt being made to detain them.

An inquest was held on the body and a verdict of wilful murder was returned against three men whose names were unknown. The jury added: 'We cannot separate without expressing a strong feeling with regard to the unprotected state of the road between Geelong and Ballarat, which is overrun with bad characters. We would respectfully but firmly urge on the Executive the immediate necessity of erecting intermediate police stations between the two places, with patrols to traverse the road from station to station, and we would also point out the necessity for strenuously enforcing the Vagrant Act.' Three men were arrested and charged with this cold-blooded murder, but were acquitted.

The great bushranging event of the year 1853 was the sticking up and robbing of the gold escort from the McIvor Goldfield. The escort was a private one travelling from McIvor to Kyneton, where it met the Government Escort which conveyed gold from Bendigo and Mount Alexander to Melbourne.

It started as usual on 28 July. At about fifteen miles from McIvor and three miles from the Mia-Mia Hotel, there was a sharp bend in the road round a point of rocks which jutted out from the range. At the bend a

One of the main tasks of police in the 1850s was escorting transportations of gold from outlying districts to the main centres. The Walhalla escort (above) carried 6,000 ounces of gold worth £73,000.

mia-mia, or shelter such as is made of boughs by the aboriginals, had been constructed, and opposite to it a big log was drawn across the track. This compelled the driver of the escort cart to pull his horses off the track and drive very close to the mia-mia. The road was very rough, and the cart swayed about badly. Just as it was passing the mia-mia a volley was fired from it, and the three troopers on the cart as well as the driver fell. The horses on which Mr Warner, in charge of the escort, and Sergeant Duins were mounted were both wounded.

Although the wounded troopers returned the fire as speedily as possible, they could see nothing to shoot at except the bushes. The bushrangers fired again, and the troopers were compelled to fall back. Then about a dozen men rushed from behind the mia-mia, seized the two boxes which contained the gold, and rushed back into the scrub. Mr Warner sent Sergeant Duins to the nearest police camp for assistance, and then followed the bushrangers, who fired at him. He replied with the three shots remaining in his revolver, and retired. Mr Warner galloped as fast as his wounded horse could go to Patterson's station for help. On his return with some of the station hands he found a man putting the wounded troopers into the cart, and arrested him on suspicion of being one of the robbers. The driver, T. Flooks, was the most seriously hurt, and he died a few days later. He and the troopers, S. B. Davis, J. Morton, and R. Boeswetter, were taken to the hospital at the police camp on the McIvor Goldfield as quickly as possible. The man who had been arrested proved that he had no connection with the bushrangers but had been acting from purely humanitarian motives and was discharged.

A party was organized to pursue the robbers, and on going to the place where the attack had been made, found three horses with packsaddles tied to the trees. It was conjectured that the robbers had been disturbed by the approach of the pursuing party before they could pack the gold on the horses, and had made off on foot into the ranges.

Some time passed before a man named John Murphy was arrested on board the ship *Madagascar*, lying in Hobson's Bay. He had booked a passage on the eve of her departure for England. When charged he admitted that he had been one of the party, and promised to turn informer. He gave some information which led to the arrest of others of the gang, but he then seems to have repented of his decision, as he committed suicide. However, his brother, Jeremiah Murphy was arrested in Queensland, and by giving the desired information, he escaped punishment. The gold stolen was valued at about £5000, and very little of it was recovered. George Wilson, George Melville, and William Atkins were charged with the murder of Thomas Flooks, and were found guilty. They were hanged in Melbourne on 4 October. Atkins died as soon as the bolt was drawn, but Wilson and Melville struggled for several minutes. The hangman was compelled to 'draw the legs of Melville down with considerable force' before life was extinct.

Occasionally the tragic events of the year were lightened by a touch of comedy, as when a resident of Ashby was returning home from his business place in Geelong. It was dark when he was crossing the dam and a man presented a pistol at him and called 'bail up'. The suburbanite was taking home with him a bottle of brandy, which, in accordance with the custom of that time, was not wrapped in paper. Paper was too dear in Australia to be used for wrapping articles which would keep together without. When challenged, the man brought the bottle from under his coat, presented it at the head of the bushranger, and cried, 'You bail up.' The would-be robber, taken by surprise, dropped his pistol and turned to run, but the man cried, 'Stop, or I'll fire,' and the fellow stopped. The suburbanite thought for a moment whether he should take the 'bushranger' to the lock-up or not, and decided that it would only entail a 'lot of trouble', so he punched his head and let him go. He kept the pistol as a trophy, and carried home his bottle intact.

I think sufficient has been said to indicate the state of the country and the character of the crimes committed during this epoch. How many men were shot while prowling about the tents on Ballarat,

The most talked-about bushranging event of 1853 was the attack on a private gold escort travelling from McIvor to Kyneton.

Bendigo, Mount Alexander, and other diggings it is impossible to say. Many of the bushrangers, after having made a haul on the roads or on the diggings, went to Melbourne or Geelong to spend their illgotten gains in riot and debauchery only to commit crimes in these towns for which they were captured and punished. Others returned to New South Wales or to Van Diemen's Land and ended their careers there. It was rarely known how many crimes even those who were captured had committed. They were placed on trial for their last offence. In some cases it was said that the prisoner had been guilty of other crimes, but the difficulty of finding witnesses in a population which was continuously shifting from one end of the country to the other as new goldfields were opened, made it impossible to prosecute for crimes committed a few months before. It was the custom therefore to inflict long terms of imprisonment to keep wrong-doers out of mischief for a time. When a prisoner was tried and convicted for more than one crime the sentences were usually made concurrent, so that there was no encouragement for the police to pile up a record of crimes against a prisoner. Captain Melville was the one exception to this rule.

# 13 Willmore, Wilson & Dido

**The last of the Van Diemen's Land bushrangers; an escape from Norfolk Island; Thomas Willmore and his capture whilst asleep; Wilson and Dido; some minor offenders.**

Transportation to New South Wales ceased in 1841, and only two vessels conveying convicts reached that colony afterwards. These brought some prisoners who were supposed to be reformed characters, and were known in Australia as 'Pentonvillains', from the name of the Reformatory in London through which they had passed. They were sent out because of agitation on the part of the wealthier settlers for the revival of transportation, but so much indignation was aroused amongst the colonists that no further attempts of that kind were made.

In the early 1850s the colony of New South Wales included the whole of the eastern side of Australia; Victoria was then the Port Phillip District and Queensland the Moreton Bay district. The southern portion, or Port Phillip district, became an independent colony about a year later, and I have dealt with the bushranging there during the gold digging era. In New South Wales robberies were also very frequent, although the condition of the colony was never so desperate as that of Victoria. In August 1853, the *Bathurst Free Press* said:

> For some time past the neighbourhood of King's Plains has been adding to a murderous notoriety . . . There bloodshed in its most awful shape, murder, appears to be reduced to a science, and the stereotyped phrase 'Murder will out' has lost its meaning. An unfortunate old man, remarkable for nothing so much as his hospitality, is slaughtered like a sheep and deposited under a heap of stones . . . Some fifteen years have rolled over his grave, his death is still enveloped in mystery. A woman in the prime of life is shot dead in her house; the walls being bespattered with her blood. A helpless old shepherd . . . who had excited the cupidity or revenge of some miscreant, is discovered in the bush, so cut, bruised, mangled, and disfigured that words are wanting to describe the tigerish bloodthirstiness of the murderer . . . A resident of Bathurst . . . starts for that bloodstained region one day in perfect health . . . and the only evidences of him, living or dead, are the merest fragments of calcined bones . . . and a few hairs which have been pronounced to be those of a human being.

The indictment was a terrible one and was no doubt true, and the paper was perfectly justified in urging the Government to take more strenuous efforts to stamp out bushranging. Nevertheless the murders spoken of here belong to a bygone age, the perpetrators having probably been attracted, like the majority of their class, to the Victorian goldfields. That was the focus to which all such enterprising scoundrels were drawn, and there the majority met the fate they so richly deserved. A few robberies were committed on the roads in the Bathurst district and in other parts of the colony, but the greatest number of such crimes took place in the Monaro district and along the road leading to Victoria.

The only bushranger in New South Wales who became notorious at this time was Thomas Willmore. He had been under butler to a gentleman in England and at the age of fourteen he was transported to 'Botany Bay' for having stolen a number of silver spoons and other plate from his employer. He was first sent to Pentonville and was then sent to the colony as a reformed character. Being among the last of the English convicts sent to New South Wales, he and his companions were known as 'Earl Grey's pets'. He was granted a ticket-of-leave soon after landing and was assigned as servant to a settler in the Wellington district. Soon after reaching the place he quarrelled with a fellow servant and fired a pistol at him. The bullet struck a button and glanced off.

The man escaped, while Willmore, to avoid a trial, took to the bush. He gained a living by highway robbery for some months. One day he met Philip Alger, near Tomandra, on the Big River. Alger was riding a very fine horse and Willmore claimed it as one which had been stolen from him, and for which he said he had offered a reward. He demanded that the horse should be given to him at once. Alger swore he had purchased the horse honestly from a man he knew, and declined to part with it. Willmore ended the dispute, by drawing a pistol and shooting Alger in the stomach. Willmore was aware that Alger had a considerable quantity of gold on him, as the man had foolishly shown it in a hut where both had stayed during the

Mounted trooper of the Victoria Police. Governor Brisbane established the first mounted police in 1825 to combat the bushranging menace. By 1838 their numbers had increased from fifteen to 166 men. They played an important pioneering role in Australia, particularly as escorts for gold coaches and pursuers of bushrangers.

previous night; but Willmore did not search the body and the gold was found on it when it was discovered. He seems to have been satisfied with the horse. He mounted it and rode towards Wellington.

At Montefiore he bargained with Malachi Daly for a cart, offering in exchange for it a quantity of gold dust which he had no doubt stolen from some other victim. They could not come to an agreement, but continued their journey towards Wellington together the next day. About nine miles from Wellington on the road to the Big River the road went down a very steep hill, and both men dismounted to lead their horses down. Daly was just starting when Willmore stepped before him, pistol in hand, and demanded his money and gold. Daly protested that he had left it at his hut, and Willmore called him a liar. They disputed for a few minutes, and then Willmore shot Daly through the head. On searching the body Willmore found only thirty shillings and a deposit receipt for £11, which

was of no value to any one except the depositor. Although Willmore boasted that he got £40 from Daly, in his last confession he said he had only asserted that he had found £40 on Daly's body because he did not wish it to be known that he had 'killed a man for thirty bob'.

Willmore was only just riding away from where Daly's body was lying when he was ordered to bail up by another bushranger. Instead of complying with this request Willmore drew his pistol and fired, both men shooting at the same time. Willmore's horse bolted and ran for some considerable distance before he could pull him up. When he had once more brought him under control Willmore wheeled his horse round, and galloped back to the scene of the encounter. He tracked his late opponent for a mile or more. He felt certain that he had not missed, and expected to find the body lying somewhere in the bush. Gradually he became convinced that he had been mistaken, and that the bushranger had escaped. He gave up the search, feeling 'very sorry' that he had not fired straight.

During the following three or four weeks he stuck up and robbed a number of people on the roads between Wellington and Mudgee, until at length it was resolved at a public meeting to hunt him down. A large party

# TICKET-OF-LEAVE.

No.

44/2528

## PRINCIPAL SUPERINTENDENT OF CONVICTS' OFFICE,

*Sydney, New South Wales,*

11 October 1844

IT is His Excellency's, the Governor's, Pleasure to dispense with the Attendance at Government Work of *John Commons* who was tried at *Galway 4th September 1835* Convict for *Life* arrived per Ship *Waterloo (4)* *Ow* Master, in tne Year *1836* and to permit *him* to employ *him*self (off the Stores) in any lawful occupation within the District of *Yass* for *his* own advantage during good behaviour : or until His Excellency's further Pleasure shall be made known.

*By His Excellency's Command.*

Registered in the Office of the Principal } of Convicts. {

A 'ticket-of-leave', issued to a convict of good behaviour who had served a portion of his sentence, enabled him to take employment and move about within a specified district. Willmore was granted a 'ticket' as a 'reformed character'.

assembled by appointment, and this was divided into several smaller bands, each of which was to travel through the district by a specified route. They were all to meet again at a certain time and place and report.

One party, under the leadership of Mr Cornish, got on Willmore's track and followed it for two days. On the third day they discovered him asleep on Ponto Island in the Macquarie River, where he had made a camp among the scrub. He was conveyed to Bathurst, tried and convicted of murder and hanged. There was great satisfaction that he had been captured without further loss of life, and Mr Cornish and the men under him were highly complimented for the skill they had shown in tracking him to his lair and their caution in effecting his capture without waking him. It was highly improbable that he would have surrendered without a fight, and his skill and coolness were such as to make it almost certain that one man at least would have been shot. In reporting his trial the *Sydney Morning Herald* compared him with 'that monster Lynch', and congratulated the colony on having got rid of 'such a savage'.

In Van Diemen's Land the interval between the two bushranging eras was shorter than in New South Wales. In fact, in spite of the assertion that bushranging had been suppressed with the breaking up of the Cash and Kavanagh gang, robberies still took place, occasionally with only short intervals between them. As a rule, however, there was nothing very

remarkable in them, and only a few seem worthy of notice here.

On 19 February 1846, Henry Ford and Henry Smart stuck up and robbed a small farmer named Robert Stonehouse, on the Tamar River. Under threats they compelled Stonehouse to accompany them to the next farm and call out his neighbour, John Joynes. When Joynes opened the door the bushrangers rushed in. They tied Joynes and Stonehouse and ransacked the house, taking everything of value. When they left they walked along the road and robbed every one they met. On 5 March they went to Mr Philip Oakden's house and rang the bell. Mr Oakden went to the door and was immediately confronted with a gun and ordered to stand. Mr Oakden informed the robbers that Mrs Oakden was very ill and requested them not to make a noise. He said he would give them all he had in the house if they would go quietly and not alarm his sick wife. He gave them three £1 notes and some silver. The robbers insisted on going in and searching the drawers for jewellery, but took nothing. They then asked Mr Oakden for his gold watch. He gave it to them and they left, taking Mr Oakden with them.

They stopped at the Rev. Dr Browne's house and made Mr Oakden inquire whether his friend was at home. When Dr Browne came to the door he was bailed up, and Ford asked him 'How much money have you got?' 'None,' replied Dr Browne. 'Take care I don't find you out in a lie,' cried Ford; 'where's your money?' They went in and began searching the drawers and cupboards, and while they were thus employed Chief District Constable Midgeley, who had heard that the bushrangers were in the town, came in with another constable. He took the bushrangers unawares and captured them, though not without trouble. When called on to surrender Ford tried to get out his pistol, but Midgeley said, 'If you stir you'll be settled quick.' Ford and Smart were convicted of highway robbery and death was recorded against them, but the sentences were commuted to imprisonment for life.

The bushrangers Wilson and Dido were the most notorious about this time. They were watching Mr James Clifford's house, at Piper's River, on 16 September 1846. When Mr Clifford came out they rushed upon him, took him inside, tied him, and took wearing apparel, ammunition and other articles out of the drawers and boxes.

In January, Mr Rees and Mr Stevenson started from Campbelltown in a gig for St Patrick's Head. On reaching the fourth gate on the road, known as Davidson's gate, they saw two men with guns. At first they took these men for constables. Stevenson got down to open the gate, and while he was doing so Rees became aware of the character of the two armed men who were approaching, and called out to Stevenson, 'Make haste! Here's the bushrangers!' Stevenson tried to jump into the gig, but before he could do so the men were upon him. They presented their guns and called

It was a simple matter for bushrangers to 'lie low' and remain undiscovered by pursuers in the rugged and dense bushland surrounding the colonial towns.

upon the travellers to surrender. They then ordered Rees to drive the gig off the road into the timber. Mr Rees objected, and the bushrangers told him he need not fear, as they intended to act honourably. 'But what do you want?' asked Rees. 'We want to rob you; we want your money,' was the reply. 'Then,' said Mr Rees, 'why not take it here and let us go on?' The bushrangers made no reply, but took the horse by the head and let him away. When the gig was in among the timber the robbers took £18, a gold watch and chain, and a gold pencil case from Mr Stevenson, and £8 and a silver watch from Mr Rees. They also took two dress suits and two top coats from the gig, and then ordered the gentlemen to take off their boots. 'What for?' asked Mr Rees. 'Because we want them,' was the reply. 'But,' cried Mr Rees, 'how are we to get home?' 'Oh, you're all right. You can ride while we have to walk,' said the bushranger. 'But . . .' began Mr Rees, when he was interrupted with, 'Oh, no more nonsense. If you don't make haste we'll strip you.' Stevenson took off his boots, and Rees thought it prudent to follow his example. They returned to their homes in Campbelltown two and a half hours after they had left, and deferred their visit to the Heads to another day.

On the 27th the police were informed that Dido, the bushranger, had been seen in a hut in Prosser's Forest. A party of constables started immediately, and reached the place at 1 a.m. Everything was quiet, and the constables walked very cautiously, fearing that if they stepped on a stick and broke it the noise would waken the bushranger should he be there. The constables took up positions round the hut to prevent escape, and then District Constable Davis, who was in command, suddenly burst in the door. Dido sprang out of the bed and fell on his knees on the floor begging for mercy. He was secured without resistance. In the hut were a double-barrelled gun and a pistol, both loaded ready for use. Mr Rees's watch and some of Mr Stevenson's clothes were found in the hut.

When brought up at the police court Dido said he had been transported in the name of William Driscoll, but his proper name was Timothy. Mr Tarleton, the magistrate, made some remarks on the folly of men taking to the bush. Dido replied that he should have been happy enough if he had not been betrayed. He might have lived in luxury for life. The man who betrayed him had been his best friend but he became jealous and gave him up. He had been in Launceston sixteen times. He had been drinking about town all day on Christmas Day. He had been drunk and had not been well since. Wilson and he had quarrelled and they had parted. Wilson was all right. He had a nice little patch of cultivation, with plenty of flour and some sheep. He was not likely to be taken.

In spite of this assertion, however, Wilson was captured a few days later while drinking at Pitcher's Inn on the Westbury road. He showed a pistol and this excited suspicion, so Mr Pitcher sent a servant to inform the police. Constable Leake came and found the man asleep in a hut at the rear of the public-house. He handcuffed him and took him to Launceston in a cart. He was identified as Dido's mate and was committed for trial at the same time.

# 14 Gardiner's gang

**A new bushranging era; cattle duffers and horse planters; the riot at Lambing Flat; Frank Gardiner, the butcher: beginnings of the Gardiner gang; reign of terror; a letter from Gardiner; the great escort robbery.**

Hitherto the bushrangers of Australia had been, as the records prove, drawn almost exclusively from the ranks of those who 'left their country for their country's good'. Those who took the most prominent share in the next outbreak of the 'epidemic' were generally native-born Australians. The *sequelae* of the old disease were not yet worked out. There were numbers of the 'old hands' scattered about the bush, some of them with farms or small cattle or sheep stations of their own who lived fairly honest and useful lives. But even among these, whatever may have been their station in life, there was the old antagonism to 'law and order', and their sympathies were all with those who waged war against society. Their children imbibed these ideas, and wherever there was a neighbourhood where this class had collected together, morality was at a low ebb.

Besides these settlers there were numbers of nomads; men who worked as shepherds, bullock-drivers, splitters and fencers, shearers, and so on. As long as the old hands formed a majority, or even a considerable minority of the bushworkers, it was the custom for men to work from shearing to shearing, or from harvest to harvest, and then 'draw their cheques', make for the nearest public-house, and indulge in a wild spree, until they were informed by the landlord that the money which their cheques represented had been expended.

There were some respectable inns in the back country where they got fair value for their money perhaps, but in too many of these 'bush pubs', the object of the landlord was to 'lam them down' in the shortest possible space of time. Perhaps when the character of the liquor sold in these places is taken into consideration, this method of cheating was not altogether an evil. It prevented the bushmen from swallowing such large quantities of the deleterious stuff as they might have done if they had received full value for their money.

During the time when they were working, their principal mode of amusing themselves was telling or listening to tales of the convict days. Some of these stories told by the old hands were of too revolting a character for repetition, but no doubt they were founded on fact. Nothing is too horrible or obscene to have been true of the convict times. The stories, however, which appear to have had the greatest influence over the minds of a certain class of Australian youth were those told of the bushrangers. In these stories there was of course much that was apocryphal, to put it mildly. Many of the exploits of the historic highwaymen of old were told as actual facts in the careers of some Australian bushrangers, with just sufficient variation to adapt them to local purposes.

One of the ancient superstitions introduced into Australia by these story-tellers was that the highwaymen robbed the rich to give to the poor. I have no desire to raise any doubts as to the generosity and benevolence of Robin Hood, but I can find no evidence of any such beneficence on the part of any of the Australian bushrangers. No doubt they got their money easily, and spent it recklessly. But they did not pause to inquire whether the person they robbed was rich or poor. There was no such class distinction in the colonies as there was in England; no very poor class not worth robbing and ready to bless anyone who gave them a penny, and no hereditary wealthy class. Every one had to work somehow for his living, though some were more successful in piling up wealth than others. But the poor had opportunities which never existed in England, and if they neglected them it was more or less their own fault if they were poor.

The Australian bushranger in fact had to obtain money or go under. He was compelled to share his ill-gotten gains with those who supplied him with food and information. He was a mark for the blackmailer, and he was compelled to find money to bribe those who were in a position to lead the troops or the police to his hiding place. But the convict bushranger was not as well off as the native-born bushranger. There was a strong feeling of camaraderie, an *esprit de corps*, among the convicts, which tended to prevent numbers of men from betraying him, even though they received no bribes. The new bushranger was more fortunate than the old one. He had his parents, his brothers and sisters, his cousins and his aunts and uncles, who

A branch bank manager on the alert in Victoria's 'bush-ranging district'. The police were strongly criticised during the 1850s for spending too much time harassing diggers for licence fees and not offering enough protection from bush-ranging and other lawlessness.

sympathized with him for family and other reasons, and who were bound to help him. It was from among these relatives and friends that the 'bush telegraphs' were drawn which informed the bushranger of the whereabouts of the police. It soon became apparent that if bushranging was to be abolished these sympathizers and bush telegraphs must be dealt with.

There were several localities in New South Wales where the conditions were favourable for bushranging; places where the morality was low and where the police, as representatives of authority, were hated with all the hatred of the old hands. One of these localities was in the spurs of the Great Dividing Range, in the neighbourhood of Burrowa. All round this district were a number of small squatters, principally cattle breeders, and among these no man's beast was safe. These small squatters were the terror of the big sheep and cattle breeders in the plains, and their principal industry was 'duffing'.

Duffing was not stealing. If a moralist had remonstrated with a Burrowa man whom he found branding his neighbour's beast, the Burrowa man would have replied, 'I'm only trying to get back my own. He's duffed many a head of my cattle.' Sheep could be duffed as well as cattle, but the ranges were generally too steep for sheep. One sheep breeder of the district adopted as his distinguishing mark, the plan of cutting off both ears. He was a most successful duffer, because his recognized ear-mark enabled him to remove the ear-marks in his neighbours' sheep. It was

no uncommon occurrence for a man to find that a calf sucking his cow had been branded by one of his neighbours, so that it might be claimed as soon as it was weaned. In such a case, if he had complained, his neighbour would probably have accused him of having 'mothered' the neighbour's calf on his cow for the purpose of cheating him out of it.

In such a neighbourhood it was impossible for any stranger to travel with horses with any degree of safety. Horses bred in the district could be duffed like sheep or cattle, and horses travelling through could be 'planted'. If a man, who knew anything of the characteristics of the settlers in this district, camped for the night there, and failed to find his horses next morning, he did not waste time in looking for them himself. He realized at once that one of 'the boys' had driven them off into some inaccessible ravine in the ranges, and 'planted' or hidden them there until a reward should be offered for their recovery. He would therefore go to the nearest station and inquire whether his horses had been seen. The answer would be 'No'. Then the traveller would say that he was willing to pay a 'note' for their recovery.

The reply of the station-owner would probably be that horses always went astray about there. There

Diggers attack Chinese miners at the Lambing Flat riot in 1861.

kind settler would even offer the use of his stock-yard if the owner could drive them into it.

This was the state of the district when the rush to the newly-discovered Lambing Flat Goldfield took place in 1860. Early in the following year there was a great 'roll up' of the diggers to drive the Chinese off the field, and the military were sent up from Sydney to restore order. In this riot the peculiar morality of the diggers, of which I have already spoken, was illustrated to a remarkable degree. The leaders of the riots strictly forbade robbery, and any person found stealing gold or any other property from the Chinese was to be handed over to the police; but burning the humpies, tents, and other property of the unfortunate 'Chinkies', cutting off their pigtails, beating or otherwise ill-treating them, as an inducement for them to leave the field, were justifiable if not meritorious acts. In later years many of the 'flash diggers' wore sashes made of Chinamen's pigtails, sometimes with just as much of the scalp attached as would prevent the hairs from scattering. However, the riots did not last long and the leader, William Spicer, was sent to jail.

There were, of course, many of the young men of the district in the goldfields and, as far as is known, these conformed to the rules laid down by the diggers with regard to property. But this did not affect their own peculiar notions as to the ownership of cattle, sheep, or horses, and the attention of the police was early drawn to the district. Warrants were soon issued for numbers of the youths on charges of horse- or cattle-stealing, and several were arrested. Later it was said that many young fellows, who might have remained at home were 'driven on to the roads' by the police. In other words, they turned to bushranging because they were interfered with in their favourite amusements of duffing and planting.

Among the residents on the diggings was Frank Gardiner, who opened a butcher's shop on Wombat Flat. Gardiner was born at Boro Creek, near Tarago, in the heart of the district in which Jackey Jackey had first won his notoriety as a bushranger. The morals of that district were very similar to those I have described as prevalent in the Burrowa district. Gardiner went to the diggings in Victoria in the 'Fifties', was arrested near Ballarat, and tried at Geelong for horse-stealing. He was sent to jail for five years. He escaped from the Pentridge stockade and returned home. Shortly afterwards he was convicted of horse-stealing at Goulburn and sentenced to seven years' imprisonment on two charges, the sentences being made concurrent. He served half the term and was granted a ticket-of-leave.

His butcher's shop at Burrangong, to give the diggings its proper name, was said to be the resort of

was such a get-away for them, and the warrigals came down and enticed them off. The story of the warrigals, or wild horses, tempting working horses away was a common fiction. Hobbled horses could not keep up with the warrigals across the ridges. But it was sufficiently plausible to serve. If the working horses broke their hobbles they might perhaps go with the wild horses; even then it was uncertain. After a few minutes' conversation, the station-owner would probably say that if any one could find the horses it was 'Jack the Kid', or some other local character, as he knew every gully in the ridges.

The wideawake traveller could understand that Jack the Kid was the man who had planted his horses, and would not return them for less than 'a note', that is £1, and on this reward for villainy being promised the traveller might go to his camp with the certainty that the horses would be brought to him in about an hour. It would be useless to look for them, because the planter would be on the watch, and if the owner was seen approaching the gully where they were the horses would be driven over the ridge into the next gully.

Cases have happened where a traveller persisted in refusing to be blackmailed and lost his horses. It would be only necessary to cut the hobbles. Then the traveller, if he wanted his horses, would have to engage two or three expert stockmen to run them in. It was useless to complain to the police. The horses had not been stolen. They were there. Let the owner come and fetch them. Nobody would prevent him and some

**Photograph of Frank (also called 'Darkie') Gardiner in the Police Museum, Melbourne.**

88

**Frank Gardiner**

all the worst characters among the young men of the district. The majority of the beasts he slaughtered and sold were said to be obtained 'on the cross'. Becoming aware that a warrant had been issued for his arrest he abandoned his shop and took to the mountains. Here he organized a band of bushrangers, and shortly afterwards reports of people being stuck up and robbed on the roads round the diggings became frequent.

In 1861 the young Australian had not taken to cricket and football as enthusiastically as he did later, and perhaps there were few opportunities for him to get rid of his superfluous energy. Whether this is so or not, it is certain that Gardiner's example had an enormous influence. Not only were those against whom warrants had been issued for cattle- and horse-stealing ready to join the gang, but numbers of young men and lads who had hitherto led blameless lives became so influenced that they too tried their hands at bushranging.

The first robberies were in the immediate neighbourhood of Burrangong, but very soon the area over which the bushrangers operated was enlarged so that it finally embraced the whole colony, and even overflowed into the neighbouring colonies. At first Gardiner and his gang claimed attention, but there were many young men who began as independent bushrangers who made their way to the Burrangong district to join the gang, and others who intended to do so who were captured on the road. It is a difficult matter to decide who did and who did not belong to this gang, as the personnel changed so rapidly. Some actual members of the gang acted independently of it for a time, and made raids into other districts, while others, after having a flutter with Gardiner, left his gang to start elsewhere.

These bushrangers did not confine their attentions to travellers on the roads. They robbed whenever and wherever an opportunity occured, and although many of the crimes committed during the 1860s were by outsiders who intended to join the Gardiner gang, the gang itself was not idle.

John Peisley was a well-known settler in the district, and as his house was said to be the resort of the bushrangers, it was closely watched by the police. On 27 December 1861, Peisley and James Wilson were drinking at Benyon's Inn, about a mile from Bigga, when Peisley challenged William Benyon to run, jump, or fight for £10. Benyon declined, and Peisley struck him several light blows on the chest and called him a coward, until at length Benyon said he would wrestle.

They went into the yard, leaving Wilson, who was drunk, on the seat in the bar. Stephen Benyon, who was at work in the barn, and several others, collected in the yard to see the wrestling match. The men stripped, and grappled, and Peisley threw the publican and then struck him in the face. Stephen Benyon called Peisley a coward, rushed forward and threw him. After getting up Peisley rushed into the house swearing he would 'do for Bill'. He seized a knife and Mrs Benyon cried out 'My God! are you going to kill my husband?' and grappled with him. Stephen Benyon picked up a spade and struck Peisley on the arm. Peisley then threw away the knife and said it was all right.

The row seemed to be all over and Peisley walked into the bar and asked Wilson where his vest was. He had taken it off when he went out to wrestle and left it beside Wilson. Wilson said he had not seen it. Then Mrs Benyon announced that she had hidden it because she found two revolvers rolled up in it. She offered to tell Peisley where it was if he would promise to go away quietly. Peisley agreed and Mrs Benyon showed him where she had hidden the vest in the garden. Peisley walked out, picked the vest up from under a bush, and went back again. He was examining the revolvers when William Benyon said, 'Surely you don't mean to shoot us?' 'You never knew me do a mean action in my life', replied Peisley, 'and I'm not going to begin now. Shake hands. We're all friends.' They shook hands all round and Peisley put on his vest and went away.

As soon as he was out of sight, William Benyon loaded his gun and took it to the barn, where his brother Stephen had returned to his work. William gave the gun to his brother and told him to take care of it, as Peisley was not to be trusted. About half an hour later, when William Benyon was in the bar, Peisley came galloping back, hitched his horse to the fence, and went into the barn. Stephen Benyon picked up the gun and Peisley said laughing, 'Why, you're not going to shoot me, are you?' 'I was told you were going to shoot me', returned Stephen. 'Nonsense', cried Peisley, 'I never did a cowardly action in my life, and I'm not going to now. Shake hands.' Stephen put the gun down and shook hands. Peisley immediately seized the gun and fired, wounding Stephen in the arm.

Stephen ran out of the barn towards the house, and Peisley, taking careful aim, again pulled the trigger, but the cap miss fired. Peisley ran to the corner of the house, and asked William Benyon's son which way his uncle went. The child pointed in the wrong direction, and Peisley ran to the other corner of the house. Not seeing Stephen anywhere he returned. He was in a great rage, and struck a man named George Hammond with the gun, which exploded without doing any damage. Peisley threw the gun away, and drew a revolver. He ordered William Benyon, Wilson, Hammond, and the servant girl into the barn. Then he said to William, 'I've got a bullet here for you. You've had your game, now it's my turn.' The servant went between Benyon and Peisley, and begged the bushranger not to hurt her master. Peisley told her to go away unless she was tired of her life. Suddenly Benyon rushed at Peisley, who fired and wounded him in the neck. As he fell Peisley rushed out to his horse, mounted, and galloped away.

William Benyon died a week later, and a warrant was issued for the apprehension of Peisley, who left his house and joined the gang. On 15 January Constables Morris, Murphy, and Simpson were searching for bushrangers in the Abercrombie Mountains, when they saw Peisley near Bigga. The bushranger was splendidly mounted. He rode up, and coolly informed the police that he was the man they were looking for. He added, 'I'd like to have a turn up with Morris if he will get down, and put his gun aside.' Morris replied, 'All right', and immediately dismounted. He placed his gun against a tree, expecting his challenger to do the same, but Peisley laughed, turned his horse round, and cantered away. Morris drew a revolver from his belt and fired. The bullet passed just under the neck of the bushranger's horse. He turned in his saddle and said 'That was a good one. Try again.' The police gave chase, but the superiority of the bushranger's horse enabled him to

**Senior-Sergeant Sanderson**

escape easily. About a week later Peisley was captured by Messrs Mackenzie and Burridge after a severe struggle. He was tried at Bathurst, sentenced to death for the murder of William Benyon, and was hanged on 25 April 1862.

On the scaffold Peisley said that he had never used violence during his bushranging career until he had had that row with Benyon. He had never taken a shilling from or done violence to a woman. He concluded with, 'Good-bye, gentlemen. God bless you.' Peisley did not appear to suffer much. He was twenty-eight years of age, five feet ten inches in height. He was described as a fine-looking man at a distance, but when examined closely there was a shifty, disagreeable look about his eyes.

In April Gardiner, with three companions, stuck up Pring's Crowther station, then went on to Crooke's and bailed up all hands there. At Pring's, one of the bushrangers played the piano while the others danced. At Crooke's one played the concertina and another sang 'Ever of thee'.

On 10 March, Mr Horsington, a store-keeper on the Wombat, was driving with his wife in a spring cart to Lambing Flat, with Mr Robert Hewitt, store-keeper at Little Wombat, riding beside them. Suddenly, James Downey, with three other bushrangers, barred the road and ordered the travellers into the bush. The two store-keepers had a large quantity of gold with them which they had purchased in the course of business, and were taking it to the bank at Lambing Flat, the main centre of the Burrangong Goldfield. Mr Horsington had a parcel containing forty ounces in his pockets, and another of two hundred ounces in the cart. The robbers took some £1100 worth from Mr Horsington in gold and money, and about £700 worth from Mr Hewitt. When pocketing the plunder, Downey said: 'You're the best gentleman I've met this month, and I've stuck up twenty already.'

Sergeant Sanderson, with detectives Lyons and Kennedy, left the Lachlan Goldfield (Forbes), on 11 April, in charge of three bushrangers who had been arrested, and who were being taken to Burrangong for the police court examinations. Near Brewer's Shanty, three horsemen with two led horses were observed, and on seeing the coach these horsemen turned into the bush. When the two detectives followed them on foot the horsemen turned round and fired. The police returned the fire, and the horses of two of the bushrangers bolted. The third bushranger remained and fired again. The police replied and the bushranger fell. He was identified as a man named Davis. He had received four wounds, none of which was very serious. He was placed on the coach with the other prisoners, and was subsequently sentenced to death. This sentence was, however, commuted to imprisonment for life.

It was at this time that the Burrangong and other papers in the disturbed area accused the Government of neglect in consequence of the non-arrival in the district of Captain Battye with his troop of black trackers. It was said that without this aid the police might ride round for months without penetrating the ranges. No doubt this outcry had the effect of stirring up the authorities, because the troop speedily arrived and was set to work without delay.

The *Lachlan Miner* of 19 April 1862, inserted the following paragraph:

We have received the following letter, purporting to be from the hand of Frank Gardner (*sic*), the notorious highwayman, of Lachlan and Lambing Flat roads. The circumstances under which we became possessed of the documents can be known, and the original copies, with the envelopes and seals, seen by the curious, on application at this office, and they can then use what judgment they choose as to the genuineness of them. We give it to our readers as we received it:

"To the Editor of the *Burrangong Miner*, Lambing Flat. Sir, — Having seen a paragraph in one of the papers, wherein it is said that I took the boots off a man's feet, and that I also took the last few shillings that another man had, I wish it to be made known that I did not do anything of the kind. The man who took the boots was in my company, and for so doing I discharged him the following day. Silver I never took from a man yet, and the shot that was fired at the sticking-up of Messrs Horsington and Hewitt was by accident, and the man who did it I also discharged. As for a mean, low, or petty action, I never committed it in my life. The letter I last sent to the press, there had not half of what I said put in it. In all that has been said there never was any mention made of my taking the sergeant's horse and trying him, and that when I found he was no good I went back and got my own.

As for Mr. Torpy, he is a perfect coward. After I

**Captain Battye**

spared his life as he fell out of the window, he fired at me as I rode away; but I hope that Mr Torpy and I have not done just yet, until we balance our accounts properly. Mr Greig has accused me of robbing his teams, but it is false, for I know nothing about the robbery whatever. In fact I would not rob Mr Greig or any one belonging to him, on account of his taking things so easy at Bogolong. Mr Torpy was too bounceable or he would not have been robbed ... Fearing nothing, I remain, Prince of Tobymen, Francis Gardner (*sic*), the Highwayman. Insert the foregoing, and rest satisfied you shall be paid."

The spelling of Gardiner's name appears to be a typographical blunder. Mr Torpy was a well-known resident of the district. This letter throws some light on the methods pursued by the bushrangers, and tends to prove that although Gardiner might not be present on some occasions, the robberies were committed under his directions. Some fresh outrage was reported almost every day, until in June when the report that the Government Gold Escort from the Lachlan diggings had been stuck up and robbed, caused a commotion throughout the colony. The escort started from Forbes on 15 June with 2067 oz. 18 dwt. gold and £700, owned by the Oriental Bank; 521 oz. 13 dwt. 6 gr., owned by the Bank of New South Wales, and 129 oz. and £3000 in cash, owned by the Commercial Banking Company, making about fourteen thousand pounds worth in all.

The report of this robbery caused intense excitement throughout the colony. Nothing like it had been heard of since the old gold-digging days in Victoria. Large bodies of police were sent out to scour the country near the scene of the outrage. When in the

**Gold-Commissioner Grenfell was supposed to leave Forbes with the ill-fated gold escort but, under special instructions, left in advance and was well ahead on the road to Orange at the time of the attack.**

the way across the ranges to Eugowra. Johnny Gilbert and Alex Fordyce were driving several spare horses which the gang had collected. They camped near the Lachlan River and Gilbert went into the town of Forbes, the centre of the Lachlan River diggings.

It was Sunday, and on his return to the camp Gilbert reported that he had had great difficulty in purchasing guns and an axe. There was only one store in the town in which guns were sold, and that was shut. He had knocked the store-keeper up, however, and persuaded him to supply him with what he wanted. Next morning the gang rode as straight as possible across the ranges, Gilbert going ahead with Charters to cut the fences on Mr Roberts's sheep run to enable them to pass through. They camped for the night between the Eugowra Rocks and Campbell's station.

On the morning of 15 June 1862, they tied their horses to saplings near the camp and walked down to the rocks. Manns was sent to McGuire's shanty at the crossing place for a bottle of Old Tom, a loaf of bread, and some cooked meat. Fordyce took too much gin and went to sleep, and Gardiner shook him roughly and told him that if he didn't wake up he'd 'cut his —— rations short'. Later Gardiner sent Charters to see if the horses were all right, and told him to stop at the camp and mind them, adding, 'You're no —— good here. You're too —— frightened of your skin.' Soon afterwards he heard firing and about an hour later the bushrangers came up leading the coach horses. They

**The Eugowra Rocks were about thirty-five miles from Forbes and about halfway to Orange. It was an isolated area where the road turned sharply to go down to the Mandagery Creek crossing, providing an ideal place for an ambush.**

ranges near Wheogo, one of these parties of police under Sergeant Sanderson, saw a man on horseback who rode away as they approached. The police followed him up the steep gully, and when he was near the top four other men joined him from behind the trees and made off too. The police followed so rapidly that a packhorse which one of the men was leading broke away and they had not time to recover him. The police seized the packhorse, but the men got away. On the captured horse were found about 1500 oz. of gold, a policeman's cloak, and two carbines which were identified as having been among those with which the troopers of the escort had been armed. It may be remarked *en passant* that no more of the property stolen in this robbery was ever recovered.

Some weeks later the police succeeded in apprehending Alexander Fordyce, John Bow, Henry Manns, John McGuire, and Daniel Charters, and they were committed for trial for having been concerned in the escort robbery. Charters turned informer, and his evidence given at the trial may be taken as a substantially true account of the method by which the robbery was effected; although, of course, due allowance must be made for the apparent efforts of the witness to minimize his own share in the crime.

Charters lived with his parents at Humbug Creek and knew the country well. One day Frank Gardiner met him near the Pinnacle and compelled him to lead

had packed the gold on them. They wiped out and reloaded their guns, and in doing so it was found that Fordyce's gun had not been discharged. Gardiner turned on the young man fiercely and said, 'You —— coward, you were too much afraid to fire, —— you. I'll cut your —— rations short for this.' They saddled up their horses and started across the ranges.

The escort was under the command of Sergeant Condell. It left Forbes about noon with Constable John Fagan driving. The other constables were Henry Moran and William Haviland. When they came to the Eugowra Rocks, near the crossing over Mandagery Creek where the road turned sharply, they found two bullock teams so placed across the road, that the escort cart had to be driven close to the rocks. The teams belonged to two bullock drivers who had been made prisoners, and had evidently been there for some time as the bullocks were lying down chewing the cud. To pass these teams the coach had to approach the rocks at an angle, and as it was passing a volley was fired and Constable Moran fell.

The horses, frightened at the noise and flash of the guns, bolted and the cart overturned when the wheels collided with a spur of the rocks. This threw the other constables out and prevented them from making any effective resistance. As the cart capsized, seven armed men, dressed in red shirts and with their faces blackened, sprang from behind the rocks shouting, 'Shoot the —— wretches.' The police fired their carbines and then surrendered. The robbers having repacked their plunder were led by Charters to the

Soon after the big escort robbery, Gardiner had a narrow escape when Inspector Frederick Pottinger lay in wait with eight other police at the house of Kitty Brown, Gardiner's mistress. The *Illustrated Sydney News*, depicting Gardiner's escape from the trap, captioned its picture: 'The Australian Dick Turpin — Gardiner's Flight'.

place near the Pinnacle where they had started. The gold and money was roughly divided, and the party separated.

Constable Moran had sufficiently recovered from his wound to be present at the trial and to give evidence. The first jury disagreed and was discharged, but at the second trial on 23 February 1863, Fordyce, Bow, and Manns were convicted and sentenced to death. Charters was acquitted according to promise, and McGuire was also acquitted on the charge of being concerned in the robbery, but was afterwards convicted of aiding and abetting the bushrangers, and was sentenced to a term of imprisonment.

From the date of this daring robbery the 'Gardiner gang of bushrangers' was the principal topic of conversation in New South Wales. After a lull of several years a new era of bushranging had started, and it lasted for about ten years before it was finally suppressed. For some time the robberies which were reported almost every day were all attributed to Frank Gardiner, but, as was subsequently proved, unjustly. Gardiner had made his *coup* and retired, but it was some time before either the police or the public became aware of this fact.

# 15 Recruits: Hall, Gilbert

**Exploits of the Gardiner gang; Gardiner's contemporaries Johnny Gilbert and Ben Hall; Inspector Norton captured by the bushrangers; the bushranger O'Meally shoots Mr Barnes; the capture of John Foley.**

Next to Frank Gardiner, the man most frequently spoken of in connection with bushranging at this time was Johnny Gilbert, alias Roberts. He was one of the gang charged with assisting in the robbery of the gold escort at Eugowra Rocks, but had not been captured. He was born in Canada, and emigrated with his uncle, John Davis, to Victoria, shortly after the discovery of gold there. Davis, it appears, soon became tired of gold digging, and went to Sydney, where he opened an hotel at Waverley. On 6 April 1854, he was found dead in his private room, and his nephew, then known as Roberts, about seventeen years of age, was arrested and charged with the murder. He was acquitted and left Sydney. He was arrested in the Goulburn district, some time later, charged with horse-stealing, and sent to jail.

He is supposed to have made acquaintance with Gardiner during their imprisonment on Cockatoo Island. Roberts made an attempt to escape from the island, but was recaptured and was punished by Captain McLerie, the visiting justice. When liberated after having served his sentence, he disappeared for a time and was next heard of in connection with the escort robbery. It soon became evident that there were more bushrangers abroad than those connected with the Gardiner gang. Robberies were reported almost every day, and over a wider range of country than it was possible for one gang to travel over. These robberies were of the most varied character.

One day Henry Stephens, innkeeper, near Caloola, was in his bar when three men walked in and called for brandy. He served them. When they had drunk their liquor they went into the breakfast room and sat down with Mr and Mrs Stephens and Mr Young. While the meal was progressing one of the strangers went out. He returned almost immediately, pistol in hand, driving the man servant in before him. Mr Stephens jumped up, exclaiming 'Hullo, what's up now?' when the bushranger fired and shot him in the mouth. The other two visitors rose, and ordered Mrs Stephens to 'hand out the cash'. As she refused they searched everywhere, breaking open boxes, smashing the furniture, and even refusing to allow the poor

**Johnny Gilbert**

woman to lift her baby from its overturned cradle, under which it was in danger of being smothered. They took away about £20 in cash, and a few small articles. As soon as they left Mr Stephens was conveyed to the hospital at Bathurst for surgical treatment. Of course this outrage was attributed to 'Gardiner's gang', but it was subsequently proved that the robbers had no connection with the ex-butcher.

On 10 December 1862, Charles Foley and John Brownlow robbed Daniel O'Brien's inn at Laggan. Another man stood on guard at the door. They tied Mr and Mrs O'Brien, and put a bag over O'Brien's head to prevent him from calling out. Foley searched the place, but only succeeded in finding 'ten bob'. Mrs O'Brien, hoping to induce them to leave quietly, offered to give them £4 10s. which she had in her pocket, but Foley said, 'We want more than that'. They ransacked the

**Victorian foot police of the 1850s**

place, and at last found a roll of about fifty £1 notes which Mr O'Brien had thrown among some empty casks in a back room on seeing them approaching the place. As they were well-known in the district they were soon arrested, and on 9 February 1863 were sentenced to seven years' penal servitude.

At the same sessions, Alexander and Charles Ross and William O'Connor were convicted of the attack on Mr Stephens. They had also robbed Mr William Webb's store at Fish River, and committed some other outrages. They were condemned to death and were hanged in March 1863.

George Willison and Frederick Britton stuck up the Hartley mail near the Woodside Inn, about five miles from Bathurst, on 16 November 1862. The driver, Owen Malone, and a passenger, Arundell Everett, were taken off the road. Their hands were tied behind them, and they were laid on the ground on their faces while the robbers searched the letters. While lying side by side Everett whispered to his companion, 'Let's make a rush'. Malone prudently declined saying, 'What could we do with our hands tied behind us? We'd only get shot'. The robbers took about £1500 in notes from the letters and immediately mounted and rode into Bathurst to exchange them. They were too late. News

96

of the robbery had reached the town, and they were arrested in the Union Bank while cashing the notes. They were sentenced to sixteen years' penal servitude, the first three years in irons. A companion who had kept watch while the mail was being robbed escaped.

The mail coach was stuck up near Mount Victoria by Charles and James Mackay and George Williams. There was nothing remarkable about the robbery. The bushrangers were closely followed and captured in a few days. The two brothers Mackay were sentenced to fifteen years' and Williams to ten years' imprisonment.

On 7 January 1863, the Yass *Courier* announced that during the week the Binalong mail had been again robbed, and Woodward, the driver, left bound to a tree. He begged hard not to be left to perish miserably through thirst, but the robbers laughed and rode away. He was released by a shepherd who happened to hear him calling. He was exhausted. The robbers took £24 10s. and a pennyweight nugget. On the same day Samuel William Jacobsen, hawker, was stuck up near the Wedden Mountains by John Healy, who ordered him to 'bail up and be quick about it unless you want your —— brains blown out'. Jacobsen and his assistant Henry Clok, were stripped and told to remain where they were for an hour under penalty of death. Their clothes were given back to them after having been searched. They dressed, and when they judged that the time allowed them had expired — their watches had been taken away with other property — they walked on. They followed the track of their wagon and came up to it about three miles away. The horses had been turned loose and were feeding near. All the drawers and boxes in the wagon had been broken open and ransacked, and everything of value had been stolen.

During the week ending 22 April 1863, a large number of people were stuck up and robbed on the road between Marengo and Burrangong. One of them, William Oakes, a store-keeper, was going on his usual round among the Fish River farms to purchase fowls, eggs, butter, and other produce for his store. He was successful in hiding his money, but the robbers emptied his horse feed out on the ground, ripped open the saddles and collars of his horses, and broke all the boxes in the cart in their attempts to find it.

On 14 January a woman was stopped at the Cherry Tree Hill, and asked for her money. She refused to give it up. The robbers tried to search her, but being unable to find her pocket, they tore the skirt off, and in spite of her cries, carried it away, leaving her to get home without it. They got about £3 in notes and silver. These fellows stuck up the Mudgee mail about an hour later. There were two passengers on board, a man and a woman. The man refused to give up his money, and one of the bushrangers said, 'If you don't hand it out we'll strip the —— woman'. As he hesitated the ruffian

During the 1860s, unescorted mail coaches carrying small amounts of gold, money and passengers were the prime target of bushrangers.

began to tear off her clothes. The man yielded but the bushrangers got only a small sum.

On 3 April the Cassilis mail was stuck up at Reedy Creek, near Mudgee, by two armed men. One of them remarked after the letters had been gone through, 'This mail never has nothing in it'. Mr Farrell, schoolmaster at Cassilis, who was riding beside the coach when it was stopped, was robbed of his gold watch and some money. He was also forced to exchange his horse, saddle, and bridle, for a knocked up horse and a very dilapidated saddle and bridle.

On the following day Mr Robert Lowe was driving in a buggy from Talbragar to Mudgee in company with Hugh McKenzie who was on horseback, when two armed men ordered them to bail up. Mr Lowe snatched his gun from the bottom of the buggy and fired. The bushrangers wheeled round and rode away, but had not gone far when one of them threw up his arms and fell. Lowe and McKenzie went over to him with the intention of taking him to the nearest town for treatment, but he died almost immediately. The two gentlemen, then continued their journey to Slapdash, where they gave information to the police and were informed that Messrs A. Brown, J.P., and Alexander Dean had just reported that they had been robbed near the same place by two men, one of whom was riding Mr Farrell's horse. Sergeant Cleary and a trooper with two black trackers, Tommy and Johnny Bein Bar,

followed the other bushranger for 260 miles and caught him near Coonamble. He was brought to Mudgee, tried and convicted, and sent to jail for ten years. At the inquest on the man Heather, a verdict of justifiable homicide was returned and Mr Lowe was highly complimented for his prompt action. He was afterwards awarded a gold medal by the New South Wales Government for his bravery in resisting bushrangers.

One day Master Willie Cadell was sent by his mother on a message a short distance away from Mudgee. He walked his pony up the hill outside the township, and was about to start in a canter when a mounted man dashed in front and shouted 'Stop'. The pony was frightened by the shout and bolted for a short distance with the bushranger galloping alongside threatening the boy with instant death if he did not pull up. At length when the pony was brought under control, the robber said, 'I don't want to hurt you, but you must come with me'. He then led the boy to a clump of trees when Mr Smith, of Appletree Flat, and two other men were lying tied on the ground.

The bushranger told Willie that he would not tie him if he promised not to run away, adding, 'If you break

*Melbourne Punch* **published this drawing in 1863, depicting bushrangers opening stolen mail, and captioned it: 'The Mudgee mail arrives at its destination (!)'.**

your word I'll put a bullet through you'. The boy promised and went and sat down on a fallen tree. The bushranger took Willie's pony 'to spare' his own horse. As he walked past Mr Smith, he gave the tied man a kick, and said roughly, 'You stopped me robbing the mail before, but I'll keep you quiet this time'. He mounted the pony and went back to the road. Presently he returned with two other men whom he tied and robbed. He fired several shots from his revolver at a mark on a tree, 'for practice' as he told Willie Cadell. Then he went back to the road again.

He soon returned with two more men, who were treated as the others had been. There were now seven men and a boy held prisoners by one man under the clump of trees. The robber had also stopped Mr Robinson with two stockriders, and had ordered them to round up the mob of fat cattle they were driving and remain on the flat until after the mail passed. Occasionally he would say to his prisoners: 'The mail will soon be here now; then you can all go.' He kept continually riding from the road to where his prisoners were and back.

About half an hour after capturing his last two prisoners, the mail coach turned off the road and came into the clump of timber with the bushranger riding behind and directing the driver where to go. There were four male and two female passengers. The women were told to go under a tree, and to 'sit down and be quiet'. The men were searched and tied. Then the bushranger coolly sat down and went through the

letters. When he had finished he mounted the pony, and took the bridle of his own horse in his hand. 'Youngster,' he said to Willie Cadell, 'you'll find your pony by the road.' He then rode away.

Young Cadell, who had replied 'All right', began to untie the prisoners as soon as the robber was outside the clump. When all were loosed they walked out to the road. The pony was hitched to a tree and the robber seated on his own horse was waiting a short distance away. He asked them whether they were all right, and after being told they were, raised his hat politely, and said, 'Good evening, ladies and gentlemen', and cantered away. The mail-man stopped to gather up the torn and scattered letters, while Messrs Smith and Martin walked to Mudgee to inform the police, and Willie Cadell cantered away to perform the errand on which his mother had sent him.

The coolness with which this robber had acted throughout induced the belief among the public that he was no common amateur bushranger, but a member of the Gardiner gang. In fact it was said that he was no other than Johnny Gilbert himself. The *Goulburn Chronicle* reported about this time that Gardiner and his gang had paid a visit to the Muswellbrook district, and suggested that one of them had committed this robbery on the way back to their own district. This was disproved later, but it was then believed that the robber was one of the numerous young men who 'turned out' with the intention of joining the gang, and endeavoured to do something on the road to prove themselves worthy of being accepted as comrades by the redoubtable bushrangers.

It was the custom of the time to attribute all highway robberies to Gardiner and his gang, but it is doubtful whether any of those recorded in this chapter so far were perpetrated by actual members of the gang. It was a time of intense excitement, and many of the more or less criminally disposed among the youth of the colony felt themselves impelled to take to the road and rob somebody. Some of these were captured; others were disillusioned and went back to their farms; while others either did join the gang or continued bushranging as independent parties.

The next story, published a few days later, involved the sticking up of the Mudgee mail on the Bathurst-Sydney road, near the Big Hill, about sixteen miles from Bowenfels. Mr Henry Edward Kater, manager of the local branch of the Australian Joint Stock Bank, was a passenger. He had with him £5000 worth of old notes, which he was taking to Sydney to be destroyed at the head office of the bank. The bushrangers had received notice from some source that these notes were on the coach, and asked for them. Mr Kater replied that they were valueless, as the numbers had been cancelled. 'Never mind', replied the bushranger. 'We can make a bonfire of them as well as you can.'

Mr Kater declined to give them up, and stooped down. The bushranger immediately ordered him to 'sit up straight and not try to come Robert Lowe on them' or he would be sorry for it. This, of course, was an allusion to the recent shooting of the man Heather by Mr Lowe. Mrs Smith, wife of a publican at Ben Bullen and a passenger on the coach, was very much alarmed. She was seated beside Mr Kater and screamed loudly. She had £200 in her pocket. The robber told her to get down and stand aside, adding 'We don't rob women'. She was only too glad to obey. She sat down on a log beside the road. The other passengers were then ordered to dismount and were robbed of their valuables. When this was done the robbers departed, one of them turning back to request Mr Kater to ask Captain Norton whether 'his spurs were getting rusty'. The robbers were well-dressed and splendidly mounted. Everybody assumed that they belonged to Gardiner's gang. A reward of £500 was offered by the Joint Stock Bank for the recovery of the cancelled notes.

In recording the principal robberies committed at this time by bushrangers who were not definitely known to belong to the gang, I have omitted to mention the robberies done by the gang itself. Now I shall return to the beginning of the year and take up the history of the gang itself.

On New Year's Day, 1863, races were being held at Brisbane Valley on the Fish River, when Frederick Lowry and John Foley made a daring attempt to stick up the crowd of more than one hundred people. A man named Foran refused to be tied and was immediately shot by Lowry. Although he was wounded in the lungs Foran rushed forward and grappled with Lowry. Several other men came to his assistance and Lowry was overpowered, while Foley, who had been engaged in tying the men, jumped on his horse and got away. Lowry was locked up in a room behind the bar of the publican's booth, but the booth was a mere shell, and he escaped before the police came.

On 27 February Mr Cirkel, publican at Stony Creek, Burrangong, was called out of his house and shot dead, after having been accused of giving information to the police. It was said that the men who committed this crime were Gardiner, Gilbert, O'Meally, and another whose name was not known. O'Meally was said to have fired the fatal shot.

The party of bushrangers rode on to Mr Myers Solomon's store at the Big Wombat. Mr Solomon, seeing them coming, attempted to run away, but was followed and brought back. A lad in the store vaulted over the counter and snatched a pistol from the belt of one of the bushrangers while the dispute was going on as to whether Solomon should be shot for attempting to 'betray' them to the police. Another of the bushrangers immediately put his pistol to Mrs Solomon's head and said to the boy, 'If you fire I'll blow her brains out'. The boy looked undecided. The bushranger cocked his pistol and swore that if the boy did not return the weapon he had taken the woman should die. The boy then stepped forward, laid the revolver on the counter, and said, 'If it wasn't for Mrs Solomon I'd stop your— run anyhow'. He was immediately knocked down and kicked.

The *Lachlan Observer* of 5 March reported that Inspector Norton, who had recently relieved Sir Frederick Pottinger as head of the police force in the district, had been captured by the bushranges. Captain Norton had been in pursuit of the robbers, and was returning from a long ride through the ranges, accompanied only by a black tracker known as Billy Durgan. He suddenly came to a camp some three or four miles from Wheogo. Billy, who was riding behind leading a spare horse, saw the fire first and shouted, 'Here they are'. Three of the bushrangers sprang up, mounted their horses, and came towards the officer. Billy advised him to 'bolt', but the captain shook his head and replied, 'No good, Billy. Horse too much knock up.' 'Mine stop it too', said Billy.

O'Meally and Patrick Daly fired as they approached, and Norton returned the fire until his revolver was empty when he said, 'I surrender'. Daly cried 'Throw down your arms' and as Norton threw away his revolver another man galloped up and fired at him. At that moment Billy the black boy, seeing the danger

Norton was in, gave a yell, jumped off his horse, and threw his empty pistol in the bushranger's face. This plucky act no doubt saved Captain Norton's life, but the bushranger turned and fired at the aboriginal. Billy kicked off his boots, sprang behind a tree, and shouted 'Come on, you ——,' O'Meally replied, 'We'll wallop you, you young ——, when we catch you.' At this threat Billy laughed, and replied, 'You catchem first.' Daly and the other bushranger chased him, but Billy dodged about from tree to tree with all the agility of the aboriginals, pelting sticks at them and laughingly telling them to 'come on'. The bushrangers fired at him several times but with no effect, and at length gave up the chase and returned to where O'Meally was still guarding Captain Norton.

After a consultation, the bushrangers told the captain that they had mistaken him for Trooper Holliston. They intended to 'do for' the trooper the first time they caught him. They detained the captain for about three hours, treating him very civilly, and then released him.

A few days later, Daly was arrested by Sir Frederick Pottinger. He was a native of the district, under twenty years of age. When brought up and charged at the police court, Captain Norton failed to identify him, but when called upon for his evidence Billy Durgan exclaimed, 'Mine know it, Patsy Daly like it brudder'. Daly was placed on trial for having, in company with others, robbed Myers Solomon, store-keeper, of property, including money, horses, guns, revolvers, clothing and food, to a large amount. George Johnson identified Daly as the man who had knocked the boy down and kicked him when he placed the revolver on the counter.

On that occasion Johnson had called Daly a coward, and was told to keep quiet unless he wanted his '—— brains blown out'. Johnson replied: 'I'd like to meet you man to man fairly.' Another of the bushrangers asked: 'Will you stand up and fight me if I give you a pistol?' Johnson replied, 'Yes', and stepped forward. The third bushranger ordered him back, and told his mates to 'quit fooling'. Johnson and the other men in the store were then made to lie on their faces, with a bushranger over them on guard, while the other bushrangers selected what they wanted, packed it in bundles, and strapped it on the packhorses. The bushranger who had challenged Johnson kicked him in the ribs savagely, and told him to keep still. The other people present gave their versions of the occurrence, but they differed little from the evidence already given. Daly was convicted, and was sentenced to fifteen years' penal servitude.

On 30 March, two men called at James Brown's hut at Wallendbeen and asked for something to eat. Brown told his wife to give them some breakfast. Such hospitality was common in Australia. Having eaten as much as they required, the travellers demanded Brown's hat and boots. After some dispute these were

handed over. The boots were too small, and the man who wanted them took out his pocket-knife to cut them when his mate said, 'Oh, come on; we'll get plenty at McKay's'. They left the boots, went out, mounted their horses, and rode away. They had only gone a few yards when they met Mr Barnes, a store-keeper at Cootamundra, and his assistant Mr Hanlow, who was in charge of a branch store at Murrumburrah. The travellers ordered Barnes to bail up. Barnes said, 'I know you, O'Meally', and O'Meally replied, 'I know you, you ——. Get off that horse; I want him'. Barnes wheeled his horse round and galloped away with O'Meally following. They galloped round the hill, back past the stockyard, and then down the gully out of sight among the trees.

In the meantime, Hanlow was conducted by the other bushranger off the road to the stockyard where they were soon joined by O'Meally. 'Where's Mr Barnes?' asked Hanlow as the robber rode up. 'Down there', replied O'Meally nonchalantly, pointing down the gully. 'You haven't shot him?' inquired Hanlow anxiously. 'Oh, no', replied the bushranger coolly, 'he hit himself against a tree and tumbled off.'

Mr Alexander McKay, the squatter who owned the stockyard and whose house was not far away, heard the galloping and shouting and went on to the veranda of his house to ascertain the cause of the noise. It was then about 11.30 a.m. and the day was Sunday. He saw one man chasing another, and thought it was a trooper after a bushranger. He watched them gallop down the gully and saw the one he took to be a trooper shoot the other, then wheel his horse round and gallop back without waiting to see whether the man who had fallen off his horse was dead or not. As O'Meally came nearer McKay recognized him and his suspicions were aroused. He started to walk down the gully to the wounded man, when he was stopped by O'Meally who ordered him to go back and open the store, adding, 'I want some boots and clothes for my mate. He lost his in a brush with the traps'.

Mr McKay went to the store and gave O'Meally the things he had asked for. The bushranger then said he wanted fresh horses. McKay replied that the horses were never brought in on a Sunday and therefore he could not get them. 'Ah', said O'Meally, 'I had Chance from you. He was a good 'un. Well, I'll come some other time and get one.' The bushrangers then went away and McKay and Hanlow walked down the gully to where Barnes was lying. They found that he was dead and sent word to the nearest police station. When an inquest was held next day, a verdict of wilful murder was returned against O'Meally and another man whose name was unknown.

A day or two later Mr Frank was riding from Lambing Flat (Burrangong) to Yass, when he was stopped by seven men whose faces were hidden by black crêpe veils. They ordered him to 'shell out'. 'I've only got thirty bob, boys', he replied. One of the robbers said, 'Oh, keep it. You'll want that to take you home again.' Some of the others said that they knew him and he wasn't 'a bad sort', so he could go. They asked him if he had seen any police on the road, and added that they wished to 'meet the —— traps'. After several minutes of conversation they rode off and Mr Frank continued his journey.

Shortly after this Constables McDonald, Lee, and Nicholls traced John Foley to Mackay's Hotel, Campbell's River, with the aid of a black tracker. McDonald pushed the door of the bedroom in which he was told Foley had been sleeping, but the man inside leaned heavily against it to prevent it from being opened. After a struggle McDonald forced his revolver through the opening and fired round the corner. He did not hit the man inside, but the shot forced him to give way a little. The constable said, 'Come along, Foley. We've got you. You can't get away'. After a moment's pause Foley replied, 'All right. Don't shoot'. He stepped back and the door swung open. The police rushed in and handcuffed him.

He was taken to Bathurst where he was charged with having looted Mrs Anne Webb's store at Mutton Falls, and with having aided and abetted other bushrangers in several robberies on the highway and elsewhere. During the trial it was noticed that Mrs Foley, the prisoner's mother, was passing in and out of the court and communicating with the witnesses who had been ordered out of court. She was cautioned, but as she persisted in spite of the efforts of the police, she was ordered to be locked up for contempt of court. Timothy Foley, a brother of the accused, was also committed for contempt of court, and was threatened with prosecution for perjury for his attempts to prove an alibi. The prisoner was convicted and was sentenced to fifteen years' imprisonment, the first three years in irons.

Another brother, Francis Foley, was sentenced at the same sessions to ten years' imprisonment for having raided the Chinese Camp at Campbell's River. Henry Gibson was also arraigned for bushranging. He admitted that he had been overseer on Ben Hall's station, but denied that he had ever joined Gardiner's gang. He was acquitted by the jury, and the verdict was received with some applause. As soon as order had been restored, the judge remarked that it would perhaps add to the general satisfaction if he informed the court that the prisoner would not go free in spite of his acquittal. He had before him a document which proved that the prisoner was an escaped convict from Victoria, and would therefore be detained until he could be returned to that colony to finish his sentence.

Hitherto the gang had continued to be known as 'Gardiner's gang', although it had been repeatedly asserted in the press that Gardiner had taken no share in the later robberies, and that in fact he had retired from 'the profession' several months ago. It was said that despite the vigilance of the police, Gardiner had

Sir Frederick Pottinger, himself only thirty-two at the height of the Gardiner gang exploits, was Police Inspector at Forbes and was instrumental in organizing most of the hunts for the elusive bushrangers. He was charged with neglect of duty after riding in a gentleman's race at the Wowingragong course when members of the early Gardiner gang were said to be present. Earlier he had arrested Ben Hall, but the outlaw was cleared and Pottinger's reputation suffered. He resigned from the police force in 1865 and shortly after died from a shooting accident whilst *en route* to Sydney.

succeeded in escaping from New South Wales, taking with him the wife of a respectable farmer in the Burrangong district named Brown. The reports, however, were very contradictory. Sometimes it was said that he had gone to New Zealand, then that he had made his way to California or to South America. In the meantime the gang continued to be as active as ever under the leadership of Johnny Gilbert and Ben Hall.

# 16 Reign of terror

**The shooting of Fred Lowry; Gardiner's gang holds Canowindra for three days; Burke, of Gardiner's gang, shot by Mr Keightley; female bushrangers; death of O'Meally at Goimbla; lively times during the Christmas holidays.**

The chief necessity for a successful career as a bushranger was a good supply of race-horses, and hence it was almost impossible for any person to keep a really valuable saddle horse during this 'reign of terror', as the newspapers of the district called it. Special raids were organized by members of the gang to obtain a supply of horses, and the bushrangers frequently travelled upwards of two hundred miles to secure a horse which had made a name on the turf.

On 18 May 1863, Harry Wilson, trainer for Mr Allen Hancock, was exercising the racer Jacky Morgan within sight of the police station in the town of Burrowa, when Gilbert rode up and said, 'I want that horse'. 'For God's sake don't ruin me, Johnny,' exclaimed the jockey. 'Hold your —— jaw and get off', was the reply, as the bushranger brought out his ready revolver. The robber specially cautioned Wilson not to 'sing out' so that the police could hear, or he'd 'be sorry for it', and in spite of his remonstrances the jockey was compelled to dismount and walk home to inform his employer. Mr Hancock told him to saddle another horse. He then took down his gun carefully, wiped and loaded it, and went away swearing that he would never return until he had recovered Jacky Morgan.

Gilbert also took a racer out of Mr Hammond's stables at Junee. He stole the racers Chinaman and Micky Hunter from the stables of Mr J. Roberts at Currawang. When leading Micky Hunter out of his stall Gilbert patted his neck and said, 'You're the —— cove we want'. Old Comus and several other horses were taken out of Mr Iceley's stables at Coombing. The old horse had had a good career on the course, and had been set apart for stud purposes, and Mr Iceley offered a large sum to the bushrangers to leave him alone, but Gilbert said, 'There's a good gallop in him yet', and led him away.

But the bushrangers did not devote their whole time to capturing race-horses. Robberies on the highway continued as frequently as ever. The police, however, were not idle. In August, Sergeant James Stephenson, Constable Herbst, and Detectives Camphin and Saunderson, traced Fred Lowry to Thomas Vardy's, Limerick Races Hotel, at Cook's Vale Creek. When asked if there were any lodgers there, Vardy pointed to the door of one of the bedrooms and replied, 'Yes, one there.' Stephenson knocked at the door but there was no reply. The sergeant knocked again and called out, 'Come out Lowry, it's no use.' As there was no answer, the sergeant placed his shoulder against the door and tried to burst it open. Immediately someone inside fired a pistol and the bullet passed through the panel of the door between the two policemen.

Stephenson again called on Lowry to come out or it would be 'the worse for him', but the bushranger replied, 'I'll fight you —— all of you.' He again fired through the door and the bullet wounded one of the police horses tied to the veranda. Sergeant Stephenson called on Vardy to take the horses to a safe place, and when they were out of sight, he and Constable Herbst again tried to force the door by leaning their combined weight against it. Suddenly Lowry threw the door open and the sergeant almost fell into the room. The bushranger shouted, 'Come on, you ——. I'll fight you fair', and fired. The police returned the fire. Stephenson, who was inside the room, took steady aim and pulled the trigger. The robber fell, saying 'I'm done for! Where's the priest?'

The police arrested Vardy and all his family, as well as a man named Larry Cummins, who was in the room with Lowry, but who took no part in the fight. When this ceremony had been completed, Lowry was made as comfortable as circumstances permitted while a messenger was sent off to the nearest town for a doctor. For more than an hour Detective Camphin sat by Lowry's side reading prayers from a Catholic prayer-book which Mrs Vardy lent him. The robber gradually grew weaker and died. His last words were, 'Tell 'em I died game.' The police borrowed a cart from a farmer who lived about a mile away from the hotel, and the body was placed in it and covered with a blanket. This extraordinary funeral *cortege* arrived at Goulburn the next day, Sunday, just as the people were leaving the churches. Frederick Lowry had been

a native of the district, twenty-seven years of age, and six feet two inches in height.

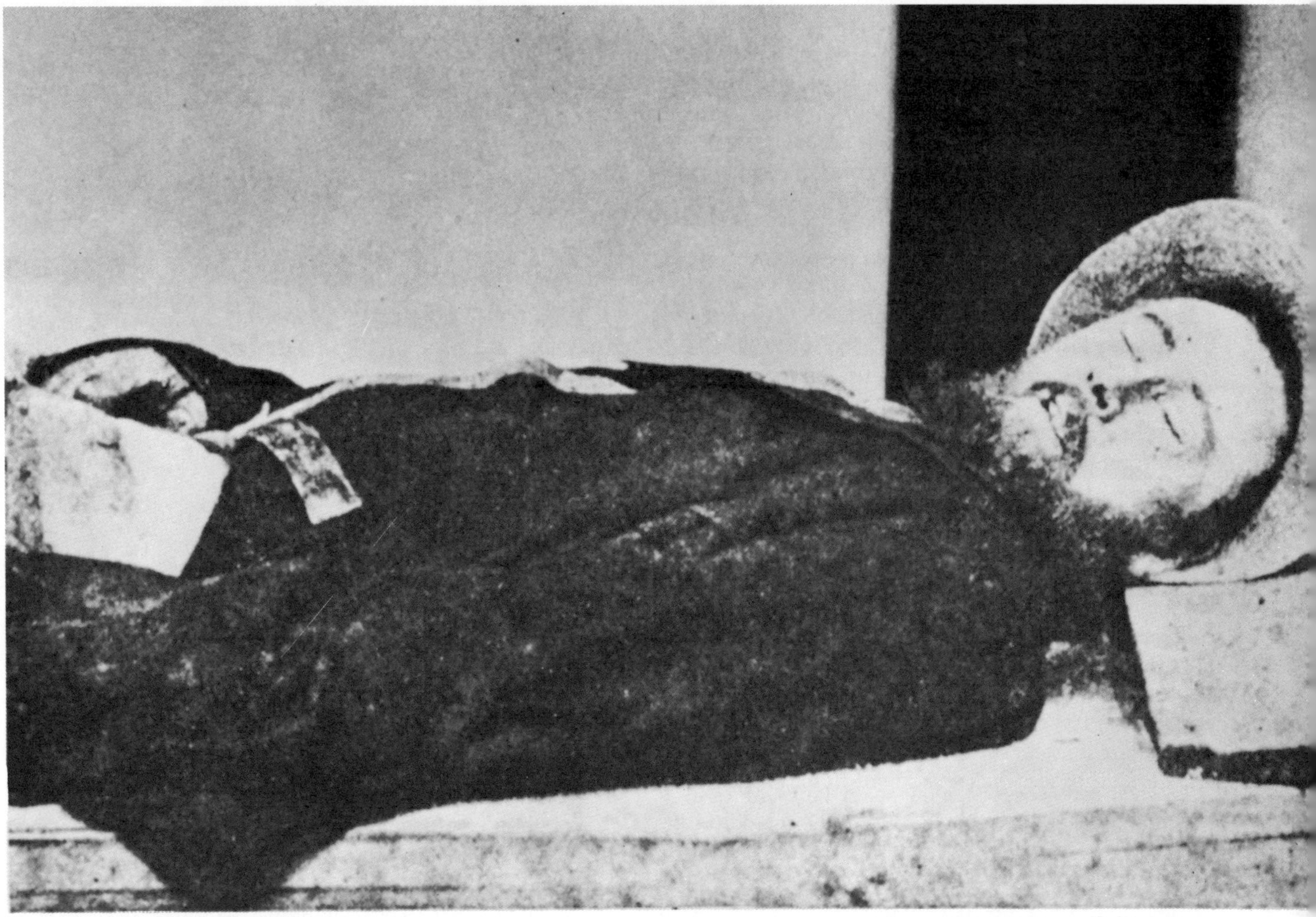

In the New South Wales Legislative Assembly, on 18 August 1863, Mr (later Sir James) Martin moved that 'the alarming state of insecurity of life and property which has so long prevailed through the country districts is in a high degree discreditable to Her Majesty's Ministers in this colony'. Mr (later Sir Charles) Cowper, speaking for the Government, said that the police authorities had full power to take all the troopers that could be spared from the more thickly-populated districts to the disturbed area. The discussion on the motion lasted for a week, when it was dismissed by forty-four to eighteen votes.

The Government was in fact doing all that it could reasonably be expected to do to preserve order, and this was generally recognized, although the Press continued to urge that more energetic measures should be adopted and bushranging stamped out at any cost.

The success of the bushrangers was largely due to the nature of the country and their knowledge of it. Had there been double the number of police in the district it is barely probable that the outbreak could have been put down much more quickly than it was. The police showed remarkable bravery, but they were unable to follow the bushrangers into the rough and

Fred Lowry maintained the bushranging tradition of holding up the Mudgee mail coach with his accomplice, John Foley. A month later he was fatally wounded by police while resisting arrest.

Ben Hall

unfamiliar country of the ranges. It was not the number of bushrangers but their activity, boldness, and more than anything their intimate knowledge of the country, which enabled them to keep so extensive an area of the colony in a ferment for so long a time.

The Carcour mail was stuck up about a mile outside the town of Blayney on 23 September. A passenger named Garland refused to 'hand out' when ordered. He was told that if he persisted in his refusal he would 'get a good hiding'. One bushranger stood by Garland's side holding a gun close to his head, while another bushranger felt his pockets. They took out two £1 notes. The coach was then taken up the ridge to about 300 yards from the road. Here there was a level spot fairly clear of timber, and in this little plain were eight men sitting in a ring with a robber standing guard over them.

The coach-driver and the two passengers were ordered to take their seats in the ring while the letters were searched. They obeyed and were detained more than an hour. One of the prisoners in the ring was a trooper. When the mail had been gone through the bushrangers, one of whom was riding Mr Daniel Mayne's horse Retriever, told them they might go. Garland said 'It's no use going without any money', whereupon a bushranger handed him ten shillings and told him not to growl. It was about five o'clock when the bushrangers rode off. They were said to be Gilbert, O'Meally, Burke, and another.

A few days later Gilbert and O'Meally went to a cattle station some miles from Burrangong and rounded up the horses. A stock-rider galloped up and ordered them to stop. Gilbert told him that they were troopers and had orders from Her Majesty the Queen to take any horses they required. The stockman then assisted them to catch two of the best.

On Saturday 23 October 1863, Ben Hall, Gilbert, O'Meally, Burke, and Vane walked into Mr Perdrotta's gunsmith's shop in William Street, Bathurst, opposite the School of Arts, and asked to see some revolvers. They were shown a number, but said they were common things and no good. Mr Perdrotta said he had sold out. There had been a run on revolvers lately on account of the bushrangers, but he expected a new stock up from Sydney in a few days. The robbers laughed heartily and said that the bushrangers required to be looked after. They promised to call again in a few days.

They walked up the street to McMinn's Hotel, and went in as the family were sitting down to tea. Miss McMinn recognized them and screamed. She was ordered to keep quiet, but as this made her scream louder the bushrangers left. The report that the bushrangers were in the town spread like wild-fire and the streets were crowded with excited people in a few minutes. It was rumoured that the bushrangers had robbed Mr De Clouett in Piper Street, and that De Clouett had recognized Johnny Gilbert as a jockey who

John Vane

had ridden for him some years before. The police hastily armed and mounted. Suddenly the bushrangers, mounted on their horses with revolvers in their hands, dashed through the crowd in Howick Street, shouting, 'Two of us is good for forty —— troopers.' The crowd scattered to let them pass. The bushrangers rode through the street at a gallop and left the town in the direction of the timbered country, avoiding the roads. The police followed close behind, but the bushrangers had the faster horses and got away.

On 17 October, Mr Robinson, of Robinson's Hotel, Canowindra, was awakened at about 1.30 a.m. by a loud knocking. He went to the door and asked, 'Who's there?' The reply was, 'The police.' Robinson opened the door and was immediately ordered to bail up. The visitors were the bushrangers Hall, Gilbert, and O'Meally. Mr Robinson gave them £3 which he took from a drawer, and said that was all the money he had in the house. He begged them to go away. They refused, and insisted on every one in the house getting up at once.

After some delay the family and Mr Kieran Cummings, a lodger, were collected in the dining-room. The bushrangers took charge and served drinks all round. When it was time for opening the hotel, the bushrangers stationed themselves one at each end of the verandah and the third in the bar. They bailed up fourteen bullock-drivers who were camped near the township and compelled them to leave their teams in the street as they arrived. The robbers took anything they required or fancied from the drays and marched the drivers into the dining-room of the hotel.

During the morning, Messrs Hibberson, Twaddell, and Kirkpatrick drove up to the hotel in a buggy. They were compelled to alight and go into the dining-room. Ben Hall, seeing that Mr Kirkpatrick carried a revolver, requested him to 'oblige by handing that thing over. Not that we want it, you know; but it might go off by accident.' Mr Kirkpatrick laughed, and gave him the weapon. Hall examined it carefully and said, 'We've got better than that. We'll leave it for you at Louden's, at Grubbenbong, so that you may get it when you pass.' Mrs Robinson and the cook were released and ordered to get a 'first-class dinner for the gentlemen, and we'll pay for it'. The prisoners were well treated. Food was brought in at intervals, and bottles of brandy were placed on the table for all to help themselves as they pleased. Several boxes of cigars were ordered, and these were opened and the cigars thrown along the table.

Robinson had promised not to 'try any hanky panky', and was allowed to go to the bar. Everything ordered was paid for without delay or dispute. Gilbert walked to the lock-up, called out the solitary policeman who was stationed in the town and made him march down to the hotel. Here he was given his musket and ordered to pace up and down before the verandah as if on sentry duty. When they grew tired of showing their contempt for 'the force' in this manner the gun was taken away and the policeman conducted into the dining-room and placed with the other prisoners to 'enjoy himself like the rest'. The robbers drank very little themselves. Occasionally they ordered a bottle of English beer, and drew the cork themselves after having examined it carefully to make sure that it had not been tampered with.

On the Wednesday morning Mr Hibberson begged hard to be allowed to go. He said that he and his friends had enjoyed themselves very much, and would have been willing to stay longer to oblige, but the river was beginning to rise, and if it came down as usual at that time of the year they might not be able to cross for a month. This would interfere seriously with their business. The bushrangers listened to this plea and then withdrew. After a consultation which lasted several minutes, Hall came back and said they thought it was 'a fair thing'. They were very much obliged to the gentlemen for their contributions towards the general amusement, and they graciously gave them permission to fetch their horses from the stable and start. An hour or so later the other persons in the dining-room were told that they might go.

This spree must have been an expensive one. The bushrangers only took a few pounds to start with, while they paid for everything that was consumed by the crowd between 1.30 a.m. on Monday and noon on Wednesday. At first there had been a feeling of

**Mr Keightley**

restraint, caused perhaps by fear or uncertainty, but this soon wore off, and the party ended by being a very merry one. Several games were started, songs were sung, and one of the bullock-drivers had a concertina and played dance music; several of the members of the party danced. The women and children were allowed to go to bed, but the men had to sleep with their heads on the table. The bushrangers only slept for short naps in turn.

On leaving Canowindra the bushrangers rode straight to Mr Grant's place at Balubula, called him out, and accused him of having given information to the police as to their movements. As a punishment they burned his house, stacks, and standing crop.

A week later, on 24 October, Hall, Gilbert, O'Meally, Vane, and Burke rode up to Assistant Gold Commissioner Keightley's house, at Dunn's Plains, near Rockley. Mr Keightley had been standing on the veranda, and on seeing them coming had rushed in and slammed the door. The bushrangers called him to come out and when he did not obey they fired some shots at the windows. Keightley returned the fire, and Burke fell, crying out, 'I'm done for.' There was very little ammunition in the house and when this was expended Keightley surrendered. He asked only that the women should not be molested. Vane swore he would avenge Burke by shooting Keightley. Mrs Baldock, wife of the camp-keeper, who was acting as general servant at the time, rushed between the men and pushed Vane back, crying at the time, 'Oh! don't shoot him! Recollect his wife and her little baby.' Dr Peechy, who was present, also interfered, but was knocked down with the butt of a revolver. Mrs Baldock again pushed Vane away,

Mrs Keightley

saying, 'Don't hurt the doctor. He never did you any harm.' Vane was very excited and swore a great deal, but he did not even push the woman away.

Presently Hall, who had been some distance away, came up and told Vane to keep cool. He added that it was impossible to say in the mêlée who shot Burke. 'Why,' he exclaimed, 'I might have done it myself.' After a short time order was restored, and the doctor then said that Burke was not dead. He offered to go to Rockley for his instruments and to return immediately. Hall said 'What's the good? Better shoot him and put him out of his misery.' A discussion followed, and at length permission was given to the doctor to go to his house for his instruments, after he had solemnly promised 'not to bring the traps' on them.

After the doctor's departure O'Meally declared his intention of taking Keightley down the paddock and shooting him. He told the Gold Commissioner 'to come on' but Mrs Keightley rushed between them and said he should shoot her before he took her husband away. Hall again interfered and order was restored.

When the doctor returned he found that Burke was dead. A lengthy discussion took place as to what should be done with Keightley. O'Meally and Vane wished to shoot him. Hall and Gilbert were in favour of holding him to ransom, and Mrs Keightley undertook to pay them £500 if they would spare his life. Finally an agreement was arrived at. Mrs Keightley was to ride to Bathurst and bring back the money by 2 p.m. the next day (Sunday). If she failed to return at that time, or brought any one back with her, her husband and Doctor Peechy were to be shot.

The distance from Rockley to Bathurst was twenty-five miles, but Mrs Keightley started without hesitation. The bushrangers refused to stop in the

house during the night in case of surprise. They took their prisoners and camped with them on a knoll, some distance away, where they had a good view of the Bathurst Road for several miles. This they declared would give them time to shoot their hostages and ride away if treachery was attempted.

Mrs Keightley obtained the necessary amount of money from her father, Mr Rolton, M.L.A., and returned home an hour before the stipulated time. She handed the money to Ben Hall, who complimented her on her endurance and pluck. Then Mr Keightley and Dr Peechy were told that they were free, and the bushrangers mounted and rode off. When this outrage was reported, the rewards offered for the capture, dead or alive, of Hall, Gilbert, O'Meally, and Vane, were increased to £1000, while £100 was offered for the capture of any other of their accomplices.

Mr David Henry Campbell was sitting in his house on the Goimbla sheep station on the evening of 19 November 1863 when he heard footsteps on the veranda. Being suspicious as to the character of the visitors, he seized his gun and retreated to an inner room, while his brother William retired by another door. Mrs Campbell was in the bedroom.

The bushrangers came to the front door, and fired into the room. Mr Campbell returned the fire, and the bushrangers retreated. First they went to the stack-yard, and fired the barn and haystack. They then returned to the house, which was illuminated by the blazing of the barn and stack. Mrs Campbell came out of the bedroom, and spoke a few words to her husband. Then she crossed the front parlour in full view of the bushrangers, took a second gun and a powder flask from the corner, and returned to her husband. The bushrangers fired at her, but missed, and they then retreated along the verandah to where the shadow cast by the blazing stack concealed them.

After waiting a few minutes Mrs Campbell, thinking, as she could hear no sound except the roaring of the flames, that the bushrangers had gone away, stealthily crossed the front room and peeped out of the window. She saw three men standing near the stack-yard, and went back to inform her husband. Mr Campbell immediately left the house by the back door, crept

Mr and Mrs Campbell

The scene of John O'Meally's death

stealthily along the fence, taking care to keep in the shadow, and approached the men as closely as possible without giving them the alarm. He recognized the man nearest to him as O'Meally, and fired. O'Meally fell. Almost at the same moment the police came galloping up. They had seen the reflection of the fire miles away, and had ridden over to discover its cause. Hall and Gilbert, the two remaining bushrangers, hastily mounted their horses and went off under cover of the darkness.

O'Meally's body was conveyed to Bathurst, where an inquest was held, and a verdict of justifiable homicide was returned. The *Bathurst Times* reported that locks of O'Meally's hair were being shown about and sold in the town, and protested against it. The paper said that the authorities had no right to allow this desecration of the body, even of a bushranger and murderer. 'The police', it added, 'would not have dared to touch his hair had he been alive. Probably Pottinger and the army of troopers that swarmed round Goimbla when the danger was passed each took a lock of his hair *in memoriam* when their enemy lay prostrate and dead.' A public meeting was held in Sydney on 3 March 1864 to consider what means should be adopted to recognize the bravery of Mr Campbell in daring to resist the bushrangers and shooting O'Meally. A number of prominent men gave addresses, and it was resolved that a public subscription should be taken up to recoup him for the loss of his barn and stacks. The amount collected at the meeting and during a few days after totalled £1100. Mr Campbell was also awarded a gold medal by the Government.

The violent deaths of Lowry, Burke, and O'Meally, in so short a time, seemed to have very little effect on the gang, which continued its rampage. Neither did these deaths prevent other young men from adopting the 'profession of bushranger'. In fact the deaths of a few bushrangers appear to have had less effect in deterring bushranging than the immunity enjoyed by the leaders offered encouragement. It was increasing instead of diminishing, although for a few months very little was heard of the Hall and Gilbert gang.

There was some comedy mingled with the prevailing tragedy. For instance, a blackfellow met Alexander Sinclair near Killoshiel, and inquired how far it was to Bathurst. Sinclair told him, and was immediately ordered to 'get off that horse'. The rider hesitated but the aboriginal pushed him off the saddle, sprang into it himself, and galloped away threatening to shoot Sinclair if he followed, although it is very doubtful whether he had any arms on him. The same native took possession of another horse in a similar manner a few hours later some miles along the road. He rode both horses until they knocked up, and then abandoned them. They were afterwards found feeding in the bush with their saddles and bridles still on. It was supposed that the blackfellow was just pining for a gallop and adopted this means of gratifying himself. He was not traced.

Sergeant Donohoe captured William Dunne after an exciting chase through the ranges. As the sergeant did not know his way back to the high road, he compelled his prisoner to lie down, and waited patiently until some other policemen went out in search of him. Neither the sergeant nor his prisoner had any food for forty-eight hours. The police also captured George Bermingham. This man was a printer, born in Sydney, and was twenty-one years of age. When taken he was full of bravado, boasted loudly of the number of people he had stuck up and talked familiarly of Vane and Johnny Gilbert. He laughed at the idea of Ben Hall having been shot as had been rumoured, and said, 'Wait till he's spent the five hundred quid he got from Keightley, and you'll soon hear of him again.' Sergeant Donohoe said he had followed Dunne because he recognized the magnificent chestnut horse he was riding as one ridden by the robbers of the Cooma mail. Dunne and Bermingham were sent to jail for ten years for having been concerned in this robbery.

In the last week for November 1863 Hall and Gilbert stuck up the Burrowa mail. Hall expressed his disgust at the number of cheques found in the letters, and requested some of the passengers to cash them. As no one volunteered to oblige him he continued: 'If I thought it would injure them (the people who posted cheques presumably) I'd burn the —— lot.' The two bushrangers sat down to open the letters, leaving the passengers perfectly free. Gilbert took up one letter which had a black border and laid it aside unopened, with the remark, 'We must respect death.' In one of the letters a piece of wedding cake was found, and Gilbert proposed that they should eat it, but Hall objected, saying 'It may be a trap.' This caution was common to all the bushrangers. They were in constant dread of being poisoned, and were therefore very cautious as to what they ate or drank. One of the passengers, Mr Robert Handley, described the two bushrangers as being well-dressed, healthy-looking, and very civil.

The following morning Hall and Gilbert went to Coffey's Inn near Burrowa, and ordered breakfast. When they had finished their meal they walked out on to the road and stopped every one who passed, compelling them to go into the bar after handing over their money. Mr Campbell, however, refused to stand when challenged. He struck spurs to his horse and galloped away. Hall fired at him and then rushed to the veranda and mounted his horse. He galloped only a short distance and then returned as Campbell had too good a start. The bushrangers 'shouted' for their prisoners in the bar several times 'for the good of the house', and paid for what they ordered. It was said that they spent nearly as much as they had obtained from the persons robbed.

On 16 December Mr Henry Morgan, one of the proprietors of the *Burrangong Star*, was driving with his newly-married wife between Bowning and Binalong, when he was ordered to bail up by Hall and Gilbert. Gilbert was in high spirits. He exchanged hats with Morgan, and put his poncho on Mrs Morgan,

declaring that she would make 'a first-rate bushranger'. The newspaper man and his wife were taken into the bush, and detained from 8 a.m. till 6 p.m. during this time Mr George Franklin and his wife and four bullock drays were stuck up. One of the bullock-drivers named Sheedy had four bottles of gin on his dray, and these were opened and the liquor served round. The robbers asked Mrs Franklin to cook breakfast 'for the crowd', taking the necessary provisions from the loading on the drays.

During the afternoon a number of other persons were brought into the camp. All except one man were allowed to move about freely. This one man was tied, and was spoken to very roughly and uncivilly. The man was supposed to be 'a telegram', and this show of harshness 'a stall'. At six o'clock the camp was broken up and the prisoners permitted to resume their journeys.

This performance was repeated near the same spot on each of the following three days. Although the individual losses were generally small, the aggregate amount of money collected must have been considerable. Only in one instance was any violence used. A bullock-driver named Lake refused to turn out his pockets. Gilbert pressed the muzzle of his revolver against Lake's face and said: 'If you don't do what you're told I'll shove this down your —— mouth.' Hall felt Lake's pockets and took out £5 in notes and some silver. At night when released, Lake asked for some of his money back to pay expenses along the road. Gilbert replied: 'If you're a —— carrier your name's good for what you want. If you hadn't been so —— jolly you'd have got something. We always divide with them that behave themselves.'

In the week ending 23 December 1863, the Molong, the Cooma, the Tuena, and the Hartley mails were stuck up and robbed, proving that either the gang was divided or that more than one party was at work in the district.

When returning home from one of the numerous race parties held during the Christmas holidays, a party including Messrs Sheedy, Bass, Hutchinson, and other residents of the district, with several ladies were ordered to 'bail up'. A lad was leading the racer Black Diamond, owned by Mr Sheedy, and let him go. Ben Hall was furious. He galloped after the racer swearing, but failed to head him. He came back and threatened the boy and Mr Sheedy, but soon grew cool. Although the ladies were treated very civilly, the robbers took watches and other valuables and all the money they could find from the gentlemen. Black Diamond was found safe in his stable when Mr Sheedy reached home.

An early Victorian trooper in the days when nearly every police station had a mounted section

# 17 Duels and deaths

**Heavy sessions at Goulburn; Ben Hall hard pushed; Gardiner's trial and sentence; Johnny Dunn; a desperate duel and death of Sergeant Parry; meeting the gold escort; deaths of Hall and Gilbert; record of the Gardiner gang; capture and trial of Dunn.**

Bushranging by no means died out with the close of 1863. On 7 February 1864, Inspector Brennan and Constables Lovett and Roche went to a sly-grog shanty, a place where strong drinks were sold without a licence, and captured George Lynam and Michael Seary. The horses of the two bushrangers were so exhausted with hard riding that although they mounted and rode away when the police came, they were soon caught. They were charged and convicted of having robbed a number of persons at William Sidwell's Governor's Arms Hotel, Towrang, two miles from Goulburn, in company with James Crookwell and Daniel Matthews. Lynam, in company with John Southgate, also stuck up and robbed Thomas Cummins, Robert Sherwood and others at Mr Cornelius O'Brien's station near Binalong. They also stuck up Mr Dwyer's place at Pudman's Creek, and after having made a bundle of all that was worth taking away, compelled Mrs Ann Dwyer to cook thirty-four eggs and a quantity of bacon for them.

They tied Dwyer, struck Mrs Dwyer, and threatened to burn the place down unless they were told where the money was hidden. Jane, daughter of Ann Dwyer, said that when they went in to search the bedroom, Lynam pointed to the crucifix and exclaimed 'There's Jesus Christ. He ought to be burned, and I've a good mind to do it.' The intruders smashed the furniture and broke open boxes and cupboards in their search for money. Lynam was sent to jail for fifteen years, while Seary, Matthews, Crookwell and Southgate were sentenced to ten years each for some offences, and to fifteen years for others. As all the sentences were made concurrent the prisoners were actually sentenced to fifteen years' imprisonment. At the same sessions Charles Jones, alias William Herbert, and Frank Stanley, alias Wright, were sentenced to twelve years for various acts of highway robbery. Some of these young men were said to have assisted in some of the robberies by the Hall and Gilbert gang, and were suspected of being on their way to join that gang.

While the police had been very successful in bringing a number of outsiders to justice, the better known members of the Gardiner gang continued to keep the district alive.

Benjamin Hall was about twenty-eight years of age. His father had come to the Wedden Mountains district in about 1840 when little Ben was about three years old. The elder Hall had worked for Mr Ranken for some years, and had always been of good character. When Ben was old enough he had been engaged as stockman with Mr Hamilton, of Tomanbil. He saved money and took up a small station for himself at the Pinnacle, about fifteen miles from Forbes and married a daughter of another settler. He had no sympathy with the bushrangers when the outbreak under Gardiner occurred and the police frequently stopped for a night at his house when looking for the bushrangers near his station. His wife was flighty and was seduced, it was said, by a police official. Hall joined the gang 'to meet the man who ruined my happiness'. Such was the story currently believed in the neighbourhood, and Ben was the only one of the bushrangers for whom the general public, apart from those who were related to or interested in them, felt any sympathy. Before 'he took to the bush' he was known as a steady, industrious, kind-hearted young man, and many could scarcely believe that it was the same Ben Hall, the noted bushranger, of whom everybody was talking.

The *Yass Courier* reported that nearly every one in the district had turned out to hunt Ben Hall, who was reported to have paid them a visit. The bushranger had been so hard pressed that he was forced to abandon the horse, Willy the Weasel, owned by Mr Garry. The horse was completely knocked up, otherwise the bushranger would not have let him go as he was a favourite. The stock-riders of the district had expressed great contempt for the police, their opinions being summed up as follows: 'They can't catch him. They don't know how to ride down a hill.' Many of the 'hills' in the district would be elsewhere considered almost as precipices.

The same week the *Young (Burrangong) Daily*

Ben Hall

*Tribune* reported that a day or two ago Ben Hall walked alone into the stables at Groggan station, Bland Plains, said 'Good morning, boys', then proceeded coolly to tie up the three men and a boy. Having secured them to his entire satisfaction, he walked to the house and asked to see Mr Chisholm. When that gentleman came to the door Hall said, 'Good morning, Mr Chisholm. I've come for Troubadour.' 'You've left him so long you might do without him now', returned Mr Chisholm. 'Oh', exclaimed Hall, 'you're getting too — — flash. If you consort with traps you'll have to be taught manners.'

They walked to the stables, where Hall put saddles and bridles on Troubadour and Union Jack. The latter had won the Champion Plate at the Wagga Wagga races on New Year's Day, and had only been brought home under police escort a day or two before. Hall also selected two other horses, which he said he 'liked the look of', and put bridles of them. He then made Mr Chisholm fill two three-bushel bags with clothing from the store, and these he packed on the spare horses. Then he mounted Troubadour and, leading the others, started away. He had scarcely moved before he pulled up again, and said to Mr Chisholm, 'That's a good looking watch of yours. I want it. Hand it over.' Mr Chisholm did so, and the bushranger then rode off. It may be explained that the reason why no opposition was attempted was because it was believed that Hall had plenty of support if he had required it. He never walked unless he was compelled, and it was thought that his mates with the horses were not far off. It was also suggested that Hall had a bad mount after he lost Willy the Weasel and that he did not wish to let Mr Chisholm see him riding an inferior horse.

When the mail coach from Wagga Wagga failed to arrive at Cootamundra at the usual time on 12 May, the contractor, Mr Burke, supposed that it had been stuck up somewhere along the road and rode up to make inquiries. About three miles from Cootamundra he found a number of letters lying scattered about the road. He gathered them up and continued his search. At length he found the mail-man, drunk in a public-house near Murrumburrah. The fellow had robbed the mail himself, no doubt with the intention of laying the blame on the bushrangers. He was convicted and sentenced to seven years' penal servitude.

The mail was stuck up at Mumble Flat, between Orange and Wellington, on 1 March. A portion of the load consisted of carbines and revolvers for the police, 'all of which', said the *Orange Guardian*, 'were borne off to be used against them.'

The Bathurst-Sydney coach was stuck up at Lapstone Hill by three armed men. The passengers were Michael Duffy, Constable McKay, in charge of a female lunatic, and three Chinamen. After having collected the money from the passengers and searched the letters, the robbers extinguished the coach lamps, took the horses out, and drove them up the hill. The driver waited for half an hour as he had been ordered to do, and then started to catch his horses. This he managed to do with some difficulty and drove on to Penrith. From there the passengers and the broken mail-bags were taken to Sydney by train. John Forster was arrested in a house at Strawberry Hills, Sydney,

**The Bathurst—Sydney coach, with armed escort, arriving at the Treasury.**

and charged with having, with others, stuck up and robbed the mail coach between Penrith and Hartley at 2 a.m. Ah Lung, one of the passengers on the coach, recognized a sash which the prisoner wore round his waist as his property, and said he carried his money in it. Forster was sent to jail for ten years.

About this time great excitement was caused throughout New South Wales by the report that Frank Gardiner had been discovered and arrested by Detective McGlone on 3 March at Apis Creek, on the road from Rockhampton to the Peak Downs diggings, Queensland. Gardiner was keeping a shanty, or roadside store, with Mrs Brown who passed as his wife. Gardiner was brought to Sydney and duly committed for trial. In connection with this case Mr (later Sir E. Deas) Thompson laid a return on the table of the Legislative Assembly showing that the amount stolen by Gardiner prior to his disappearance was about £21,000. Of this total, £13,694 had been stolen in the robbery of the Lachlan Escort, and £5335 had been recovered by the police under Sir Frederick Pottinger. No murders were charged against Gardiner, but he was convicted on three counts for highway robbery. On each of these counts he was sentenced; on the first to twelve years and on the other two to ten years each, the first three years in irons in each case. The sentences were made cumulative, and aggregated thirty-two years.

Despite the constant vigilance of the police (above), there were not enough of them, nor did they have sufficient knowledge of the mountain areas, to ambush the well-mounted, clever Gardiner. Eventually he retired from bushranging to Apis Creek, near Rockhampton in Queensland, as 'Mr Christie', the part-owner of an inn and general store (below). Unfortunately for him, his mistress, Kitty Brown, wrote home proudly to tell of their new life and soon afterwards Detective McClone with two other police and a dozen Queensland native police arrived and captured the outlaw.

It will be remembered that Captain Melville, the bushranger, was sentenced to a similar term of imprisonment in Victoria about twelve years before, and there were many people in New South Wales who thought that Gardiner had been too harshly dealt with. Such a sentence, they said, deprived a man of all hope, and rendered him desperate. They would not be surprised if Gardiner rebelled abainst it as Melville had done. However, those who held this view were in the minority. The majority said bushranging must be stamped out at any cost, and until this was effected the sentences could not be too severe.

On 20 May Ben Hall, Gilbert, and a new recruit known as 'the Old Man', rode up to McGregor's Inn at Bong Bong, where a number of men were on the veranda. The bushrangers ordered these men to 'throw your arms up', enforcing the order with revolvers. There were some twenty visitors on the veranda and in the bar, and these were ranged along the wall in the dining-room with Hall on guard. Gilbert and the Old Man walked down the yard to the stables where several race-horses were in the stalls under the charge of constables Scott and Macnamara who were escorting them to Burrangong for the races on Queen's birthday. Gilbert called to the constables to 'leave those horses'. The constables drew their revolvers, and fired. The bushrangers fired, and Hall left the dining-room to take part in the scrimmage. For some minutes the shooting was very brisk, but no one appeared to be hurt. The police were on foot and under cover of the stables; the bushrangers were mounted and in the open yard. Suddenly the firing ceased as if by mutual consent, and Gilbert shouted that they would be back presently. The bushrangers then rode away.

As Hall went out of the gate his cabbage tree hat fell off, and a cry was raised that he had been hit. He rode off, however, without showing any symptoms of injury. Believing that the bushrangers had gone for reinforcements, the two constables barricaded the stables, and sent a messenger to the nearest police depot for assistance. About midnight Sir Frederick Pottinger arrived with four troopers, but the bushrangers did not return.

On the following afternoon the mail coach was stuck up at Emu Flat, between Burrangong and Yass. Although a passenger named Michael Curran saved his gold watch and chain by dropping them among the straw in the bottom of the coach, a valuable gold ring and £21 in notes were taken from him. Ben Hall also exchanged an old poncho for a valuable rug, and an old clay pipe for a very fine meerschaum. Some distance away Mr Barnes met the coach. The driver, J. Roberts, who knew him, warned Barnes that the bushrangers were on the road. Barnes laughed and went on. He was stopped and robbed, and as he did not hand out his money very readily when ordered to do so, he was very roughly treated and was threatened with death.

Several teams were also robbed. The bushrangers were riding the racers Teddington, Harkaway, and Troubadour.

During this 'reign of terror', the Press, especially in the country districts, continued to urge the necessity for suppressing the bush telegraphs and other sympathizers of the bushrangers. It said that while so many who aided them either by giving them information of the movements of the police or providing them with hiding places when they were hard pressed were at large, the police had little chance of making headway against the evil doers. The *Yass Courier*, for instance, spoke of 'the wealthy relations — of the bushrangers — with whom the police are afraid to interfere, but whose places never have and never will be stuck up'. The paper 'perforce refrains from publishing the names of these people on account of the state of the libel law', but it charged them with 'comforting and assisting the bushrangers'. It seems difficult to understand what the police were expected to do, or to see what action could be taken against a settler because his place was not raided and who had some more or less distant relative 'on the road'. But this serves to show how closely the Press inquired into the antecedents and relationships of the bushrangers.

A man believed to be Johnny Gilbert, accompanied by a lad named Ryan, stopped to dinner at the Korowatha Inn. They talked freely of bushranging, and laughed at the report that Hall had been hit at McGregor's, as the newspapers had reported. They affirmed that 'the traps could not fire straight enough to hit a haystack'.

On 22 June 1864, the *Bathurst Times* said:

After an immunity from bushranging crimes in this district for some months, the gang has appeared once more and commenced operations. On the 18th, the mail coach for Orange and the Lachlan started an hour late from this town in consequence of the heavy mail. There were on board James Nairne and seven passengers. About eighteen miles out, near the turn-off road to Guyong, three men jumped out of the bush and ordered the mail-man to bail up. The coach was taken off the road, where the passengers were robbed and the letters torn open. The driver and passengers were then told that they would be detained until the down mail came. While they were waiting a little boy was stopped and one pound of tea and 1s. 6d. in money were taken from him. The boy's father, a farmer living near, came out to look for his son, and was run in among the crowd. After some dispute the tea and the 1s. 6d. were given back, but the father and son were compelled to remain until the other coach came by. The down mail, driven by John Fagan, arrived about midnight and was stopped. Fagan was asked what made him so late, and replied that the roads were bad with the rains. The letters were opened, except those in the registered bag, which the robbers missed. About 2 a.m. the robbers told their prisoners that they might go, and walked away.

Titled, 'Sticking Up the Goulburn Mail' this drawing depicts how easily bushrangers robbed unprotected travellers.

It was said that this was not the Gilbert and Hall gang, as the robbers had no horses. The police started in pursuit from Bathurst and Orange as soon as news of the robbery reached these towns.

Ben Hall and his gang stuck up and robbed Pearce and Hillier's store at Canowindra, and held the town for the day as on a previous occasion. The following afternoon, 23 June, they called at Mr Rothsay's station, took four horses from the stables, and set fire to a stack containing about fourteen tons of hay as a 'caution to traitors'.

Ben Hall, Johnny Gilbert, John Dunleavy, and James Mount (known as the Old Man) stuck up the Carcour and Cowra coaches. They then rode on to the Half-Way House Hotel and compelled the landlord to hand over £76. They held the road for several hours, robbing all who passed and bringing them to the hotel, where they 'shouted for all hands' several times. This time the bushrangers drank port wine. They took several well-bred horses from the stables. One of these got loose and galloped along the road. He was followed by Dunleavy, who failed to head him. The horse was caught next day and sent to Bathurst for safety.

Hall and Mount went to Mr Jamieson's station on the Bland River and informed the proprietor that they intended to stop for the night. They called the men up, asked their names and how much money each one had. Having obtained this information they announced that they did not intend to take anything from any one. Possibly this decision may have been due to the fact that the total amount was small. They ordered supper to be served, and made all present sit down to the table in the dining-room.

When the meal was over and the table cleared, Mr Jamieson was asked to bring out some rum from the store. A pint pot, filled with hot water with plenty of salt in it, was placed on the table, and Hall announced that if any one present refused to sing or to contribute in some other way to the general amusement, he would be compelled to swallow the contents of this pannikin. Then they made a night of it. In the morning half the men were lying on the ground in a drunken sleep, but the bushrangers were quite sober, having drunk very little. They spent half an hour in the stable cleaning their horses, had breakfast, and rode away, declaring that they had enjoyed themselves immensely, and thanking Mr Jamieson for the entertainment he had afforded them.

They called at the next station and took the race-horse Plover out of the stable. Mount ordered the stockman to fetch the horses out of the paddocks as he wanted to select one or two of the best stock-horses. While they were talking, the stockman moved round from Mount's right-hand side to the left. The bushranger immediately shifted his revolver from the right hand to the left, remarking quietly: 'I can shoot just as straight left-handed as right.' Hall said he had enjoyed many a good laugh at the newspaper yarns about himself. He added that Brown's men were 'jolly good fellows'. In the evening they stuck up the Gundagai mail near Jugiong. When opening the letters Hall found a bulky roll of bank notes. 'Ah!' he said, 'This is what I like.' He took a number of newspapers

away with him, 'just to see what they say about me.'
From there they rode straight to the Chinese camp at
Wombat, 'to give the Chinkies a lesson'. The Chinese
were very slow in producing their gold, and the
bushrangers fired in among them, killing one and
wounding another.

The next day, Sunday, they stuck up a number of
Chinamen on the road and took their gold but did not
ill-treat them. In the afternoon they went to Mr
McCarthy's store in Jugiong and compelled him to open
the door. They selected a quantity of clothing and
drapery, which they placed on a spare packhorse they
had with them. In the evening they stuck up the
Gundagai mail within a mile of the place where they
had stuck it up a few days before. Hall took out a roll
of half notes from one packet. 'This is a green trick,
this is,' he said, holding them up. 'It's little trouble to
us to match half notes.' This series of outrages,
following so closely one on the other, naturally stirred
the police to increased activity, and the bushrangers
were so closely followed that a brush took place
between them and the police in the last week of
October. In this fight, which lasted only a very short
time, Dunleavy was severely wounded and
surrendered, while Mount was captured.

James Mount was an escaped convict, out on a
ticket-of-leave. He was forty-five years of age, but had
been called the Old Man before his name was known,
to distinguish him from the young men and boys who
formed the body of this gang. Mount was tried and
convicted of highway robbery in Bathurst, and was
sentenced to ten years' imprisonment.

In commenting upon the capture of Mount and
Dunleavy the *Goulburn Herald* announced that their
loss to the gang had been to some extent compensated
for by the accession of Johnny Dunn, who was born in
Murrumburrah. Earlier in the year 1864, Dunn had
won the principal prize at the Yass race meeting with
the Binalong horse, Ringleader. He was an excellent
rider and would no doubt give the police some trouble.

'Messrs Hall, Gilbert, and Dunn seem to have
obtained a lease of the Main Southern road,' said the
*Yass Courier* of 19 November. They robbed the up and
down mails from Gundagai two consecutive weeks. On
the last of these four robberies the coach was bailed
up at Deep Creek, near Jugiong, at about 4 p.m. Messrs
Bradley and Sheahan, passengers, had alighted to walk
up the steep hill and were some hundred yards or so
ahead of the coach when three men suddenly appeared
from behind the scrub and ordered them to bail up. 'All
right', replied Mr Sheahan, holding his hands above his
head. Hall said, 'That'll do. We've got a little township
of our own up there. Come on'. He pointed up the hill
as he spoke. They followed him until they came to a
small, clear spot, surrounded with high trees and
scrub. Here they saw twelve bullock drays and a
number of men. Several horses were hitched to the
trees round the clearing, and the men who owned

**Johnny Dunn**

them, as well as the bullock-drivers and some footmen,
were seated on the ground.

When asked for his money Sheahan replied, 'Got
none. Search if you like.' 'Oh, you're not a bad sort',
said Hall, 'we'll take your word for it.' Bradley took out
a cheque for £1, saying, 'That's all I've got. I brought it
to pay my way on the trip.' Hall put his hand into
Bradley's pocket, and finding nothing there told him to
keep the cheque. A cask of port wine which was found
on one of the bullock drays, was tapped, and the wine
was handed round to all present in a quart pot in
which tea had apparently been made. When the letters
had been searched, the bushrangers told the company
that they might go.

Expecting that the return mail would be robbed
again next day Mr Ross, police magistrate, and
Constable Roche in private clothes went as
passengers, while Inspector O'Neil and Sergeant
Edmund Parry rode beside the coach on horseback. At
Black Springs near Jugiong, the bushrangers appeared
as anticipated, and on emerging from the bush one of
them shouted out, 'Hullo, here's the bobbies.' Hall said,
'There's only two. Rush the ——.' The three
bushrangers then rode forward shouting 'Come on, you
——, fight like men.' Sergeant Parry rode forward and
encountered Gilbert, and a desperate duel on
horseback with revolvers took place until Parry fell.

In the meantime Inspector O'Neil had kept under
cover of the coach and managed to keep the other two
bushrangers at bay until Parry fell, when he
surrendered. Mr Ross fired several shots, but what

became of Constable Roche is not known. He was not captured or wounded. He simply disappeared in the scrub. When all was quiet Gilbert dismounted, turned over Parry's body, and remarked coolly, 'He got it in the cobbera. It's all over with him. Well, I'm sorry for it. He's the bravest trap I've met yet.'

The coach was taken off the road to where several bullock teams, two horse carts with their Chinese owners, a buggy with Mr and Mrs Hayes, and several footmen and horsemen — among whom was Constable McLaughlin, who had fired away his ammunition before he surrendered — were collected together. The robbers searched the letters as usual, took all the police horses and arms, collected the money, watches, and other valuables from the crowd and rode away saying 'We'll rob the mail tomorrow if all the —— traps in the colony are here.' Whether this was merely an empty threat, or whether the bushrangers intended to draw the police here so that they might operate in safety elsewhere, has been frequently argued without any definite result. The police were on the road, and the bushrangers did not put in an appearance. On the following day, however, the gang stuck up the Binalong mail. After searching the mail they burned letters and papers to 'put a stop to the —— English correspondence'.

A day or two later, 'Messrs Hall & Co.' took possession of the road between the Fourteen Mile and the Fifteen Mile rushes at Burrangong and bailed up about thirty men, women, and boys. A bridle took the fancy of one of the gang, and he insisted on taking it and giving his own in return. With this exception, and the taking of a quantity of bread and butter found on the drays bailed up, nothing was stolen. The bushrangers explained that they expected some gold buyers along the road and when they came the camp would be broken up. In the meantime they wanted every one to enjoy the picnic. The women were set to work to cut up and serve out the bread and butter. Fires were lit and tea made. Then races and other sports were organized for the boys. One of the bailed-up men was a newsvendor, and the bushrangers 'borrowed' his papers and took it in turn to lie down and 'read the news'. At last one of the boys contrived to sneak away unseen, and as soon as his escape was discovered the camp was broken up and the robbers rode away.

On 19 December, the Hon. William Macleay, M.L.C., was driving in a buggy from Towrang to Shelly's Flat, when he noticed a large crowd a little way ahead. He sent his coachman on with the buggy and got down to make inquiries. As he drew near he saw that a number of people were standing round two bullock drays, while one or two men were breaking open the boxes on the drays. Mr Macleay asked a man what was the matter, and the man motioned to him to keep quiet. Mr Macleay conjectured that it was the bushrangers robbing the drays, and withdrew as quietly as he had joined the crowd. He walked on to Plum's Inn, where he found people enjoying a wedding party. He told the

**Ben Hall and his followers hold up the Gundagai mail coach near Jugiong in November, 1864, and Johnny Gilbert shoots Sergeant Edmund Parry.**

landlord what he had seen and advised those present to take precautions to avoid being robbed.

Some time later the bushrangers came up, and seeing a number of men on the veranda with guns and revolvers in their hands, they fired. Mr Macleay immediately returned the fire. The bushrangers drew together some distance away and held a consultation. They apparently decided that the risk was too great, as they went off along the road. For beating off the bushrangers and proving that a show of resistance might prevent robberies, Mr Macleay was awarded a gold medal by the New South Wales Government. On the other hand, the fact that the bushrangers robbed the drays openly in the main road in this instance instead of taking them into the bush, was cited as evidence that they were growing bolder and more careless of the police.

Hall, Gilbert, and Dunn rode up to a store at Binda, owned by an ex-policeman named Morris, on 21 December, and took about £100 from his cashbox. They informed Morris that a ball was being held at the Flag Hotel, and insisted on himself and Mrs Morris dressing themselves and accompanying the bushrangers to the ball. Morris at first objected, but finally gave way.

When they reached the Flag Hotel the bushrangers mixed freely with the crowd, dancing and otherwise enjoying themselves. Presently some bush telegraph informed the bushrangers that Morris had been sounding several of the men present as to the probability of effecting a capture. Gilbert and Dunn drew their revolvers and started to look for Morris who, having been informed of what had transpired, jumped through an open window, and ran towards where the bushrangers' horses were tied to the trees. His intention was to take one and ride for the police. The bushrangers caught sight of him and divining his intention ran and fired at Morris. This compelled him to turn aside and take refuge behind a tree. The bushrangers made no attempt to follow him. They removed their horses to a safer place, then walked to the store where they piled a quantity of brushwood on the veranda and set fire to it. Then they mounted their horses and sat and watched the blaze until the house was well alight before riding off. There were more than a hundred people at the ball, but no attempt was made to prevent the bushrangers from burning down the store.

In connection with this 'act of vengeance' Christina McKinnon and Ellen and Margaret Monks were arrested and charged with having aided and abetted in burning down Morris's store. The girls had been dancing with the bushrangers, and had accompanied them when they went to the store. The police said that they were well known as bush telegraphs, and cited instances in which it was supposed that they had given notice to the bushrangers of the approach of the police. Margaret Monks was discharged, but the other two

were sent to jail, the evidence showing that they had assisted the bushrangers in piling wood on the veranda of the store.

Mr D. Davis, auctioneer of Yass, had been conducting a sale at Murrumburrah and was returning home on 30 December when he was stuck up. He had on him £109 1s. 5d., the proceeds of the sale, principally in cheques. When these were handed out Ben Hall was in a furious rage and threatened to burn them. Gilbert proposed that he should gallop on and 'change them before they're stopped'. There was £1 5s. 6d. in cash, and of this they kept £1, returning the silver. They then rode rapidly away. Nothing more was heard of the cheques; they were never cashed.

During the first week or two of 1865 very little was heard of Messrs Hall & Co., but on 26 January the three principal members of the gang (Hall, Gilbert, and Dunn), stuck up Mr Kimberley's store in Main Street, Collector. Dunn was stationed on guard on the veranda while Hall and Gilbert went inside to select such

**To the *Melbourne Punch* of 1864 there seemed no limit to the daring of the bushrangers, calling on settlers as they chose and robbing them of all their valuables.**

articles as they required or fancied. Constable Nelson, the only policeman stationed in the little town was at the lock-up, and on being informed of what was going on he loaded his carbine and walked down the street towards the store. Dunn saw him coming and withdrew out of sight behind the fence at the corner of the veranda.

When the constable was only a few yards distant the robber fired at him. The constable fell and Dunn, coming out of his hiding-place, walked to where he was lying, put his revolver close to the constable's head, and fired again. Hearing the shots Hall and Gilbert came out. On seeing what had been done they held a whispered consultation and then mounted their horses and rode away. They went straight to Alfred Cramp's farm at Binda and ordered dinner. While they were still at the table a party of police galloped up, dismounted, and rushed into the front door of the house as the bushrangers went out the back door. A few shots were fired but the bushrangers mounted and escaped, owing to the superiority of their horses. The news of Constable Nelson's death had been conveyed to the police at once, and they had followed close on the tracks of the bushrangers.

In February, a number of people were stuck up near Illalong, on the road between Yass and Burrangong. The robbers were said to have no connection with Hall & Co., as they robbed their victims of their coats and vests. The Hall gang never did this. If they saw a man with a coat or vest, or any other article of clothing to which they took a fancy, they would exchange with him, but they only stole clothes from the stores. However, while the police were out in search of these plebeian bushrangers, they happened to come across Hall and Gilbert at Lodge's Inn, Breadalbane Plains, and captured their horses. It was supposed that the two robbers had been sleeping in the barn. They rushed out when the police came, and went across a cleared paddock, both parties firing their revolvers. Constable Wiles was wounded, and Ben Hall fell. He was up again in a moment however, and succeeded in reaching the timber where the ground was too rough and heavily-timbered for the police horses to make their way through it.

A daring attempt was made by Hall and three others to stick up the Araluen escort on 16 March. The bushrangers fired from behind trees as the escort cart was going up Major's Creek Mount, at the same place where a similar attempt had been made about two and a half years previously. Constable Kelly fell wounded, and died a few days later. Constable Burns, who was driving, jumped off the cart, put a stone behind the wheel, and then fired, shouting 'Come on.' Mr Blatchford, J.P., who had been riding beside the driver, remained on his seat until a voice from behind the trees cried out, 'Shoot the —— on the cart'. He jumped down quickly but was wounded in the leg. He fell, but got up again immediately and ran down the hill

Before Ben Hall took over, Johnny Gilbert was the right-hand man of Frank Gardiner. He was always a flash dresser, had plenty of money to spend and had a keen eye for horses.

to Noonan's Hotel for assistance.

Constable Stapleton and his companion forced their horses up the steep cutting which bordered the road, and disappeared among the trees. Burns, thus left alone with the cart, sheltered himself behind it as well as he could, and kept blazing away coolly from his cover. Suddenly Constable Stapleton and his companion attacked the robbers from the rear. Gilbert turned sharply and said, 'You're a —— good shot, take that', and shot the constable's horse. The two policemen kept up the firing and the bushrangers mounted their horses and rode away. Mr Blatchford presented Constable Burns with a cheque for £50 as a reward for the pluck he had shown in defending his charge.

It was at about this time that Sir Frederick Pottinger, who was in command of the police in this district, was charged with having neglected his duty. Sir Frederick had ridden in a gentlemen's race on the Wowingragong course. It was rumoured that the bushrangers for whom he was supposed to be looking had been on the course too, and had not been recognized. Sir Frederick was called to Sydney to attend an inquiry, and resigned his position in the force. About a month later he died from the effects of a wound from a pistol accidentally fired by himself.

The gang yarded a mob of horses at a station near Murrumburrah and picked out several of the finest horses which they took away, leaving their own knocked-up horses in their place. They rode to Wombat where they stuck up a mob of Chinamen, one of whom was shot to make the others 'shell out' their gold more quickly. Then the bushrangers travelled to Forbes, and on the following day robbed Mr Jones's store of £81 in cash and a quantity of clothing and drapery. Information was given to the police in the town as soon as the robbers left the store, and a party of police with two black trackers followed them.

On the following evening, 5 May, they came on two hobbled horses feeding near the Billabong Creek. These were recognized as horses which had been ridden by the bushrangers, and the police watched them carefully without allowing themselves to be seen. This was not difficult as there were thick patches of scrub about the flat.

Half an hour later a man came out of one of these patches of scrub, unhobbled the horses, and led them about two hundred yards away to where there was better grass. It was too dark to distinguish him. He rehobbled the horses and retired into the scrub once more. The police drew up closer to this patch with great caution and watched till morning. At daybreak the man appeared again and looked round to ascertain whether the horses were in sight, and Inspector Davidson immediately recognized him as Ben Hall and called on him to stand.

Hall turned to go back into the patch of scrub and the inspector fired at him. Sergeant Condell and the four policemen also fired. Hall stopped and leaned on a sapling for support. Then Constable Hopkiss took steady aim and fired again and Hall let his revolver fall from his hand. The police went forward and Hall said 'I'm hit. Shoot me dead.' He relaxed his hold on the sapling, staggered forward and fell. The police rushed up, but he died before any attempt could be made to staunch the blood.

When his body was examined one rifle and six revolver bullet wounds were found, any one of which should have proved fatal. The bushrangers' horses were soon caught, the body was strapped on one of them, and the party returned to Forbes. The police were very surprised to have found Hall alone, but guessed that Gilbert and Dunn had gone down the Lachlan River to some of the great stations to procure horses as all the race-horses about Burrangong had been pretty well exhausted. The two captured with Hall were in very poor condition and had evidently been ridden hard. He thought he was quite safe in the scrub so far away from his usual haunts.

The death of Ben Hall no doubt had a depressing effect on the bushrangers generally, but it by no means put an end to their crimes. On 11 May, a horse was stolen from Murrumburrah. On the following day the horses at Mr Furlonge's station were rounded up and a

Ben Hall, shortly before he was shot

After parading the body of Ben Hall through the streets of Forbes and souveniring most of his clothes, the police hurriedly buried the body for fear somebody might steal the head. In the 1920s, the original rough wooden grave (above) was replaced by a stone headstone (below). It was rumoured that a woman had done this, but romantics believe that an aging man, Ben Hall's abducted son, was responsible.

The newspapers of May, 1865, carried contrasting but equally
dramatic representations of the death of Ben Hall under fire
from six troopers.

race-horse taken away, the Murrumburrah horse being left instead of it. Information was immediately sent to the police, and a party with the aid of a black tracker, followed the tracks towards Binalong. The place was near the house where Johnny Dunn's parents lived so the police camped near and watched the little township all night but saw nothing to excite their suspicions.

In the morning a lad named Thomas Kelly, brother of convicted bushrangers, was asked whether any one was staying at his grandfather's house and replied, 'No.' Constables Hales and King walked up to old Kelly's place and pushed the door open. Gilbert and Dunn were in the front room, and immediately fired at the police, who retreated. A few minutes passed, during which the police were looking to their revolvers. Then the two bushrangers were seen to emerge by the back door and walk steadily down the paddock. The police followed, and some shots were exchanged.

Near the fence the bushrangers made a stand, and there was a pause for a second or so. Then constables Hales and Bright fired together and Gilbert fell. Dunn jumped over the fence and dashed in among the trees. Some of the police followed but he soon disappeared. On examination it was found that a bullet had entered Gilbert's breast and passed out below the left shoulder-blade, having travelled through the left ventricle of the heart. He was then about twenty-five years of age. Old Kelly was arrested, charged with having harboured bushrangers, and sent to jail.

John Dunn, the last of this notorious trio, did not long survive his two mates. His record as given in the *Yass Courier* is very instructive. He joined Hall and Gilbert a few days after the capture of Mount and the wounding of Dunleavy, and on 24 October robbed Mr Chisholm on the highway near Goulburn. On the 28th, in company with Hall and Gilbert, he stuck up Mr Macansh's station and robbed the Albury mail near Jugiong. On 8 November they robbed Mr Rossi's station, near Goulburn. On the 9th they robbed the Southern Mail six miles from Goulburn, and on the 11th they robbed the Gundagai mail near Jugiong where they had a desperate fight with the police, and Sergeant Parry was shot by Gilbert. On the 19th they robbed Mr Clarke's station at Bolero and stuck up the Goulburn mail near Towrang. On the 27th they stuck up Mr Morris's store at Binda, forced Mr and Mrs Morris to go to a ball, and finally burned his store and house. On the 30th Dunn and his companions stuck up Mr Davidson and others on the Murrumburrah Plains; on 19 January 1865, they robbed Mr James Christie's store and on the 25th stuck up Mr Ross and others on the Gap Road. On the 27th they stuck up a number of carriers and the hotel at Collector, and shot Constable Nelson. On 6 February they bailed up the Goulburn mail twelve miles from Goulburn, and on the 18th stole race-horses from Messrs McAlister and Browne. On

the 23rd the trio had a desperate fight with the police on Breadalbane Plains, where several were wounded and the robbers lost their horses. On 13 March they stuck up the Gundaroo mail near Geary's Gap, and on the 14th attempted to rob the Araluen escort at Major's Creek, where one policeman was mortally wounded, two others put to flight, while the fourth beat off the bushrangers and saved the gold. On the 22nd they were seen at Gardiner's old haunt near the Pinnacle whilst on the 24th they went to Mr Atkin's place near the Billabong Creek, had a good dinner and enjoyed themselves, as well as feeding the horses stolen from Mr Morton the day before. They left on the 25th, taking clothes for winter wear and about £90 in cash from Mr Jone's store in Forbes. On April 1 they stuck up Mr Sutton's station at Boramble and on the 10th robbed Mr Watt's Inn at Newra. On the 11th they robbed Mr Gallimore's store and the White Horse Inn at Black Rock and on the 18th bailed up the Newbiggen Inn, organised a *soirée dansante*, and compelled all hands and the cook to take part in it; afterwards they robbed Mr Lee's station at Larras Lake. On the 25th they robbed Mr Cropper's station on the Lachlan whilst on 8 May they robbed two travellers on the Cowra Road, eighteen miles from Marengo. On the 11th the three bushrangers robbed Mr Furlonge's station and on the 14th four policemen attacked them near Binalong, where Gilbert was shot and Dunn wounded.

On the 15th Dunn alone stuck up Julian's station and took a race-horse, a saddle and bridle and some food. He was not heard of again until 18 December, when he was recognised and pursued by the police near Mr McPhail's station at Walgett. He escaped, but two days later a man in whom he had confided gave information to the police as to his whereabouts. A desperate

After the depressing news that Ben Hall had been shot, Gilbert and Dunn sought refuge at the farmhouse of an old man named Kelly. The police caught up with them there and after a short shoot-out (opposite), John Gilbert was shot dead (above). Dunn escaped into the scrub, although wounded in the leg.

struggle took place in which Dunn was wounded in three places and Constable McHale was also severely wounded; Dunn however, was captured.

This record of the achievements of the gang during the time that Dunn was a member — namely, from 24 October 1864 to 15 May 1865, less than seven months — although not quite complete, serves to give a very vivid idea of the terrible scourge which the bushrangers were to the country. The gang was not more active during the time covered by this record than it had been before, or since it was first organized by Frank Gardiner in 1861, although some of the most extensive robberies committed by the gang belong to the earlier period. However, with the capture of Johnny Dunn this gang ceased to exist, and we have only to finish the story of his life before turning back to take notice of the proceedings of other gangs of bushrangers in other parts of the colony.

Constable McHale and John Dunn were conveyed as carefully as possible and by slow stages, from Walgett to the lock-up at Dubbo, to be nursed back to health. After some weeks, Dunn appeared to be growing strong, and as his character was well known, it was thought wise to put him in irons. He resented this treatment, very naturally perhaps, and refused to eat. He groaned so continuously that he prevented McHale, who was in bed in the same room in the watch-house, from sleeping.

The police were taken in by this shamming, and thought that Dunn was dying. They therefore took off his irons. The watch-house was an ordinary four-roomed weatherboard cottage with a veranda. It had been built as a residence for the local policeman. Behind, was a stronger building divided into two or three cells for the safe-keeping of the few evil-doers likely to be arrested in this settlement on the borders of civilization. The sick men were in bed in the cottage, the window of which was only a couple of feet above the level of the plain on which the town of Dubbo stands.

Dunn was not altogether shamming. He was very weak, but he was strong enough when his irons were removed to watch for an opportunity to escape. He placed his pillow length-ways in the bed, covered it with the sheet, which was the only covering required in that district at that time of the year, and placed a red silk handkerchief where his head was supposed to rest, as if to keep the flies or mosquitoes off his face. This was no doubt done to convice McHale, and any one else who came into the room, that he was still sleeping. When daylight came, McHale saw that the thing in the other bed was not Dunn and pounded on

Dunn was eventually captured by Trooper McHale (above) in the Lachlan district and hanged on 19 March, 1866.

the floor with a boot, being too weak to shout. At the time the police on duty in the next room were laughing and joking about something, and it was some minutes before McHale could make them hear. At length one of them came in, and on being told that Dunn was gone, gave the alarm.

The tracks in the dust outside showed that the robber had simply stepped out of the window which was kept open on account of the heat, and had made for the bush. It ws Sunday morning, 11 January 1866, and very few people were about in the little town. The tracks were lost among the number of tracks in the roadway and there was no one to give the police any information as to the direction in which the bushranger had gone. Search parties were organized and sent out in all directions.

About two miles away a brickmaker was watching his kiln and gathering brushwood for his fire, although it was Sunday morning, when a man crawled out from behind a log and begged for a 'drink of water, for God's sake'. It was Dunn. He told the brickmaker who he was and begged the loan of a horse to get away. 'Only save me from hanging and I'll make it up to you,' he cried, but the brickmaker refused. He went and caught his horse and rode into Dubbo to inform the police, who returned with him and recaptured the runaway. Dunn was forwarded to Bathurst without delay and was lodged in the jail, while Smith the brickmaker, was rewarded for the assistance he had given in recapturing the noted bushranger.

By the end of February Dunn was sufficiently recovered from the effects of his wound to be placed on trial. He was charged with the murder of Constable Nelson. The evidence showed that a number of people had been stuck up on the road between Taradale and Collector. They were marched to Kimberley's Hotel and taken inside by Hall and Gilbert, while Dunn

remained outside in charge of the horses. Dunn called a boy, who was standing in the street and who chanced to be the son of Constable Nelson, and told him to hold the horses and not let them go unless he wanted his brains blown out. The party in the hotel were singing and dancing. Hearing the noise the constable walked from the watch-house to where his son was and asked him what was going on. The boy told him the bushrangers were there and the constable returned to his house for his gun.

When he came back he did not see Dunn, who was hiding behind the fence, and was walking towards the front door of the hotel when he was shot, as already related. Gilbert came to the door immediately and Dunn cried out 'I've shot the —— trap.' Gilbert walked to where the body was lying, turned it over and took off the belt, saying 'This is just what I wanted, I've lost mine.' At that moment Hall came up and the three bushrangers took their horses and went off. Dunn was found guilty and sentenced to death. He was hanged on 19 March 1866. He was of slight build and only twenty-two years old when he died.

Of the chief members of this gang, Gardiner was sentenced to thirty-two years' penal servitude; Vane surrendered owing to the influence of Father McCarthy and was sent to jail for fifteen years; Bow and Fordyce were sentenced to death, but their sentences were commuted to fifteen years' imprisonment; Manns, Peisley, and Dunn were hanged; Lowry, Ben Hall, and Gilbert were shot by the police, and Burke and O'Meally by civilians; Mount or the Old Man was sent to jail for ten years.

There were others who either claimed or were supposed to be members of this gang, but it is difficult to say with certainty how far these claims were justified. Some of these have already been referred to, and others will be mentioned farther on. Probably some who intended to join the gang were captured before they had an opportunity to do so. Others merely said they had been out with Ben Hall or Johnny Gilbert on account of the glory they gained among their fellows. However this may be, the majority of the members of this gang were quite young men, many of them little more than boys. Several were under twenty years of age, and all were under thirty with the exception of Mount, the Old Man. Their lives may have been exciting, but they were short and none of them, with the exception of Gardiner perhaps, made any money by their robberies. They all died poor.

# 18 Bloodthirsty Morgan

**Bloodthirsty Morgan: murder of Sergeant McGinnerty; murder at the Round Hill station; Morgan shoots Sergeant Smyth; accepts a challenge to enter Victoria: his fate at Peechelba.**

Daniel Morgan began his career as a bushranger shortly after the Great Escort Robbery, by sticking up travellers on the roads about Wagga Wagga. His headquarters were said to be in the huge patch of scrub which stretched away southward from the Murrumbidgee River across the low ranges between Wagga Wagga and Narrandera. He was credited with being the most bloodthirsty of the New South Wales bushrangers after Willmore. We have seen that some of the members of the Gardiner gang held human life very cheaply, but it was the general opinion that, except in the case of a few Chinamen, these bushrangers murdered only when on the warpath. In many cases they met the police boldly and fought with some degree of fairness; while Morgan, on more than one occasion, fired on unarmed, and in some cases, sleeping men.

For some months he pursued his career without much interference from the police. When it became apparent that he had no connection with the Gardiner gang and continued his robberies alone, a party of police was detailed to hunt him down about the middle of 1863. In August of that year, this party of police tracked him for several days and came on his camp on the 22nd. A desperate fight took place in which Morgan's mate was severely wounded and crawled into the bush to die. This man was known as 'German Bill'. On the other side, Mr Bayliss J.P., a volunteer who accompanied the police, was severely wounded. He recovered, however, and was awarded a gold medal by the New South Wales Government for bravery in opposing bushrangers. Morgan made his escape in the scrub.

Later on the same day a shepherd was shot dead on Brookong station, and it was supposed that the murderer was in league with Morgan. About Christmas Morgan, with three companions, watched the road near Narrandera, with the intention of sticking up several wealthy squatters who were in the habit of travelling to Melbourne at about that time of the year. Fortunately, that year they took a cross track and escaped the meeting. While waiting, Morgan took about 2lb. of cheese from a bullock-driver named John

Daniel ('Mad Dan') Morgan, born at Campbelltown, New South Wales, was the illegitimate son of a Sydney prostitute and a former London barrow-boy. He took the name of his hero, Morgan the pirate, and by the time he reached his teens had served six months in Berrima jail for assaulting a policeman. A second term, in Pentridge, embittered him against squatters (one had given false evidence against him) and on his escape, he sought vengeance on settlers in the Narrandera district of New South Wales.

Cole. There were several cheeses in the dray, and when Morgan said he should 'like a bit' Cole offered him one and told him to 'take the lot'. Morgan replied that 'the —— traps would risk their necks climbing over the area railings for a leg of mutton. I don't know what they'd do for a whole cheese, but this lump's enough for me.' Afterwards he remarked that the police generally were 'a sour milk lot'.

During the next few months robberies occurred in various parts of the extensive tract of country between Wagga Wagga and Deniliquin, and were all attributed to the Morgan gang. On 16 April 1864, Mr George Elliott of Burrangong, with a stockman named Donnelly, reached Deniliquin with a mob of horses for sale. Because of rumours in the town, Mr Elliott was closely questioned by the sergeant of police, and after some hesitation admitted that he had been stuck up by Morgan on the road between Narrandera and Jerilderie and robbed of £127 17s. and a bay horse with saddle and bridle. He said that when he got rid of his horses he would have to return home by the same route, and thought it prudent to hold his tongue as there was no saying whom he might meet on the road.

In June, Sergeant McGinnerty and Constable Churchley were riding along the road to Tumbarumba when they overtook a horseman near Coppabella. McGinnerty civilly said 'Good day' as they passed, in the usual Australian fashion. The man looked at him and replied, 'Oh, you're one of the —— wretches looking for bushrangers, are you?' and hastily drew a revolver and shot McGinnerty through the breast. The sergeant's horse bolted and the bushranger galloped after him into the bush. Constable Churchley rode back to Coppabella for assistance. On his return with a party and fresh horses he found McGinnerty's hat lying in the road, and opposite to it some distance away, the body. It was supposed that the bushranger had placed the hat on the road to indicate where the body was and to facilitate its discovery.

The robber must have ridden straight from the scene of this cold-blooded murder to the Round Hill station, where he mustered all the men and drove them into the carpenter's shop. He then went to the house, called out the proprietor Mr Watson, and led him to the door of the carpenter's shop. He inquired whether the men had sufficient rations. 'If they haven't', said Mr Watson, 'they've only got to say so and they'll get more.' 'Well, I'm Dan Morgan, I just wanted to know, and you'd better give them a nobbler,' replied the bushranger. Mr Watson said he'd no objection to the men having a nobbler, and sent to the house. The messenger returned with four bottles of spirits, and each man was given a nobbler in a pannikin.

The men laughed and took it as a good joke. One of them asked the bushranger whether he had 'stolen his stirrup irons from Mr Johnstone?' Morgan with a curse immediately drew his pistol and fired into the room. The men ran out. Morgan followed them, shouting,

'You —— wretches, do you want to give me away?' He fired several times, until John McLean fell wounded. By this time the men had sheltered themselves behind trees. Seeing no one to shoot at Morgan dismounted, lifted McLean carefully on to his horse, and led the animal to the house. Mr Watson and some of the women took McLean in and Morgan mounted and rode away. Then it was discovered that another man, John Heriot, was lying wounded in the carpenter's shop. Heriot had a broken leg, and he was placed in a buggy and conveyed with as little delay as possible to the hospital at Albury. McLean's wound was too serious to allow his removal, and he died after lingering in pain for two or three days.

At the inquest held on the body, Edward Smith, stockman at the Round Hill station, said that Morgan had called at the station two days after the attack to inquire how McLean was, and had sat at the bedside for several hours. At that time there were numerous parties of police and civilians searching the country round in all directions in hopes of finding him. A verdict of wilful murder was returned against Morgan on 23 June, and a few days later a proclamation was issued by which the reward offered for his capture dead or alive was increased from £500 to £1000.

A man walked into the bar of the Five Mile Creek Inn, near Bogolong, and called for a nobbler of brandy, which was supplied him. He then demanded another, which the barman refused to give him until he had paid for the one he had drunk. 'Be careful what you do', exclaimed the customer, 'I'm Dan Morgan.' He drew out a pistol, and the barman rushed from behind the counter, jumped through a window, and ran. The customer followed him to the window but the barman ran right round the house. When he returned to the window through which he had made his escape, he saw the bushranger's pistol lying on the sill. He grasped it, and having recovered from his momentary panic, walked into the bar in time to see the pseudo Morgan helping himself out of a bottle. The barman at once grappled with him and the cook, the only other man in the house at the time, hearing the scuffling, came in. The man was soon secured, and in due time was handed over to the custody of the police. He was identified as a fiddler who travelled about the country playing for a living. He was sent to jail for a few months as a caution not to obtain grog again under false pretences by impersonating a bushranger.

Morgan, with three mates, visited Yarribee station, stuck up Mr Mate the overseer, with two bushmen and the bullock-driver, and tied their hands behind them. He demanded the key of the store which was given to him. He opened the door and selected a quantity of articles which he packed on a horse. He served out tobacco, gin, and beer to the men whom he had made prisoners. The liquor had its effect, and some of the men became uproarious. Morgan swore at them and ordered them to be quiet. As they did not obey he

**Morgan shoots Sergeant McGinnerty**

brought out the station brand — P.T. — put it in the
fire, and swore he would brand every one of them on
the cheek. Whether the threat frightened the men into
quietness, or whether the bushranger thought better of
his purpose, is not known, as Morgan rode away with
his plunder without using the branding-iron.

Under the heading 'Comforting Bushrangers', the
*Deniliquin Chronicle* of 18 December said: 'Mr —— we
hear has given orders that whenever Morgan calls at
his station he is to be given everything he wants, and
when he does not call food is to be taken into the bush
and left for him.' The paper goes on to accuse the
unnamed squatter with 'holding a candle to the devil'.
It is difficult to see where the blame comes in. The
stations were from twenty-five to fifty miles apart, and
except at lambing and shearing times had few men
employed on them. There were not many police in the
district and even if they had been very much stronger
than they were they could not have prevented a
daring, reckless man like Morgan from setting fire to
the grass. It was so easy at that time for even an
offended bushman to have revenge by starting a blaze
which would destroy the grass over hundreds of
square miles before it could be stopped, and could ruin
a squatter. In face of this danger a few clothes or a
quantity of food was a trifling loss. Certainly Morgan
never did fire the grass, because perhaps there was no
profit in it for himself, but there can be no doubt that
he would have done it had he desired to have revenge
on any particular run-holder.

One of the many stories told about the brutality of
Morgan was that he went to a cattle station near
Jerilderie and asked to see the overseer. The
overseer's wife informed him that her husband was
away at a back station mustering and branding, and
that she and the children were the only persons at
home at the head station. Morgan replied that he was
sorry for it. He'd travelled to the station specially for
the purpose of shooting the overseer, who was too
friendly with the police. He then demanded a sum of
money which he said he knew the overseer had
recently received. The woman declared that her
husband had no money at the station, or if he had that
she was not aware where he kept it.

Morgan refused to believe her. He made her boil him
a number of eggs, declaring that he would eat nothing
else as there was too much strychnine and arsenic
about these stations. When these were ready he
examined them carefully, rejecting all which had
cracks in the shells and eating only the sound ones. He
then made up the fire until there was a big blaze, when
he once more asked her for the money. When she
persisted in declaring that she had none he seized her
by the shoulders, forced her back until she was seated
on the blazing logs, and held her there until her clothes
were on fire. Then he allowed her to get up and
seizing a bucket of water standing near he dashed it
over her to put the fire out. She was severely burned.

When he mounted and rode away he said he would soon be round again and hoped then to find the overseer at home.

Sergeant Smyth and Constables Cannon, Baxter, and Reed, who were out seeking for the bushranger Morgan, camped one night in September near Kyamba. They had put up a tent and were seated inside. They had a candle, and this threw their shadows on the canvas and afforded a magnificent mark, which the bushranger could not resist firing at. The shot wounded Sergeant Smyth, but he and the constables rushed out of the tent and blazed away, without seeing their assailant. It was supposed that this attack was made by Morgan, although nothing was seen of the bushranger. Sergeant Smyth fired twice after being wounded and then he fainted. He was taken without delay to Doodal Cooma station and a doctor was found, but he never rallied and died a fortnight later.

It was said that Morgan was on the Wagga Wagga racecourse at the Christmas races, had lunch at the booth where the magistrates, the police inspectors, and the leading merchants and shopkeepers of the town went, and that afterwards he rode into the town itself without being recognized by the police.

On 18 March 1865, he stuck up Mr Rand's station at Mohanga, collected all the men in one room, and ordered Mr Rand to fetch some grog from the store. When this was done, Morgan asked one of the men whether he could play the concertina and when told he could, asked him to get his instrument and 'amuse the company'. When all was ready the bushranger said to Mr Rand: 'I understand you are a good dancer. Will you favour the company with a reel?' Mr Rand said he should be only too pleased, and began at once. Morgan watched him critically and applauded every now and then, but when Mr Rand stopped, he raised his pistol and said: 'Once more, please, you dance very nicely,' and kept the squatter jigging till midnight when he was allowed to retire. In the morning Morgan took from the store a quantity of clothing and some other articles including a gun. He then asked for a horse, saddle and bridle, to pack his plunder on, and got them.

At Jerilderie, when engaged in one of his usual robberies, he spoke in the most contemptuous terms of the police. He said that the Victorian police had been boasting that they would soon catch him if he crossed the border. He declared that he would soon show them that they were no smarter than the New South Wales police who were 'frightened to go near any place where they thought they might find him'. A Beechworth paper, commenting on this report, challenged Morgan to cross the Murray and prophesied that if he dared to do so he would be either dead or in jail within forty-eight hours.

This challenge, it was said, greatly offended the bushranger, who had apparently, owing perhaps to his long immunity from arrest, developed the belief that he was invincible. He was reported to have referred to it

frequently, and to have asserted his intention to cross the Murray River and 'take the flashness out of the Victorian people and police'. Accordingly, early in April, he made a raid south of the Murray. Mounted on Mr Bowler's racing mare, Victoria, Morgan stuck up Mr McKinnon's station on the Little River. He crossed the King River, and set fire to Mr Evans's barns and granary for 'having shot my fingers off', an event which had taken place some time previously in one of his many encounters on the 'other side'.

Morgan then stuck up and robbed a number of carriers on the road between Wangaratta and Benalla. He also stuck up Mr Warby's station, and on the evening of 8 April arrived at Peechelba station, owned by Messrs Macpherson and Rutherford. Morgan rode up and knocked at the door of Mr Macpherson's house. It was opened by Mr Macpherson's son. Morgan, pistol in hand, ordered him to bail up. Then all those in the house were called in and compelled to range themselves in line along the wall of the dining-room. A housemaid named Alice Macdonald, thinking he was joking, refused to stand up against the wall 'like a child'. Morgan took her by the arm to force her into line when she smacked his face. Raising his pistol he said, 'My young lady, I must take the flashness out of you. Do you know who I am?' 'No', replied the girl. 'Well, I'm Morgan. Will you take your place?' The girl pouted but did as she was told.

Morgan placed two revolvers on the table and sat down. He said he had had no sleep for three nights, but he hoped to return to New South Wales next day and have a good sleep. He asked a servant to make him some tea and allowed her to leave the room. Then he said that he had heard music as he approached the house, and he asked which of the ladies played? On being told 'Miss Macpherson', he asked her to favour him with a tune. She replied, 'Certainly, Mr Morgan.' 'Call me Morgan', he said, 'I hate to be Mistered.' Mr Macpherson asked him what had induced him to lead such a life? 'I was forced to it,' he replied. 'I was tried at Castlemaine for a crime of which I was innocent and received a heavy sentence. Well, I escaped from the stockade and there you are. What else could I do?'

The party sat all night, and Morgan chatted freely, but his vigilance relaxed so that Alice Macdonald contrived to slip out without being seen. She went to Mr Rutherford's house, about a quarter of a mile away, and informed Mr Rutherford of what had taken place. She went back again immediately in case the bushranger should miss her. Morgan informed the company that he was born at Appin, in New South Wales, and that his parents were still living.

**After dining, wining and listening to music all night at Peechelba (above), Morgan stepped out early next morning without knowing that Alice MacDonald had given the alarm during the night; he was shot in the back (below) by John Quinlan.**

In the meantime Mr Rutherford mustered all the men on the station and dispatched a messenger to the police at Wangaratta. He posted sentinels all round Mr Macpherson's house, hiding them behind bushes or any other cover. In the morning Morgan ate a hearty breakfast and then walked out on the veranda. Mr Macpherson invited him to take a glass of whisky and poured out some for himself. Morgan replied that he rarely drank; he was almost a teetotaller. However, not wishing to appear churlish, he accepted half a glass. He went into a bedroom to wash his hands and face and comb his hair and Alice Keenan, one of the servants, took advantage of the opportunity to carry a can of coffee to the watchers outside.

When Morgan had washed he stepped out on the veranda again and reminded Mr Macpherson that he had promised to let him have a fresh horse. Mr Macpherson replied that he had not forgotten it. He called to his son and they walked together towards the paddock to catch the horse, while Morgan waited on

the veranda. They had not gone far when Morgan started to follow them, and John Quinlan shot him from behind a bush. The bushranger fell, crying 'Why didn't you challenge me?' He was carried indoors. Every attention possible was paid to him, but he died at about half-past one — roughly forty-eight hours after he crossed the Victorian border.

The £1000 reward was divided as follows:— John Quinlan £300; Alice Macdonald £250; James Frazer, who rode into Wangaratta and back — forty-two miles — in three hours and a half, £200; Donald Clarke, who fetched guns from the school house, cleaned and loaded them, £100; Alice Keenan, who communicated between the parties inside and outside the house, £50. The remaining £100 was given to Mr Rutherford and Inspector Singleton (£50 each) to be divided among the civilians and the police who took part in the capture, according to the merits of their performances.

The news of the death of Morgan was received generally throughout Australia with satisfaction. There

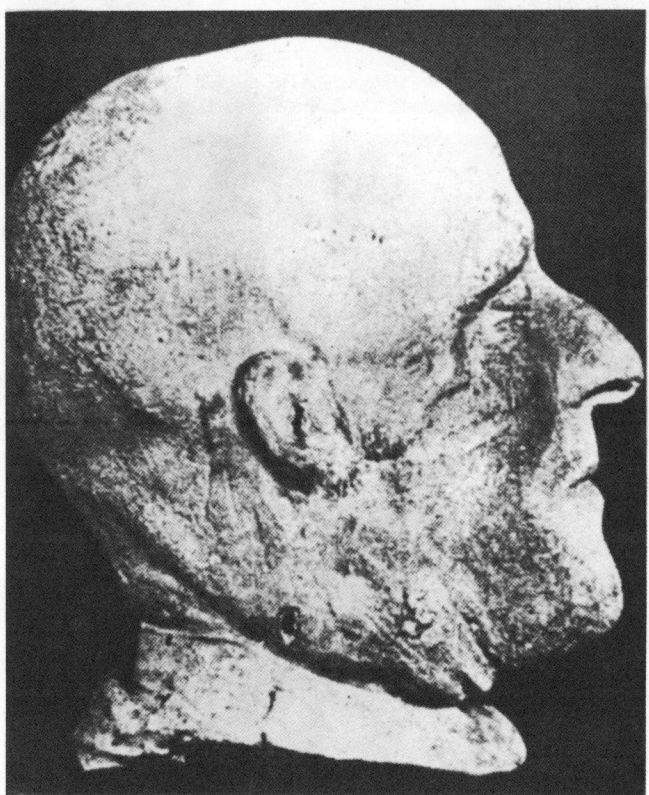

After Morgan's death at 2 p.m. on the day he was shot, his eyes were opened and his body propped up on public display in a stable next-door to the Wangaratta jail, with one of the two Colt revolvers found on him placed in his hand.

Later, a Benalla doctor shaved the bushranger's beard which he wanted for a souvenir, and numerous locks were cut from Morgan's hair for curios. The outlaw's head was severed, preserved and sent to Melbourne University where a death mask (above) was made.

were a few people whose love of fair play impelled them to express the opinion that he should have been challenged, but the majority held that he was little better than a wild beast, and should be treated accordingly. He had given no notice to Sergeants McGinnerty and Smyth, nor to the unarmed men among whom he had fired at the Round Hill station. It is doubtful whether those who declared that he should have been accorded 'fair play' would, knowing the character of the man, have risked their lives by challenging him in circumstances similar to those in which he was captured.

There was a tendency among a portion of the people of Victoria to glorify themselves at the expense of New South Wales over the capture of Morgan. It was said that bushrangers would never receive the public sympathy and support in Victoria which they did in New South Wales. This was attributed to the fact that Victoria had never had a penal settlement within its borders. However only a few months after the paeon of self-glorification had been sung by the Victorian press over the death of Morgan in that colony, the same papers lamented the fact that while bushranging appeared to have been stamped out in New South Wales, it still flourished in Victoria.

Over page:
Morgan's killer, the stockman John Quinlan, proudly posed for photographs.

# 19 Clarke brothers captured

**The Clarke brothers of Manaro; the raid at Nerigundah; murder of four special constables at Jinden; capture of Thomas and John Clarke; some daring robberies.**

The Clarke brothers of Monaro, although they did not belong to the Gardiner gang, were more or less closely connected with it. There were three of them. Thomas, James, and John, and their education was on similar lines to that which was prevalent in the Western Ranges. They were cattle duffers and horse planters until the police began to inquire too closely into their mode of life, when they 'took to the bush'.

James was probably saved from the fate of his elder and younger brothers by being arrested on suspicion of having been concerned with Ben Hall, Johnny Gilbert, and others in the robbery of the Cowra mail. As the evidence of his presence on that occasion was inconclusive he was acquitted and charged with having received stolen property because a number of the bank notes stolen from the mail had been found in his possession. He was convicted and sentenced to seven years' penal servitude on 12 January 1865. He was probably kept out of mischief during the troublesome times by this imprisonment.

Thomas and John, the eldest and youngest of this interesting family, operated over the district in which the redoubtable Jackey Jackey first earned his notoriety as a bushranger. As they did not confine their operations within any strictly defined limits, they overlapped with the Hall and Gilbert gang. The elder brother Thomas was arrested in October 1864 on a charge of highway robbery, but escaped from the Braidwood jail. He stole several racedhorses from residents in the neighbourhood of Jembaicumbene and Mericumbene, stuck up the Araluen mail, robbed the Post Office at Michelago, and stuck up and robbed numbers of travellers on the roads about Braidwood and Moruya. On 12 January, the very day on which his brother James was being tried, he stuck up Mr George Summer's store at Jembaicumbene, and on the following day he bailed up John Frazer and Kenneth Matheson on Major's Creek Mount robbing them of £36 10s. in money and a bank draft for a large amount. In these enterprises he was assisted by several young men and lads residing in the district.

In April, Thomas Clarke, Patrick Connell, Tom Connell, William Fletcher, and two or three other

**John Clarke**

young men were returning home from the racecourse at Bega, where races had been held, when Clarke stuck up a Chinaman, who was travelling from the Gulph diggings, and took his gold and money. A little farther along the road the party met the mail boy, and Clarke compelled him to exchange his horse, saddle, and bridle for those stolen from the Chinaman. Some miles from the scene of this outrage the party met Mr John Emmott, and ordered him to bail up, but he wheeled his horse and started to gallop away as he had a considerable amount of gold and money on him. By this time others of the party had become excited and several of them chased Emmott, firing their revolvers at him. Emmott fell wounded and his horse was killed. About £100 in money and a parcel of gold dust was taken from him, and the party went on, leaving Mr Emmott to make his way to where he could obtain surgical aid as best he could.

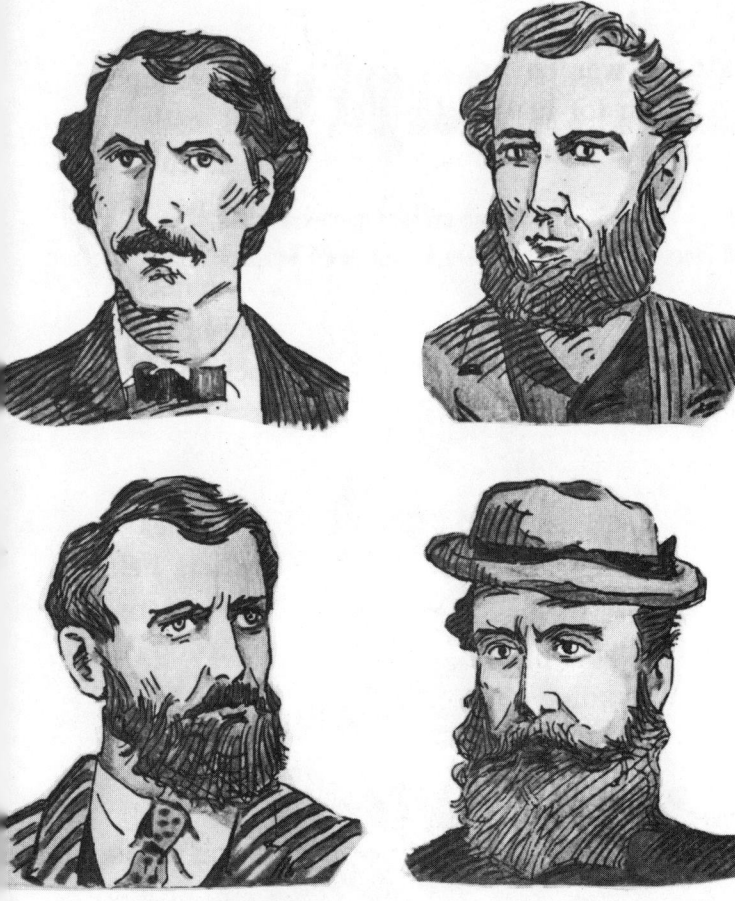

The four police constables sent to capture the Clarke gang; from top left: Patrick Kennagh, John Phegan, Eneas McDonnell, John Carrol.

On the following day they arrived at the Gulph diggings, stuck up Mr Pollock's store, and stole between two hundred and three hundred ounces of gold, besides all the money that they could find. On leaving the store they met Charles Nash in the street, and Clarke greeted him with 'Hullo, Charlie, back from the Bega races?' 'Yes,' replied Nash. 'Then fork out,' cried Clarke, bringing out his revolver. Nash at first thought this was a joke and began to laugh, but when the remainder of the gang crowded round and presented their revolvers in a threatening manner, he put his hand in his pocket, took out about thirty shillings, and handed it over with the remark, 'That's all I've got.' He was then permitted to pass on.

Fletcher then led the way to the butcher's shop owned by R. Drew, and putting his revolver to the butcher's head, told him to 'shell out'. Drew put his hands behind him and made no reply. Then the rest of the gang crowded in and called for a light, declaring their intention to search the place. Drew told them to 'clear out'. They refused, and threatened to shoot him. The dispute grew so loud that it reached the ears of Constable Miles O'Grady, the only policeman stationed on the little diggings, who was ill in bed. O'Grady got up and dressed, and went to the butcher's shop. He inquired what the row was about, and ordered the crowd to leave the shop. Fletcher turned round and fired at the constable, but missed. O'Grady immediately returned the fire and Fletcher fell dead. One of Fletcher's mates shot O'Grady, who died a few days later. The bushrangers rushed to their horses, mounted, and galloped away out of the township.

The *Moruya Examiner* said that William Fletcher was little more than a boy, and was born in the district. He had ridden in the St Patrick's Day races on 17 March at Mullenderee only a few weeks before. His father was a farmer in the district, and had always been of good character. The boy had been digging for gold at Araluen, Nerrigundah, the Gulph, and other diggings in that neighbourhood. It was his first attempt at bushranging. His mind had probably been inflamed by the stories told of Gardiner, Ben Hall, and Johnny Gilbert, and he had been induced to endeavour to emulate their actions by the boastings of Thomas Clarke.

Several young men who had taken part in this fray returned home afterwards, and were arrested by the police. Some of them were acquitted on account of their previous good character, and because there was no evidence to prove that they had done more than accompany the robbers. Thomas Clarke, his uncle Patrick Connell, his cousin Tom Connell, with Bill Scott and one or two others who escaped to the ranges, continued to commit crimes similar to those described in the previous chapter.

In September 1866, John Carrol, Patrick Kennagh, Eneas McDonnell, and John Phegan were sent by the police authorities to the Braidwood district to assist the police in the capture of the Clarke gang. Phegan had been mining in the district and was well acquainted with the ranges. He paid a visit to Mrs Clarke, and was received with some suspicion as a stranger.

On his second visit Mrs Clarke and her two daughters became quite friendly, and asked Phegan to write out a petition in favour of her second son James, who was a prisoner on Cockatoo Island. The party camped as if engaged in surveying, and Phegan said that Kennagh knew more about writing out petitions than he did. He therefore took Kennagh to the place and introduced him to Mrs Clarke. They wrote out the petition and left. During the next few days they saw the girls frequently. In the absence of their brothers these girls looked after the cattle, and were riding about the ranges every day. They passed the camp several times and spoke in a friendly manner.

On 4 October, the party had been pretending to survey a flat, and under this pretence had searched a gunyah hidden among the timber. This gunyah was believed to be one of the rendezvous of the bushrangers, and was closely watched in the hopes that the bushrangers might visit it. On the day named,

This 'wanted' photograph, issued to Victorian police in 1866, showed Tom, eldest and most vicious of the Clarke brothers, mounted on a stolen horse, 'Boomerang'. £5,000 was offered for his capture, dead or alive.

the special constables had finished their work and were standing round the camp fire when a gun was fired. The bullet passed between the men and struck the tree against which the fire was built. The party had their guns ready and returned the fire, although they could not see what they were shooting at. In the morning a flask half full of powder was picked up, but this gave no indication as to who had attacked the party. After this no pretence of friendship was made, and Carrol and the party under his charge openly took up the pursuit of the bushrangers, penetrating the mountains and searching everywhere where they thought it probable that the bushrangers might camp.

In January 1867, the bodies of the four men were found near their camp on the Jinden station in the Jingera ranges, in the Braidwood district. How or when they were shot is not known, but it is supposed that they were somehow drawn into an ambush and shot down. Carrol's body was lying on its back, and a handkerchief thrown across it with a one pound note pinned to it. The bodies of Carrol and Kennagh were close together, while the other two were half a mile away. Three revolvers were lying beside Phegan. One of the men had £14 on him, and another £19. The bodies were found by Mr Edward Smith's stockman when riding through the ranges after cattle, on 9

January, and as they were in an advanced state of decomposition, they must have been there for several days.

The Governor, Sir John Young, immediately issued a proclamation calling upon magistrates, freeholders, and all other of Her Majesty's subjects resident in the police districts of Braidwood, Browlee, Queanbeyan, Eden, Bega, and Cooma to assist the police in the capture of 'the notorious outlaw, Thomas Clarke, whose life is forfeit to the laws of his country.' The colonial Secretary, Mr (later Sir Henry) Parkes, offered a reward of £5000 for the capture of the persons guilty of murdering the four special constables. A free pardon was also offered to any accomplice not being the actual murderer.

Carrol, Kennagh, and Phegan had been warders in Darlinghurst jail and had volunteered to attempt the capture of the bushranger Clarke; McDonnell was an ex-policeman who had accumulated a considerable sum of money in business. Although he was about to visit Ireland, his native country, he volunteered to join this

135

**Thomas Clarke**

party before going home. The firing had been heard at Jinden station, three miles from the camp, but no notice had been taken as it was attributed to possum hunters. According to the medical evidence, the men were killed with rifle bullets fired at close range — not more than twenty yards. Phegan and McDonnell were shot first, McDonnell only having one wound which was fatal. Phegan was shot in the right side. He appeared to have turned over after falling, and to have been then shot on the other side to finish him. Carrol and Kennagh appeared to have been kneeling when shot, and had perhaps surrendered. The ostentatious disregard of the money on the bodies showed, said the *Sydney Morning Herald*, that revenge and not plunder was the object of the murderers.

It was never definitely established how these men came to their deaths. According to rumour, three of them were shot by Thomas Clarke and the fourth by Bill Scott, who was afterwards wounded in a brush with the police. It is assumed that Scott was later killed by Clarke just as the bushranger known as German Bill had been killed by Morgan to prevent him from falling into the hands of the authorities and being induced to give evidence against his former companions. In both cases, however, the fate of the missing bushranger is uncertain.

At the Criminal Sessions held in Goulburn in April 1867, Thomas Cunningham, Charles Hugh Gough, alias Wyndham, alias Bennett, James Baldwin, and Harry Brown were each sentenced to fifteen years' imprisonment for various acts of bushranging in various parts of the district. For robbing and shooting at a man, William Johnson received a sentence of only two years. Several of these bushrangers came from the

neighbourhood of Braidwood, and the *Yass Courier* reported that Annie Clarke, one of the sisters of the bushrangers, stayed in Goulburn during the time that the sessions lasted. Her visit was doubtless one of sympathy with some of the prisoners. She was about twenty years of age with a fine figure and good features. She was observed to change her costume four times in one day. In the morning she was very quietly dressed, whilst later she came out in a second costume, also very quiet and neat. In the afternoon she walked about the streets in blood red silk, with red hat and feathers to match, and towards evening she came out in a bright blue silk dress, white shawl, and a hat with white feathers.

At Wellington, in the same month, John Kelly was sentenced to fourteen years' hard labour, the first two in irons, for highway robbery.

At this time the reward offered for the capture of Thomas Clarke was raised to £1000, while £500 was offered for his brother John who had just 'turned out'. A similar sum was offered for the capture of Bill Scott, whose death had not then been ascertained, or for any other member of the gang.

On 26 April, Senior Constable Wright, and Constables James Wright, Lenehan, Walsh, and Egan, with the assistance of a black tracker known as Sir Watkin Wynne, tracked the bushrangers to a hut not far from where the four special constables had been murdered. The hut or cottage stood in a small cultivation paddock in which there was a small haystack. The constables watched the hut from behind this haystack until morning. At daybreak two race-horses were seen feeding behind the hut, and Constable Walsh, making a detour round the hut so as not to be heard by the occupants, walked down and caught these horses. He was leading them towards the haystack when the door opened and the two Clarke brothers came out of the house and fired at him.

The other troopers immediately rushed forward from behind the stack and summoned the Clarkes to surrender. They made no reply but went inside and shut the door. The police then took up positions, Constable Lenehan with Sir Watkin stopping at the stack with the horses at about two hundred yards from the hut and nearly facing it. The Senior Constable and Constable Wright went to a fallen tree about fifty yards to the right of the hut, while Constables Egan and Walsh went to about the same distance to the left, where there was no cover.

The paddock in which the house stood had been recently ploughed, and the heavy rains which had fallen made the ground difficult to travel over. The hut was built of slabs, and these had shrunk away from each other, leaving cracks through which the bushrangers could point their guns and revolvers. The bushrangers kept up an irregular fire until Constable Walsh was wounded in the thigh and Sir Watkin in the shoulder. The other four troopers then made a rush, forced upon the door, and entered. The bushrangers surrendered. They had two revolvers, two double-barrelled guns, two revolving rifles, one single-barrelled gun, and a horse pistol.

The black tracker's wound was so severe that he had to have his arm amputated, and he bore the operation with the stoical indifference of his race. He walked downstairs from the upper ward of the Braidwood Hospital to the dissecting room, and after his arm had been cut off and the stump bound up he walked up again as coolly 'as if he had merely had his finger punctured', said the *Braidwood Dispatch*. He was supposed to be about fifty years of age, and was well-built and 'handsome for a blackfellow'. He was promoted to the rank of sergeant-major, and had two stripes placed on his arm, of which he was very proud. Senior Constable William Wright was made sub-inspector, and the other constables engaged were promoted and rewarded.

Thomas and John Clarke were placed on trial, charged with having wounded Constable Walsh and black tracker Sir Watkin while in the execution of their duty. In two years Thomas Clarke had committed nine mail robberies, and had stuck up and robbed thirty-six individuals, some of whom had been wounded. He was also suspected of having caused the deaths of at least two persons. John Clarke had taken part in twenty-six of these robberies. They were found guilty, and the Chief Justice (the late Sir Alfred Stephen) in his address said:

I never knew a bushranger (except one who is now suffering sentences aggregating thirty-two years) who made any money by it . . . I will read you a list of bushrangers . . . many of them young men, capable of better things, but who died violent deaths. Peisley executed; Davis sentenced to death; Gardiner sentenced to thirty-two years' hard labour; Gilbert shot dead; Hall shot dead; Bow and Fordyce sentenced to death, but their sentences commuted to imprisonment for life; Manns executed; O'Meally shot dead; Burke shot dead; Gordon sentenced to death; Dunleavy sentenced to death; Dunn executed; Lowry shot dead; Vane a long sentence; Foley a long sentence; Morgan shot dead; yourselves, Thomas and John Clarke, about to be sentenced to death; Fletcher shot dead; Patrick Connell shot dead; Tom Connell sentenced to death, but sentence commuted to imprisonment for life; Bill Scott, a companion of your own, believed to have been murdered by you. . . . The list shows six shot dead and ten wounded. . . . Unfortunately there were seven constables shot dead and sixteen wounded in three years . . . since 1863. . . . the murders believed to have been committed by you bushrangers are appalling to think of. How many wives have been made widows, how many children orphans, what loss of property, what sorrow you have caused! . . . and yet, these bushrangers, the scum of the earth, the lowest of the low, the most wicked of the wicked, are occasionally held up for our admiration! But better days are

Mounted police and black trackers. After the brutal murders of the four special constables, public opinion turned strongly against the Clarke brothers and nothing was spared in the hunt for the bushrangers. A black tracker, 'Sir Watkin Wynne', eventually led the troopers who captured Tom and John Clarke.

coming. It is the old leaven of convictism not yet worked out, but brighter days are coming. You will not live to see them, but others will.

Sentence was then passed in the usual form, and the brothers were hanged on 25 June 1867.

Meanwhile robberies were frequent in other districts, Mrs Colonel Pitt, with her daughter and Mrs Colonel Campbell, were driving along the Mechanics' Bay Road, near the domain, Forbes, when a servant who was leading the horses at the time was knocked down by an armed man. Another robber tried to seize the reins, but Mrs Pitt stood up in the buggy and raised them out of his reach. She brought the butt of the whip so heavily down on the bushranger's head that he fell. Mrs Pitt shouted and whipped the horses, and they galloped up the hill and did not stop until they reached Parnell, where the police were informed of what had occurred. A couple of troopers immediately started down the road and found the servant lying where the outrage was said to have been committed.

He had been severely beaten, but was still alive. He was taken without any unnecessary delay to the hospital at Forbes, where he subsequently recovered. The robbers were tracked, followed and captured next day, 5 March 1865. They were Richard Middleton, alias Ruggy Dick, John Wilson, and Thomas Travey. They were tried, convicted, and sent to jail for long periods.

The Bathurst mail was stuck up and robbed on 2 February 1866, near Pulpit Hill, by two young men. Seymour and John Ford, who were followed and captured next day.

Sergeant Grainger and Constable Carroll chased a young man on the Carcour Road on suspicion that he was a bushranger. When asked by the sergeant where he was going, he replied, 'Looking for work.' The sergeant made him unstrap a coat which was fastened across the pommel of his saddle, and a small revolver was found in it. 'What do you carry that for?' inquired the sergeant. 'For protection,' was the reply. The sergeant then snatched away the coat and saw that the man had a large revolver in his hand. He was told that if he attempted to raise this weapon he would be shot at once. Seeing that escape was impossible he surrendered and allowed the police to handcuff him. Then the sergeant opened his vest to ascertain what caused a protuberance there, and found a pair of false whiskers and moustaches. The man was identified as John Miles, who had raided the Chinese camp at Mookerawa, besides committing several highway robberies on Evans' Plains and in the neighbourhood of Orange. He was sent to jail for ten years, the Judge saying that the prisoner had used less violence than was usual with bushrangers, and had not ill-treated the Chinamen further than by taking their gold.

Mr Kelly's store on the One Mile Creek, Emu Creek Goldfield, was stuck up by John Kerr, alias Maher, and John Shepherd. Kelly, with his wife and children, and a man named Gibbons, were locked up in a back room while the robbers were making a bundle of clothing, drapery, and other articles in the store. Gibbons succeeded in forcing open a back window without being heard by the robbers, and making his escape. He ran to the police station and gave information, but the robbers discovered his escape before the arrival of the police, and decamped without their booty. This, however, did not save them. They were followed and captured by Sergeant O'Donnell and Constable McGlone. They were convicted of more than one robbery on the Cowra road.

On Saturday night, 8 June, a bushranger called Cummings made an attempt to escape from the Bathurst Jail while awaiting trial for highway robbery. He filed a link of the chain of his leg-irons with a small pocket-knife, which he had somehow procured, tore up two boards from the floor of his cell, crawled under the joists and scraped away the mortar so as to loosen several bricks in the jail wall. The opening was only about ten inches square but he managed to squeeze through. Of course, when his cell was found empty on the Sunday morning, there was great excitement in the jail. Mr Forbes, the head jailer, soon found the prisoner seated in the summer house in his private garden. 'Here I am,' cried the bushranger; 'I did my best, but could not succeed.' The prisoner had found some pieces of scantling in the outer yard, but they were not long enough to enable him to reach the top of the wall which encloses the jail yard. An examination into the state of the jail showed that the boards were quite rotten and that the walls themselves were not very strong, the bricks being quite soft and rotten.

Several bullock-drivers were stuck up by John Egan and Patrick Ryan on the Orange road, in August 1867. On the 16th Robert and John Tait, father and son, and Edward Barrell were camped together when the bushrangers rode up and ordered them to 'fork out'. The robbers took all their money and some articles from the drays. On the 19th they repeated the operation on some other bullock-drivers. They were followed by Sergeant Rush and Constable Lawrence and arrested about forty-five miles from where the robberies were committed. At the Bathurst Assizes the prisoners called seven witnesses to prove an alibi, but they contradicted each other under cross-examination. When the prisoners were found guilty, his Honour, Judge Hargrave, directed that the witnesses should be prosecuted for perjury. The prisoners were sentenced to fifteen years' imprisonment. Another bushranger, John Foran, who was convicted on three charges, was also sentenced to fifteen years.

Patrick Fitzgerald, alias Paddy Wandong, was charged at Wellington on 21 October 1867, with having on 21 December bailed up Thomas Goodall, a free selector, on the Castlereagh River. The prisoner rushed into the house in the night and ran into the bedroom. Mr Goodall was sitting in another room and heard his wife scream and cry 'Don't kill me.' the prisoner, who was a half-caste, seized her by the throat and pulled her out of bed. The other man, Ted Kelly, stuck up Mr Goodall. The prisoner said he was at Curbin, five miles away, but as he was positively identified and was well-known in the district he was convicted and sentenced to fifteen years' hard labour. The judge said that Kelly had been tried for his share in the crime and had been sentenced nearly twelve months since. Circumstances connected with bushranging had greatly altered since then and this would naturally induce him to be less severe; yet, having passed a sentence on one man, he could not now pass a lighter sentence on an accomplice who was no less guilty.

On 24 November 1867, a party of forty or fifty shearers and others had assembled at Mr William Whittaker's store on the Willandra Billabong, about a mile and a half from Mossgiel station, for the purpose of holding a race meeting when they were bailed up by

During the long gun battle before the Clarke brothers surrendered, John (second left) was wounded in the shoulder.

John Williams, William Brookman, Edward Kelly, and John Payne, and robbed of a considerable amount.

Afterwards Michael McNamara, a constable stationed at Booligal about sixty miles from Mossgiel, but who was at Mossgiel on duty at the time, was talking to Mr Dobbins on the veranda of the store, when Williams and Brookman came up and asked Dobbins if he was Constable McNamara. Dobbins replied 'No.' Brookman then turned to the constable and asked him the same question. The bushrangers each had a revolver in his hand, and so the constable also said 'No' and made a rush at Brookman. In the struggle they got inside the store, and Brookman's pistol exploded, the bullet shattering McNamara's wrist. Brookman was shouting for help, and another shot was fired, wounding Constable McNamara in the back of the head. Mr Peerman, overseer of the Mossgiel sheep station, and Mr Edward Crombie rushed up and secured Williams and Brookman. They were placed in a hut and watched by Messrs F. G. Desailly, Robertson, and others. The two bushrangers had five revolvers all loaded, except two barrels which had recently been fired. Williams had £82 1s. 10d. and Brookman £34 8s. 8d., making in all £116 10s. 6d.

The two bushrangers were charged on 14 January 1868, at Deniliquin, with having wounded with intent to kill Michael McNamara, a constable, in the execution of his duty. Williams, it was said, was a bullock-driver, who had recently sold his team for the purpose of turning bushranger. Brookman was under seventeen years of age, and very boyish in appearance.

Mr George Milner Stephen, who appeared for the prisoners, pleaded hard for a light sentence on Brookman on account of his youth and also because his family were respectable people. The Chief Justice said that in a recent case of a bushranger who put a pistol to the head of an advancing constable, the jury had found that there was no intent to kill. In the present case the arresting constable had not been killed, and the jury must decide as to the intent. With regard to the youth of one of the prisoners, it was an ascertained fact that lads when they became bushrangers were more bloodthirsty, brutal, cruel, and fiendish than grown men. The prisoners were sentenced to death, and the boy when he heard the sentence said 'Thank you'. His sentence was afterwards commuted to imprisonment for life.

Edward Kelly and John Payne pleaded guilty to the robberies at Whittaker's and to two other charges of bushranging. They had been followed by the police, and Payne was captured while Kelly got away, although wounded. Subsequently Payne led the police to the camp, and thus assisted them to capture his wounded mate. For this act of humanity, the judge sentenced him to ten years' imprisonment on two charges, the sentences to be concurrent, while Kelly was sentenced to two terms of fifteen years each, or thirty years in all.

Walter Maher, another bushranger, also pleaded guilty to a charge of highway robbery, and was sentenced to ten years' imprisonment.

Charley Johnson and Miller, alias Slater, who had been arrested and lodged in the lock-up at Denison Town on 3 April 1868, made a rush on the watch-house keeper when he entered their cell, knocked him down and took his revolver. They fired two shots at him and walked away. They called at the blacksmith's shop and made the blacksmith take off their irons. Then they left the town, to resume their bushranging career. On the following morning they stuck up and robbed Mr Ashton of about £10. On the 6th they stuck up the Green Swamp Inn, kept by Mr McNaughton.

In the evening they walked into Mr Tuckerman's hotel in Mudgee, and called for drinks. When these had been served they ordered all in the bar to bail up, and began collecting the money. When they had obtained all they could they walked away, no attempt being made to detain them. They went into Langbridge's Hotel, and collected the money in the same way. Then they returned, mounted their horses, and left the town by the Green Swamp Road. They stopped for supper at Landell's Hotel, about a mile from the town.

In the meantime a party under Constable Campbell, composed principally of those who had been robbed, started in pursuit. They rode rapidly, and as they came up to the front of Landell's Hotel the bushrangers left by the back door as the horses they had ridden had been captured.

On the following morning Mr Farrar was returning from Gulgong to Mudgee when he saw three mounted men, whom he took to be bushrangers. He started to gallop away, when he recognized Constable Webb's voice, and pulled up. He informed the police that he had stayed at Matthew Horner's Inn on the previous night, and had been suddenly wakened by a blow on the head from the butt of a revolver. He was ordered to keep quiet and to get up. He did so, and was compelled to lead the way to the stable, saddle and bridle his horse, and give the animal to the bushrangers. He had no idea who they were, and had been too much confused by the blow on his head to notice their appearance. Afterwards they roused up Mr Horner and compelled him to supply them with horses, giving Farrar his horse back again.

On obtaining this information the party in pursuit rode on to Horner's Inn to make further inquiries, while at the same time the bushrangers must have been riding through the bush to Mudgee, and so passed their pursuers. They called at Tuckerman's Hotel, and had breakfast. As soon as their presence in the town was known, another party was made up to capture them. When the bushrangers left the town they were again followed, and were overtaken near Bambera Hill, where a fight took place. When the pursuers had expended all their ammunition they returned to Mudgee, while the bushrangers proceeded to stick up and rob the Barragon mail. They were captured subsequently, and sent to jail.

On 20 April 1868, Robert Cotterall, alias Blue Cap, was tried at Wagga Wagga for having stuck up and robbed Carl Seeman at Rock Station, Reedy Creek, in June 1867; and William Marshall, Jeremiah Lehane, and several others at various places, between 15 July and 24 October. The prisoner had put up a hard struggle when run down by the police, and had been wounded. He was still very ill when brought to trial. Being deathly pale, and wearing a green shade over his eyes, he looked very little like the popular idea of a bold bushranger. He was convicted and sent to jail for ten years.

# 20 Captain Thunderbolt

**Bushranging in the northern district of New South Wales; Captain Thunderbolt and his daring exploits; a Chinese bushranger; Captain Thunderbolt's desperate duel with Constable Walker and his consequent death.**

It must not be supposed that while the southern and western districts of New South Wales were harried by bushrangers, the great northern district escaped from this scourge. In fact, although bushranging began rather later than in the western district, it was prevalent in the northern district at this time.

In April 1864, Peter, James, and Acton Clarke, with John Conroy and a boy of twelve named Samuel Carter, were riding together towards Culgoa, near Warland's Range. The boy had cantered some distance ahead, when he was ordered to bail up by a mounted man who suddenly came out from behind a clump of trees. The boy took no notice and the man fired at him and missed. The boy galloped away and the man started to follow him when he caught sight of the other travellers who had just appeared round a bend in the road. The bushranger stooped his horse, turned to meet them, and ordered them to dismount. They did so. The bushranger also dismounted and came towards them. He demanded their money and they felt in their pockets to get it out.

Just then Peter Clarke made a rush, threw his arms round the bushranger, and tried to throw him. There was a short struggle, and a pistol went off. Peter Clarke fell dead and the bushranger broke away from him. The other travellers had come forward and endeavoured to assist Peter, but had been unable to grasp hold of the bushranger as the wrestlers shifted so rapidly. Now, however, they caught him as he was trying to reach his horse. In the struggle both James Clarke and Conroy were wounded, but the bushranger was overpowered and disarmed. They tied his arms and took him along with them. About two miles along the road they came upon two men tied to trees, who said that they had been stuck up and robbed by the prisoner about two hours before. The prisoner was handed over to the police and identified as Harry Wilson, twenty years of age. He was taken to Maitland and charged with wilful murder. He was convicted, and hanged on 4 October. A public meeting was held at Murrurundi and a committee was appointed to raise a subscription for the purpose of erecting a monument to Peter Clarke, who had 'sacrificed by life in the cause

of order and justice'. This project was duly carried out.

Mr Samuel Turner, travelling from Bingera Goldfield to Newcastle in a buggy, put up for the night at Britten's Hotel, Willowtree. Next morning (Sunday, 19 October) he started early, intending to breakfast at Wallabadah. He had gone barely ten miles when he was stuck up by a man riding a fine-looking horse. The robber took him off the road, tied him to one tree and hitched his horse to another. He robbed Mr Turner of about £12, a gold watch and chain, and a bunch of keys, then rode away. Mr Turner struggled desperately and succeeded in getting loose. He was leading his horse through the scrub towards the road when the robber returned, tied him up more securely than before, and cautioned him not to 'try that dodge again'.

This time Mr Turner remained quiet, and about an hour later the bushranger returned again, directing Mr McShane where to drive his mail coach. When the coach had been placed in a satisfactory position the robber tied McShane and a passenger back to back with a sapling between them, and laid them on the ground. The bushranger then sat down to go through the letters. McShane said, 'You'd better leave them alone, you'll get nothing out of them.' 'Won't I,' replied the bushranger. 'What do you call this? It's a hundred and forty quid anyway.' He held up a roll of bank notes as he spoke.

Having finished the letters he told them to remain quiet until he 'got the other mail', and went away again towards the road. It was fully two hours later when he again returned, directing Smith, the driver of the other mail, where to stand. Smith said his horses were young ones and would not stand. 'All right', replied the bushranger, 'stand at their heads, but, mind, no hanky panky.' The only passenger was Mrs O'Dell. she was politely requested to take a seat on a log and was not interfered with or asked for her money. By a strange coincidence her husband had been a passenger on the coach a week before and had been robbed at the same place, presumably by the same bushranger. By the present transaction the Bank of New South Wales lost

£274, and it was doubtful whether this included the 'hundred and forty quid' or not.

On 16 December a toll-keeper named Delany was 'sitting at the receipt of custom' in the toll-house on the road between Maitland and Rutherford, when a man pushed the door open, presented a pistol at his head, and cried out 'Give me your money.' Delany was of course considerably startled by the suddenness of this attack, but he replied 'I've got none'. 'No —— nonsense!' cried the bushranger. 'Give it here!' 'I tell you', exclaimed Delany, 'there's no money here. My mate's just taken it to Maitland.' The bushranger stepped into the house, pushed Delany aside, opened the cupboard, and took out the cashbox, saying at the same time, 'I'm Captain Thunderbolt.'

Delany made no attempt to resist this violence, and the bushranger put the box under his arm and walked away up the road to where he had hitched his horse to the fence. He mounted and rode away. A few minutes afterwards O'Brien, the lessee of the toll-bar, returned from the town. Delany told him what had occurred, and leaving O'Brien in charge walked towards the Spread Eagle Inn at the Rutherford Racecourse. Near the Inn he came upon the bushranger, who exclaimed, 'Hulloa, come after me?' 'No', replied Delany, 'I'm going to the pub.' 'Has your mate gone for the crusher?' asked the bushranger. 'No', was the reply, 'he's minding the bar.'

Captain Thunderbolt kept silence for a moment as if thinking, then he said, 'I was told that young Fogarty, the flash fighting man, was keeping the bar, and I wanted to take it out of him. I didn't want to hurt you. You'll find your cashbox behind that clump of trees and here's your money.' He handed Delany about four shillings, mostly in coppers, and Delany walked away, picked up the cashbox, which was uninjured, and went back to the toll-house. The bushranger walked into the bar of the inn and asked if he could have something to eat. Mrs Byrne, the landlady, replied 'Certainly', and went out to cut him some bread and meat. He sat down and waited, and on her return ate the bread and meat as if he was very hungry. When he had finished he asked 'How much?' 'Oh nothing', replied Mrs Byrne, 'we never charge for a little thing like that.' 'Well', said the robber, 'I came here to stick you up, but as you're so —— hospitable, I won't.' He then asked for a bottle of rum, paid for it, and went away.

About half a mile away he met Godfrey Parsons, who was taking his sick wife to Maitland to see the doctor. Thunderbolt ordered him to 'bail up and hand out'. Parsons replied, 'We've only two pounds, and we want that for the doctor.' The bushranger asked what was the matter with Mrs Parsons and how long she had been ill. Parsons told him. 'Well', said the robber, 'I'm a bushranger, but I don't rob sick women; pass on.' Mrs Parsons had £30 in her pocket and was crying at the prospect of losing it.

Farther along the road Thunderbolt met a man and four women, and stopped to joke with them. He said he thought it —— unfair that one man should have four women, while he could not get one. As they were laughing a trooper rode up, and the bushranger immediately challenged him to fight; the trooper, however, said he had no ammunition with him. 'I've been chased by you —— traps near Armidale,' exclaimed Thunderbolt, 'but they pulled up at the Black Rock. They were afraid of getting bogged in the Green Swamp if they followed me.'

He stopped a number of other people during the afternoon, robbing some and letting others go, and in the evening went back to the Spread Eagle for tea. He chatted for some time with Mrs Byrne, telling her of his exploits. Just after his departure four troopers rode up. Information as to the proceedings of the bushranger had reached Maitland, and these troopers had been sent out to catch him if possible. They made some inquiries, and then followed in the direction in which Thunderbolt had gone, overtaking him as he was talking quietly to a man on the road.

The foremost trooper presented his pistol at the bushranger's head, and said 'You're my prisoner.' 'Am I?' cried Thunderbolt with a laugh, as he put spurs to his horse and galloped away. After a long chase, and the expenditure of a large quantity of government ammunition, the bushranger escaped in the dark. The

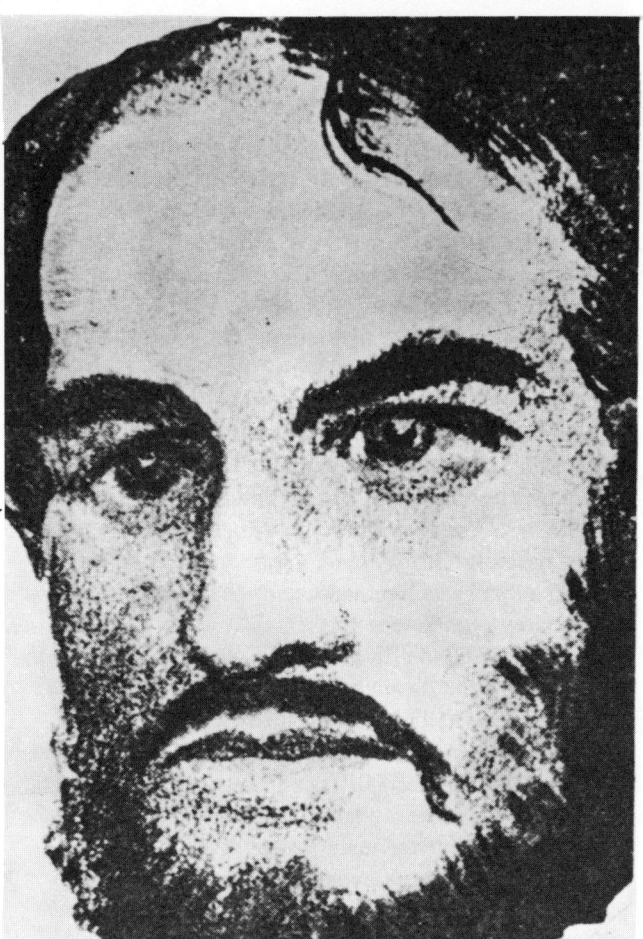

Frederick Ward, *alias* 'Captain Thunderbolt', was born in 1836 at Windsor, New South Wales. Although he won local fame as a jockey, he was sentenced to a long term in prison for horse-stealing. Embittered by what he claimed was a wrong conviction, Ward escaped in 1863 and began his career as 'Captain Thunderbolt'.

*Left:*
Ward was at times wrongly blamed for holding up the Northern mail. In fact, he directed most of his attention to toll-gates and single travellers.

troopers' horses were almost too tired to return to Maitland. In its comments on this escapade of the new bushranger the *Maitland Mercury* inquires: 'Is this hitherto quiet district to be disturbed as the western district has been for so long a time?' and events proved that it was.

Within a few days the Northern mail was stuck up by two armed men. One of the robbers was said to be in a state of trepidation the whole time. Perhaps this may account for the bushrangers missing two registered letters, one containing £60 and the other £30, and a small bag of gold-dust in a package. A gentleman who was accompanying the mail cart on horseback was allowed to continue his journey because he said he was on a visit to a sick friend. He was required to promise 'as a gentlemen' not to give any information to the police. He kept his word, but on his arrival in Tamworth he made a bet that the mail coach would not arrive by 3 p.m. The mail was delayed less than half an hour, however, and the driver nearly made up the lost time by fast driving. The gentleman therefore lost his bet in spite of the special knowledge he had acquired.

The robbers were followed at once, and on 6 January 1865, William Mackie and Robert Johnstone were committed for trial for this robbery. Mackie was identified as a bushranger who had been previously convicted at Bathurst for robbery under arms, but had

made his escape while being conveyed to Sydney to be sent to Cockatoo Island. The prisoners had been taken from Bathurst to Penrith by coach. From there they went to Sydney by train. They were handcuffed in the guard's van with the door open, as the day was very hot. As the train was running along the embankment near Fairfield, between Liverpool and Parramatta, Mackie, ironed as he was, had jumped out. The train had been travelling at a fast rate, and it ran some distance before notice could be conveyed to the driver and the train stopped.

It was expected that the prisoner would be found dead at the foot of the embankment, but nothing could be seen of him. It was then believed that he had crawled somewhere into the scrub to die, but although diligent search was made no body could be discovered. After their recapture, Mackie and Johnstone were sent to Cockatoo to undergo their original sentences. It was

143

thought that they had intended to join Captain Thunderbolt.

An attempt was made on 7 January to stick up the Northern mail about twelve miles north of Singleton. A shot was fired from behind a culvert on the road as the coach was passing, and a voice called out 'Bail up'. Instead of obeying the driver lashed his horses, took his foot off the brake, and the coach plunged down the hill at a tremendous rate, at the imminent risk of capsizing. Two robbers came out from behind the culvert and fired. The passengers declared that they heard the whizz of the bullets, but no one was hurt and the coach reached the level ground safely.

On the same day the branch mail from Bendemeer was stuck up and robbed near Stringy Barks, proving that more than one party was raiding on the Great North Road. There were no passengers, but a number of half notes were taken. The robbers handed the driver several cheques to 'take care of', one being for £1000. No violence was used.

The Northern mail was robbed again on 30 January, at Black Hill about two miles from Muswellbrook, by four armed men. There were three male and one female passengers. The amount stolen was estimated at between £700 and £800. These and several minor robberies on the road were all credited to Captain Thunderbolt, or to men who were trying to join him.

It was said that the immunity enjoyed by him encouraged other criminals to take to the road, and in one case at least a Chinaman turned bushranger. Constable Ward was returning to his station at Coonabarabran from Mudgee on 21 February, when he was informed that a Chinaman had recently stuck up and robbed a number of persons in the neighbourhood. The constable followed him into the bush, found his camp, and called on the Asiatic to come out and surrender. Instead of obeying the Chinaman exclaimed, 'You —— policeman, me shootee you!' and did so. The constable, though wounded, returned to the nearest farm. From there news of the occurrence was sent to the police-station. A party was organized and the Chinaman was soon hunted down. He was convicted of attempting to murder a constable while in the execution of his duty, and was hanged. Constable Ward recovered from his wound.

On 6 April, 1865 Mr Hughes, of Bourke and Hughes, squatters, informed the police at Dubbo that the hotel at the Fisheries had been stuck up and robbed, and volunteered to assist in the capture of the bushrangers. They tracked the robbers to Canonbar, about a hundred and twenty miles away where Mr Hughes's horse knocked up. There they were informed that the bushrangers had passed three days before, and had stolen fresh horses from Mr Baird's station, Bellerengar, leaving their knocked-up ones in exchange. The black trackers were thrown off the trail by this manoeuvre and followed the tracks of the abandoned horses for several miles before they

discovered their error. They soon picked up the new tracks although the bushrangers had kept off the road as much as possible, as if aware that they were being followed. They rode through the scrub and across arid or rocky patches wherever they could find them, but the black boys followed them with unerring skill and little delay.

At Martell's Inn the police were informed that the bushrangers were only twelve hours ahead. The bushrangers stuck up and robbed several people on the road and took fresh horses, provisions, and other necessaries from the stations as they went along. They stuck up Mr Strahan's station and then went on to Gordon's Inn, where they called for drinks like ordinary travellers, 'shouting' for all those in the bar. Then the leader, Daniel Sullivan, produced his pistol while his two mates went to the door to prevent any of the men inside from running away. They collected about £4 from the landlord and those in the bar, then they put their pistols in their pockets and began 'shouting' again.

When the £4 was spent they again produced their pistols, compelled the landlord to hand over the cash, and proceeded to spend it as before. The money had been spent some three or four times when Sullivan left his mates, Clarke and Donnelly, to 'keep the game alive', mounted his horse and rode into the bush. Mr Gordon was compelled to remain in the bar to serve out the liquor called for, but Mrs Gordon went on to the veranda to see whether she could find any one to send to Molong to give the alarm.

Presently she saw three dusty, weather-stained travellers walking towards the inn and thought that they were more bushrangers. Fortunately she did not go into the bar to tell her husband, and when Sergeant Cleary, with Constables Brown and Johnston, came up they quickly told her who they were, and were informed that the men they had ridden so far to arrest were inside. The police entered the bar and, covering the two bushrangers with their revolvers, called on them to surrender. Instead of obeying, Clark put his hand to his belt and was immediately shot. Donnelly made a rush towards the corner of the bar where their guns were standing against the wall, and he also was shot just before he reached them. A moment later Sullivan rode up to the front of the hotel, unconscious of the change which had taken place during his absence.

When he found himself covered by the police weapons he was so dumbfounded that he permitted himself to be pulled from his horse and handcuffed without resistance. The police had left their horses some distance away in charge of the black tracker. Now they went for their horses and fed them as well as themselves. Later on a cart was brought and the body of Donnelly was placed in it. Beside it, wrapped in a blanket, was the wounded man Clarke. Sullivan, being uninjured, was mounted on horseback, and the whole party proceeded to Molong where an inquest was held on Donnelly's body. Sullivan and Clarke, who recovered from his wound, were subsequently tried and convicted.

On 29 April, the *Tamworth Examiner* said:

A week ago we reported that Frederick Ward, alias Captain Thunderbolt, had stuck up the Warialda mail. He afterwards went to Mr Lloyd's Manilla station, and took two first-class horses. Then he stuck up Cheeseborough's and Lethbridge's stations. From the 20th to the 24th nothing was heard of him, but on the last-mentioned date he and another stuck up Munro's Inn, at Boggy Creek. Mr Munro challenged them to fight singly, either with fists or pistols, but they laughed at him and shot a valuable dog. They drank a large quantity of spirits, and collected between £70 and £80. They went on to Walford's Inn at Millie, sticking up Mr Baldwin on the road. Mr Walford, having been informed of their approach, had hidden away everything of value, so that they got very little, except more grog. The police also had been informed, and three troopers, with a black tracker, soon arrived on the scene. As they approached, the bushranger on guard outside whistled, and the other man came out and mounted, Thunderbolt waving a revolver and pointing to a field behind the house as a challenge. He led his men to the clearing and made a stand. The police followed, and a number of shots were fired on both sides. The police closed up, and Constable Dalton shot one of the bushrangers, a mere lad, and he fell. Dalton shouted to Constable Morris to 'look after him,' and turned towards Thunderbolt, when the boy raised himself on his elbow and fired. Constable Lynch shot the boy in the neck, probably in time to save Dalton's life. Ward made a dash forward, perhaps with a view to driving the police away from the boy and carrying him off, but the police fire was too brisk, and after a few more rounds the robber turned and rode into the bush. The police followed, but as their horses had travelled fifty miles that morning, they were obliged to give up the chase. The robber who was killed, was identified as John Thompson, aged sixteen.

In December 1865, Ward, riding Mr Duff's racer, Eucalyptus, stuck up Cook's Inn at Quirindi on the 18th, J. M. Davis's Inn at Currabubula on the 20th, and Griffin's Inn at Carroll on the 23rd. At the last place he pulled up and said to his mate in a loud voice, 'Let's have a glass of brandy. We want it this wet evening.' They dismounted, and stepped on to the veranda.

As he entered the door Thunderbolt raised the corner of his mackintosh to display his pistols and said 'I'll trouble you, ladies and gentlemen, to bail up.' The women began to scream, and Ward said, 'Don't be afraid. We shan't hurt any one. We only want a little money.' A traveller who had entered some time before drew away from the bar and joined the bushrangers. The other men present were ranged in single row along the wall, and when all were in position each man was called up in turn to be searched. The proceedings

The mounted troopers of the day were a smart-looking lot but had often proved ineffectual in capturing wrong-doers. The Police Act of 1862 established the New South Wales Police Force and after that their activities were better organized, although they still lacked sufficient numbers to effectively control bushranging.

were very suggestive of the 'next, please', in a barber's shop. While this was going on several people entered, and were compelled to take their places at the end of the queue.

The bushrangers held the bar from 5 to 9 p.m. pausing in their work every now and then to order drinks for all hands. Shortly after nine o'clock two men rode up to the veranda and shouted 'Landlord'. The two robbers looked out and recognizing the horsemen, retreated into the back room. Mr Griffin went to the door, and said in a low tone to Constable Lang, 'We're all stuck up here.' 'Which are the bushrangers?' asked the constable, and on being told that they were in the back room he strode to the door and fired. The shot was returned, and the shooting continued until the constable was wounded in the arm and his horse in the neck. The bushrangers went out through the back door, and escaped in the darkness into the bush; but they left their horses behind.

Early in 1866 Ward and his gang made a raid across the Queensland border, robbing stations, hotels, and travellers in the Curriwillinghi district. He soon returned to his own district, and in March the Tamworth and Wee Waa mail was stuck up near

145

Bullingall by two armed men supposed to be Ward and another. The driver of the Northern mail was also ordered to bail up near Murrurundi, and as he did not obey with due alacrity he was speedily brought to a standstill by one of his horses being shot dead. After going through the letters the bushrangers rode into the town and took a quantity of clothes, some money, some jewellery and other valuables from Barton's and Johnstone's stores and Humphries's Hotel.

James Booth, William Willis alias Dunkley, and Thomas Hampton were arrested in a public-house at the corner of Goulburn and Pitt Streets, Sydney, by Detectives Camphin and Finigan on 17 April 1866, and charged with having robbed the Singleton mail on the previous day. The coach had arrived at the Red Post Hill, between Muswellbrook and Singleton, when the men sprang out from behind the trees bordering the road and sang out, 'Bail up, stand and deliver, throw up your arms.' Mr Moore, one of the passengers, jumped out of the back of the coach, and Hampton chased him and brought him back. Mr Button, a government railway guard, also tried to get down, but Willis told him that he would blow his '—— brains out' if he didn't sit still. The passengers were all tied up and robbed. One of them, George Beved, said that Willis was the man who threatened to 'Blow the roof of his —— skull off' when Moore was wrestling with Hampton. The prisoners were also charged with having bailed up and robbed the mail near Campbelltown, on 10 April. The proceedings were of the usual character. The prisoners were convicted on both charges and were sentenced; Willis to ten years' and Booth and Hampton each to eight years' imprisonment.

The April Sessions at Bathurst were unusually heavy. John Weekes was sentenced to death for the murder of Mr Scheffts at Grenfell, and John Connors for attempted murder in another bushranging exploit. Besides these, Patrick Foran and James Kelly were sent to jail for ten years for sticking up the Halfway House on the Carcoar road, and other acts of bushranging; James Kennedy, alias Southgate, to fifteen years for sticking up John Edwards, William Woodley and Henry Rodwell, at Murdering Swamp on 1 January — Kennedy also pleaded guilty to robbing John Fawcett and John Eaton; Charles Rutherford, who had been engaged in several robberies in company with William Mackie (who, as aready related, had jumped out of the train while being conveyed to Sydney, and was afterwards captured in the northern district) was sentenced to seven years' penal servitude; Smith and Moran sentenced to seventeen years each, and Kerr to ten years.

These, with other prisoners sentenced for minor offences, were being conveyed to Sydney to jail on 25 April 1867. There were fifteen prisoners in all, guarded by eight troopers. Sergeant Casey, in charge, was seated on the box seat of the Cobb's coach. The prisoners were inside chained together in two gangs of seven and eight respectively. Constables Madden and Kennedy were seated, unarmed, with the prisoners, while the other five troopers rode beside the coach fully armed. Despite the heavy guard the prisoners made a desperate attempt to escape at Pulpit Hill. In the mêlée Constable Holmes was killed, while Rutherford and another prisoner got away in the bush.

Rutherford immediately returned to his old haunts and recommenced his crimes. In December 1867, he was captured by Sergeant Cleary of Bourke, and was conveyed to the lock-up where again he escaped. In January 1868, he stuck up the Boggy Creek and Galathera Inns, and robbed numbers of people on the road. He then went to Mr Beauvais's inn at Canonbar and called on the landlord to bail up. Mr Beauvais, however had a pistol in the till and knew how to use it. On pretence of taking out the money to hand over as commanded, he got out his revolver and shot the bushranger. He was awarded a silver medal by the Government for this act.

The districts raided by Rutherford and Thunderbolt overlapped, so that it is difficult to decide which of these two bushrangers were responsible for many of the outrages. Ward, however, was not idle. In company with a boy named Mason, he stuck up and robbed the Northern, the Walcha, and several other mails in the district. He was frequently chased by the police, but being a magnificent rider with an intimate knowledge of every gully, ravine or hill in the extensive district over which he ranged, he always managed to escape. Sometimes he was very hard pressed; for instance, when he was compelled to abandon Talleyrand, a race-horse Mr Wyndham had offered a reward of £100 for its capture.

Ward's companions were captured one after the other; they were generally boys of from sixteen to twenty. Thunderbolt continued his career unchecked. No doubt he owed many of his hairbreadth escapes to the superiority of his horses. He would travel two hundred miles to steal a noted race-horse. Thus he stole Mr Samuel Clift's horse, John Brown, from Breeza. The horse had run on the Maitland and Sydney courses.

One of the stories told about Ward was that he stuck up a German band at Goonoo Goonoo Gap, and made the musicians play for him, besides giving him their money. The Germans pleaded hard. They said they were only poor men, and that their wives and children would suffer if they were robbed. Thunderbolt told them that he must have money. He was waiting for the principal winner at the Tamworth Races, he added, and he promised that if he caught him he would return the Germans their money. He took down their names and addresses. The Germans departed very sorrowful, never expecting to see their money again. Nevertheless, on their arrival at their home in Warwick, Queensland, they found a Post Office Order

for £20 awaiting them. They guessed therefore, that Thunderbolt had captured the winner.

On 25 May 1870, Ward met Mr Blanche, innkeeper near Uralla, returning home with his wife from a drive, and called on him to bail up. Blanche laughed, taking no notice of the order. Ward exclaimed, 'No humbugging. You wouldn't let me have a bottle of rum the other night, though I offered £5 for it.' Blanche replied that he never served any one after hours. He then took four shillings and sixpence from his pocket and said, 'This is all the money I've got. You can have that.' The robber said, 'The missus has more than that.' 'No', cried Mrs Blanche, 'I've no money. We only came for a drive.'

Ward seemed to consider for a moment, and then told Mr Blanche to drive on. Several men came up the by-road from Carlisle Gully and Ward stopped and robbed them. An old man named Williamson and an Italian dealer named Giovanni Cappisote were also stopped. After handing over a gold watch and chain, a small nugget of gold, and £3 13s. 6d. in money, the dealer was allowed to depart. The other men were taken to Blanche's Inn where Williamson was ordered to 'shout'. He did so, then Ward did likewise. They danced, and sang, and enjoyed themselves.

Becoming quieter, Ward asked Blanche whether he remembered a fight between a bushranger and the police seven years before at the Rocks, about three hundred yards away. Blanche said he remembered it well. 'Well', cried Ward, 'I'm the man; I was shot in the leg.' Ward went on to relate more of his exploits and the narrative was interspersed with songs and dances.

In the meantime, Cappisote drove on to a selector's farm about a mile and a half along the road. Here he told Mrs Dorrington what had happened. He borrowed a saddle and bridle, took his horse from the cart, and rode to Uralla; making a wide detour round Blanche's house. He told the police where the bushranger was, and Constables Mulhall and Walker armed and mounted at once. Mulhall had the faster horse and he reached Blanche's first. As he rode up he saw Ward and a young man, both mounted on grey horses, riding along the road. He followed them, and as he approached Ward turned round in his saddle and fired. Mulhall returned the fire but his horse bolted. The trooper soon pulled him up. He wheeled and seeing one of the men on the greys gallop away, followed, shouting to Walker to 'look after the other fellow'.

The 'other fellow' was Thunderbolt, and he turned off the road and rode down the steep hill towards the Rocky River, followed by Constable Walker. Both men fired a shot occasionally when an opportunity offered but neither spoke. On reaching the bank of the river, Ward plunged in, intending to cross and escape up the opposite range, but Walker shot his horse. Ward fell into the river, which was shallow there.

Walker galloped along the bank past a deep hole and crossed. Then he returned to where Ward was standing in the water and called on him to surrender. 'Who the —— are you?' inquired Ward roughly. 'Never mind who I am', replied Walker, 'put your hands up.' 'Are you a trooper?' asked Ward. 'Yes', replied Walker. 'Married?' continued Ward. 'Yes', said Walker. 'Well, remember your family', said Ward. 'Oh, that's all right', returned the trooper. 'Will you come out and surrender?' 'No', cried Ward, 'I'll die first.' 'Then it's you and me for it,' said Walker.

The trooper urged his horse into the river. The animal objected at first and then entered with a rush into deep water. Walker raised his revolver above his head to keep it dry. Ward fired several shots, none of which took effect. When the horse steadied Walker fired again and Ward fell. He rose immediately and tried to scramble up the bank. Walker struck him with the butt of his revolver and the bushranger fell back into the deep hole and sank. The trooper slipped from his horse, and reaching down grabbed Ward's shirt and pulled him up. He dragged the bushranger out of the hole, up the steep bank, and laid him out on the grass, believing him to be dead. Then he remounted and rode to Blanche's Hotel for assistance to bring the body in.

Several of the men about there volunteered to help, but on their reaching the river they found that the bushranger had disappeared. A search was made, but it was too dark to look for tracks. The next morning at daybreak the police and several civilians went to the spot and found a trail of blood. They followed it and found Ward hidden under some bushes. He was placed in a cart and taken to Uralla, but died before night. The young man chased by Constable Mulhall said he had gone after Ward to try and get back a horse which the bushranger had stolen from him, and as nothing detrimental to his character was known he was discharged at the police court.

Constable Walker was highly complimented for the pluck and determination he had shown in this desperate encounter alone with the noted bushranger in a deep water hole in a mountain stream. Of the many brave actions recorded of the police, this was perhaps the bravest and the most tragic. The constable was promoted and paid his well-earned reward.

In referring to this duel the Melbourne *Argus* spoke of Ward as the last of the 'professional bushrangers' of New South Wales, and said: 'With a much more compact territory than New South Wales, and with a population which can entertain no ancestral or traditional sympathies with burglars or highwaymen, we are nevertheless amenable to the same reproaches as those with which the neighbouring colony was assailed a few years ago.'

Thunderbolt was shot by Constable Walker after the struggle in the Rocky River (top right), and although help was fetched and he was taken to Uralla, he died that day.

Constable Alex Walker (right) was highly commended for his bravery in capturing the famous bushranger even though it was discovered that Thunderbolt's gun was unloaded during the encounter.

The grave of Captain Thunderbolt, *alias* Fred Ward, at Uralla (above), and a sketch made after his death (far right).

# 21 The Governor's mercy

**The end of bushranging in New South Wales; a raid into South Australia; agitation for the release of Frank Gardiner; Gardiner and other bushrangers released; he leaves the country for California.**

Bushranging in New South Wales practically ceased with the death of Frederick Ward, alias Captain Thunderbolt. Prior to his tragic death after the encounter in New England River, the few stragglers from the big gangs had been captured. Any new men who attempted to revive the 'reign of terror' were speedily dealt with by the police. There were a few robberies besides those already related which were distributed over a wide range of country. One party even crossed the border into South Australia, where the bushranger had previously been known only by hearsay. But these later bushrangers did not inspire the terror which those who had passed away had done. They were very small fry as compared with Gardiner, Gilbert, Hall, Dunn, Morgan, Thunderbolt, and their companions.

In December 1869, a number of people were bailed up and robbed in the Paroo and Warrego districts. Although the "Wild Paroo" had not been very long reclaimed from its original desert state, this did not prevent an enterprising bushranger from finding his way there, though he did not continue his career for very long. He stuck up Messrs Lyons & Martin's station and made the men sit on the top rail of the stockyard fence while he rolled up a parcel of goods which he had selected from the store.

Messrs Browne, Zouch, and Bradley drove up in a buggy while he was doing this, and were ordered to dismount and take their places on the fence with the station hands. The robber escorted them, pistol in hand, from where the buggy stood to the stockyard. While walking across this intervening space, the bushranger inadvertently, or carelessly perhaps, stepped rather too near to Mr Browne, who stood six feet five inches in his socks, and was proportionately strong. With a whoop Mr Browne pounced on to him and held him in a vice-like grip. This turned the tables completely. The men on the fence got off, and the bushranger was in his turn securely tied to the fence and kept there until the police could be brought from the nearest town, Bourke, about a hundred and fifty miles away. After this, bushranging does not appear to have been popular in this district.

On 9 May 1869, Mr Henry Kidder Gillham, manager of the Australian Joint Stock Bank at Braidwood, returned home at 8 p.m. He was entering by the side gate when a man sprang out from the shadow and called on him to stand. The bushranger presented a revolver which Mr Gillham pushed aside. Then another man struck him with a life preserver and knocked him down. Two shots were fired from revolvers.

Michael Collins, a gardener living on the bank premises, was in the kitchen when the two bushrangers entered. One of them called out: 'Not a word, or it will be the worse for you.' The tall man had a 'Northumberland voice — that is, he could not pronounce the r.' They tied Collins and went out of the kitchen. In the meantime the firing had been heard, and Mr Finnigan, a teacher, with Sergeant Duffy and Constable Luke Dacy, ran to the bank. When they got there two men ran out of the garden, and after a chase during which several shots were fired, Joseph Horne was captured. He had no boots on. The other man, John Bollard, escaped at the time, but was later tracked and captured.

At his trial, the Chief Justice, Sir Alfred Stephen, said that Horne had been sentenced to seven years' hard labour at Maitland. He was afterwards convicted in Melbourne and had escaped from Pentridge stockade, although shot in the shoulder. Horne said that punishment had made him what he was, and pleaded hard for Bollard, who was young and had been enticed from the right path by him. Horne was sentenced to fifteen years' imprisonment and Bollard to ten years.

John Baker and William Bertram divided their attentions between New South Wales and South Australia. In May 1869, warrants were issued for their arrest for horse-stealing from the Mount Murchison station. They took to the road and stuck up a number of people. In October they bailed up a hawker named Charles Young, who resisted and was shot dead. This occurred at the Barrier Ranges, not far from where the Broken Hill silver-lead lode was afterwards discovered. Bertram was followed and captured, and

One of the first 'paddy wagons' in Australia. By the 1870s, police methods of transporting prisoners had vastly improved.

was subsequently tried, convicted, and hanged at Bathurst.

Baker escaped for the time and made his way to Koringa. Said the *South Australian Register*, 'He showed a remarkable want of caution in returning to a district where he had passed his hobbledehoy years and was consequently well known.' He had been employed as a horse-breaker at the Cross Roads Grounds, Burra Burra, about seven years previously and had afterwards worked for Messrs Macdonald & Hockin, mail coach proprietors, on the Great Northern Road.

On his arrival at Koringa he went into a barber's shop and asked to have his hair cut and dyed. The hairdresser refused to dye it. Baker swore at him but could not change his determination. The bushranger also grumbled at the time spent in cutting his hair, and continually urged the barber to 'hurry up'.

When the job was completed Baker walked to Redruth, and sat down in the main street opposite the Court House, where the police sessions were being held at the time. There were a number of people about, but Baker sat and cut his tobacco with all the nonchalance of innocence. He filled and lighted his pipe, and was smoking comfortably, when Corporal Smith and Constable Walker came up and said 'You're our prisoner.' 'What for?' asked Baker. 'Bushranging', was the short reply. Baker sprang up from his seat, and raced away at a great rate along the road. He was speedily followed by the police on horseback and brought back. He struggled furiously, slipping his hands from the handcuffs with the greatest ease. The police, however, carried him into the lock-up, and put him into a cell. When questioned, he said he had brought a mob of horses down country for sale, and

carried a revolver for his own protection.

In the same cell was a man named Dobson, arrested for horse-stealing, who had been quiet until Baker came. But the door was barely closed and locked when the jailer heard a suspicious noise in the cell. On opening the door he found that Baker and Dobson were trying to make a hole in the roof with a heavy board seat which they had wrenched from its mortice, and were now using as a battering-ram. Baker was placed in another cell and ironed.

He was a small wiry man, very active, and a daring rider. In company with Bertram he had stuck up the Mount Murchison station, stuck up Mr Cobham's station two hundred miles from Wilcannia, and taken money, a revolver, and several horses; stolen the horse he was riding from Mr O'Leary, of Poolamacca; robbed and murdered a hawker at the Barrier ranges, and stuck up and robbed a number of people on the roads about Tiers, Gumeracha, and other places near the Murray River, on both sides of the New South Wales-South Australian border. When Bertram was captured, Baker endeavoured to induce a young man whom he met to join him, telling him they could easily raise £200 to £300, but the young fellow replied that he 'didn't want to be hung yet'. Baker was extradited to New South Wales, and was tried and hanged at Bathurst early in 1871.

One day, about this time, a man walked into the branch bank at Cassilis, pointed a pistol at the head of the cashier, and ordered him to 'bail up, or I'll blow your brains out'. 'Will you, by G—?' cried the cashier as he placed his hands on the counter and vaulted

151

over. The would-be robber was so startled by this unexpected action on the part of the cashier that he dropped his weapon and ran. The cashier immediately gave chase along Main Street. He soon captured and brought back the pseudo bushranger. The news spread rapidly, and in a few minutes the whole population of the little township was in the Main Street.

It was soon learned that the only policeman stationed in the town had gone to Mudgee 'on a case', the would-be robber was therefore treated to a good cuffing and some threats, and turned adrift. The revolver was found to be old, rusty, and useless, but for some time it hung in the bank chamber as a caution to bushrangers. This attempted bank robbery appears to have been conducive to thirst, as the bars of the two hotels were crowded for the rest of the day by a laughing and jeering mob of citizens.

This little comedy furnishes a very appropriate finish to the story of the many tragedies which were enacted during this the most serious outbreak of bushranging which occurred in New South Wales. During the following two or three years the people were gradually becoming convinced that the crime of bushranging had been thoroughly stamped out, and a sort of reaction set in; letters appeared in the newspapers, in which the writers urged that some clemency might safely be shown to some of the young men who were still in jail. In spite of the brutal indifference which many of the bushrangers had shown for human life, it was almost impossible to help admiring the reckless courage exhibited by them. One thought was frequently expressed in various ways. It was that these bushrangers would have made magnificent soldiers if they had been properly trained and made amenable to discipline. There was in fact a disposition to regard them much as the philosopher regards dirt as 'matter in the wrong place'.

The convict system, which was regarded as the basis of bushranging, had long since passed away. The convicts themselves had almost died out and had ceased to be a prominent class in the community. Here and there one of the old fellows lingered and told stories of the barbarous times which had once existed in the colonies. But they were generally too incapacitated by age to do much harm. There had been a time when horror and detestation of the convicts were very general, but even these feelings had gone now, and there was a prevalent opinion that the convicts had been made worse by the brutal discipline to which they had been subjected.

The very papers which were most strenuous in their exhortations to the Government of the day to stamp out bushranging at any cost, and which urged the police and all orderly citizens to slay and kill any person who interfered with the mails or who molested travellers on the high roads, now admitted that the bushrangers had been harshly dealt with. Those who had been convicted of murder, or of attempts to murder, had

been hanged or shot, while the lesser criminals had been sentenced to penal servitude for life or for very long periods. The juries all over the country had shown no leanings towards mercy or clemency, and the judges had treated the bushrangers with great severity. The people generally, it was asserted, had given ample proof that they would not tolerate a reign of terror such as the bushrangers had striven so hard to establish. If there should ever be another outbreak, which was not considered probable, it would be crushed out long before it could possibly assume such vast proportions as it had gained during the past era. If there were wrong-doers in the colony they would be aware that public opinion was opposed to them and would hesitate before they decided to adopt bushranging as a profession.

The spirit of mercy was abroad. Public meetings were held in all centres of population, petitions were sent to the Governor and the Legislature, and the Press was full of letters praying that mercy might be shown to the evil-doers. The prisoner most frequently mentioned was Frank Gardiner. It is true that he had organized the first gang, and had given a vent to the evil passions of a class; but for him this terrible bushranging era might never have been inaugurated. However he had never committed murder, and had retired from the country and endeavoured to lead a lawful life after only a few months on the road. It had been said that he was engaged in sly grog selling, even when he was ostensibly keeping a store on the road to the diggings in Queensland. If so it was for the Queensland authorities, not those of New South Wales, to punish him for this offence against the licensing laws. However, the Queensland authorites had never made any charge against him, and the report might not be true.

**Sir Alfred Stephen, Chief Justice of New South Wales**

At length the Chief Justice, Sir Alfred Stephen, wrote to the Sydney newspapers. His letter appeared on 23 June 1874. Sir Alfred said that the aim of all punishment was first, the prevention of individuals from committing crimes, and secondly, the deterring of the other individuals from the committing of similar crimes. Gardiner's sentences, aggregating thirty-two years, had been passed in a time of great excitement and the punishment seemed to have been measured more in view of the crimes he was supposed to have committed than with reference solely to those which were proved against him. Sir Alfred could not say whether the reported reformation was sincere, but he thought that the prisoner had been sufficiently punished and therefore recommended a conditional pardon.

Emanating from such a source, this opinion carried great weight. Almost coincidental with its publication, the Governor, Sir Hercules Robinson, (later Lord Rosmead) laid before the Executive council six petitions signed by a number of well-known and responsible persons in various parts of the colony praying for the release of the convict Gardiner. He said it was true that no hope of an absolute remission of his sentence had ever been held out to him, but in the Governor's minute of 5 December 1872, it had been implied that if the prisoner continued to conduct himself well he might hope for remission at the end of ten years.

Official returns were laid on the table showing the number of prisoners still in penal servitude for highway robbery. The prisoner whose case attracted most attention next to Gardiner was William Brookman. His parents were said to be respectable. He was only seventeen years of age when he was charged on 16 January 1868 with wounding with intent to murder. He was convicted and sentenced to death, but his sentence was commuted to fifteen years' penal servitude. It was said to have been his first and only attempt at highway robbery, and he had never previously been arrested or charged with any offence against the law. At the time of this inquiry he had served six and a half years of his sentence.

The other bushrangers in jail at this time were:

Samuel Clarke, sentenced 18 April 1866. Served five years, one month. No previous conviction.
Daniel Shea, sentenced 6 November 1865. Served eight years, six months. Previously sentenced for two years for horse-stealing.
William Willis, alias Dunkley, sentenced 16 May 1866. Served eight years. Three previous convictions for horse-stealing, of nine months, eighteen months, and six months respectively.
Alexander Fordyce, sentenced 23 February 1863. Served eleven years, nine months. No previous conviction.
John Payne, sentenced 14 January 1868. Served six years, six months. No previous conviction.
James Jones, sentenced 31 March 1864. Served ten

Sir Hercules Robinson, Governor of New South Wales 1872—79, signed a pardon for Gardiner.

years, one month. No previous conviction.
Robert Cotterall, alias Blue Cap, sentenced 29 April 1868. Served six years, one month. No previous conviction.
James Boyd, alias McGrath, sentenced 24 February 1864. Served nine years, three months. Previously sent to jail for five years for horse-stealing.
Thomas Cunningham, alias Smith, sentenced 9 April 1867. Served seven years, one month. No previous conviction.
Charles Hugh Gough, alias Wyndham, alias Bennett, sentenced 9 April 1867, served seven years, one month. Previously sentenced to three years for assault with intent to rob.
Thomas Dargue, sentenced 28 March 1867. Served seven years, two months. No previous conviction.
Henry Dargue, sentenced 28 March 1867. Served seven years, two months. No previous conviction.
John Kelly, sentenced 11 March 1867. Served seven years two months. Previously sentenced to two years for embezzlement.
Edward Kelly, sentenced 14 January 1867. Served six years, seven months. No previous conviction.
James Smith, sentenced 15 April 1866. Served

153

seven years, one month. Previously sentenced to three years for horse-stealing.

John Foran, sentenced 18 October 1867. Served six years, seven months. No previous conviction.

John Williams, sentenced to death 14 January 1868. Sentence commuted to fifteen years' penal servitude. Served six years, four months. No previous conviction.

William H. Simmons, sentenced 6 April 1868. Served six years, one month. Previously sentenced to ten years on two charges of larceny.

William Taverner, sentenced 5 April 1867. Served five years, one month. No previous conviction.

Daniel Taylor, sentenced 24 October 1865. Served eight years, one month. No previous conviction.

John Bow, sentenced 26 February 1863. Sentence death, commuted to imprisonment for life. Served eleven years, six months. No previous conviction.

John Bollard, sentenced 19 October 1869. Served four years seven months. No previous conviction.

All these prisoners were very young men, little more than boys, when they were convicted. Of the twenty-three, sixteen had had no charges brought against them prior to their arrest for highway robbery. The four others who had been previously convicted of horse-stealing were cattle duffers and horse planters. A few years before, these were scarcely considered to be crimes by the residents of the districts in which these young men were born; although the law, when it came to be enforced in these districts, called these acts criminal. It was said that if Gardiner was to be released these young men, who had been led away principally by his example, should also have their sentences remitted.

The reports, with such comments as had been made on them by the Executive Council, were placed before the Legislative Assembly. On 3 July 1874 a debate began relative to the cases of Gardiner and Brookman, it being understood that the decision in the case of Brookman should apply to the other twenty-two named in the reports. On a division being taken the vote stood twenty-six for and twenty-six against a remission of the sentences. The Speaker gave his casting vote with the ayes, and it was consequently resolved that the two prisoners should be released on 8 July 1874.

The Governor extended the prerogative of mercy to the others named above, and they were all released at the same time. In the case of Gardiner the pardon was coupled with the condition that he should leave the colony forthwith. Consequently, a short time after his release he sailed to California, and was reported to have died there about nine years later. Mrs Brown, his paramour, had died in New Zealand during his imprisonment.

The release of the bushrangers was not carried without opposition, however. A monster meeting of diggers was held at Grenfell to protest against any mercy being shown them. Large meetings were held elsewhere and it was said that remitting the sentences

154

Frank Gardiner was released from Darlinghurst jail on 20 July, 1874, after serving ten years of his thirty-two year sentence, on condition that he left the country. He was then forty and his mistress, Kitty Brown, had died in New Zealand. Gardiner eventually opened a saloon in San Francisco where he adopted the name 'Frank Smith' and died nine years later.

of the bushrangers was tantamount to encouraging other wrong-doers to rebel against the laws. The speakers deplored the action of the Governor, the Executive and the Legislature, and prophesied a new outbreak of lawlessness. But the spirit of the opposition was less active than that of the people in favour of mercy, while the majority of the population were more or less indifferent. And so ended the great outbreak of bushranging in New South Wales.

## Harry Power

# 22 Bushranger Power

**Bushranging in Victoria; Harry Power's capture and escape from Pentridge; captured while asleep; a peacock as 'watchdog'; the Power procession at Beechworth; his trial, sentence and eventual death.**

While New South Wales was the chief centre of bushranging during this epoch, the neighbouring colonies were not entirely free from the scourge. In those cases where bushranging extended over the borders of the mother colony — as when Morgan, Thunderbolt, and Bertram crossed into Victoria, Queensland, and South Australia respectively — the inroads have been dealt with in connection with the careers of these particular bushrangers in order not to break the continuity of their stories. Having described the rise and fall of bushranging in the older colony, it is now necessary to return to Victoria and continue the narrative there. Bushranging in this colony during this epoch was rather a survival from the past than a new development. With one notable exception, the police dealt promptly with the lawbreakers. The exception will be noticed in due course.

In July 1864, a sensation was caused in the Kilmore district by a report which gained currency, that Gardiner and his gang had stuck up a number of people near Yea. A party of volunteers was speedily organized to assist the police in hunting down the bushrangers. The pursuers were divided into small parties, and on the evening of the 20th one of these, composed of Mr Grant and Constable Buck, came upon three suspicious-looking characters camped on Pack Bullock Flat with a mob of horses. When Constable Buck asked where they were going one replied 'To Melbourne', and another 'To the Jordan'. Buck called on them to surrender, whereupon one man sprang forward and clutched him by the throat. Another rushed at Grant who was unarmed.

Grant turned and ran to where they had left their horses, calling on Buck to come away. Buck broke loose and joined him, losing his revolver in the struggle. They rode away to find help, and returned with Mr Grant's brother, George Grant, and Mr Walker. Grant shot one bushranger dead, Walker stunned a second with a blow on the head with the butt of his gun, while Buck captured the third after a smart run. The captured men were convicted of robbery by violence and it was said that the horses

they had with them had been stolen from various stations.

The central figure in Victoria of this era was undoubtedly Harry Power. This notorious bushranger arrived in Victoria from Ireland shortly before the proclamation of the discovery of gold at Ballarat, and went to the diggings. In March 1855, he was seen near Daisy Hill, in the Maryborough district, riding a valuable horse, the description of which tallied with that of a horse which had been stolen and for which the police were seeking. He was stopped and challenged to show his receipt for the horse.

Instead of producing it or saying where it was deposited, Power disputed the right of the police to stop him on the highway and drew a revolver. The police, very naturally perhaps, took this as a tacit admission that he could not show any rights to the horse and tried to apprehend him. Several shots were fired and at last one of the troopers fell wounded. Power put spurs to his horse and galloped away. A warrant was immediately issued for his arrest and he was followed and captured. He was convicted of 'wounding with intent to do grievous bodily harm', and was sentenced to fourteen years' penal servitude.

A short time before the expiration of his term he was employed in drawing refuse from the Pentridge Jail to the rubbish heap in a cart. A number of other prisoners were similarly employed. While the cart he was helping to draw was being tipped, Power managed to hide himself under a corner of the heap. He was not missed until evening when the prisoners employed at this work were mustered. The prisoners at work with him must of course have been aware of his evasion, but professed ignorance in accordance with convict etiquette.

A search was made and his hiding-place was discovered, but Power was gone. He stole some clothes from a farm not far from Pentridge, and with the blade of an old pair of sheep shears to defend himself, he declared that he would not be captured alive. Shortly after his escape on 7 May 1869, he stuck up the mail coach near Porepunkah and continued to

155

rob in the Ovens and Beechworth districts for several months. Then he made a raid into New South Wales, going as far as Adelong. He returned about the end of September to his old district and stayed there for the remainder of his career.

Commenting on his actions, the *Ovens and Murray Advertiser* said: 'Possessed of a thorough knowledge of the country, this scoundrel has made periodical descents to the settled districts, and afterwards, like a hunted dog, betaken himself to the ranges. *From a certain portion of the population he — or whoever else has been masquerading in his name — has received succour and information, while the police have been misled and deceived.*'

The article from which this extract was made was copied and italicised in the Melbourne *Argus*, and made the subject of a leading article in which it was contended that if bushranging was to be stamped out the sympathizers and bush telegraphs must be restrained from aiding the bushranger with food and information. The Government was urged to pass a special Act to enable the police to contend with the difficulty. It was said on the other hand that the Outlawry Act, if strictly applied, would meet the case.

William Moore, of Buffalo, was returning from a trip to Eldorado, where he had sold his load of farm produce, when a young man rode up and asked him 'Where have you been?' 'What's that to you?' returned Moore. The young fellow said 'I only asked a civil question.' 'Well,' said Moore, 'I've been to Eldorado, and I'm going home. Will that satisfy you?' The young man nodded and cantered on. As he passed, Moore noticed that he had pistols in his belt. He hastily took a roll of notes worth £35 from his pocket, and thrust it into an empty flour sack in the dray. The young man only rode on about fifty yards, then wheeled round, revolver in hand, and cried 'Bail up.' Moore stopped and willingly turned out his pockets, displaying a half-crown, which he handed to the robber who rode away.

In reporting this robbery Mr Moore said that he believed that this was the young man's first attempt at highway robbery, as he trembled violently and seemed glad when it was over. The *Ovens and Murray Advertiser* of 7 May 1870, in commenting on this case, said: 'It shows the necessity of more determined efforts to capture Harry Power, who has for more than a year robbed rich and poor alike in this neighbourhood, and it is the immunity which he has for so long enjoyed that encourages young lads to imitate him.'

Shortly before, in April, Patrick Stanton otherwise known as Jack Muck, was captured after a smart run. He was convicted of having stuck up and robbed a coloured man, a well-known splitter and timber cutter, on the Black Dog Creek. The splitter had been to town to be paid for a number of posts and rails and was returning home along the Rutherglen Road when he was bailed up.

The Kilmore *Free Press* reported that Power had been seen in Mr Dunlop's paddock at Mount William. He was firing at a mark on a tree. No one interfered with him.

On 2 May, Edward Kelly was arrested at Greta and was charged with having assisted Power in some of his robberies. He was not identified by the witnesses, and was therefore discharged.

On the 27th Superintendents Nicholson and Hare, Sergeant Montford, and black tracker Donald left Wangaratta and made a journey into the ranges near the head of the King River. It was believed that they had received special information from a friend of the bushranger. At the head of the glen near where Power's camp was, a family named Quinn resided, and it was said that Power would never be caught while they were there. The Quinns owned several dogs and a peacock, which apparently would never allow any person to pass up the ravine without giving notice. The peacock was reported to be the 'best watch dog of the lot'. His screams could be heard far away whenever a stranger approached the hut; he generally gave the first signal and thus roused the dogs.

On this occasion, however, the police passed without either the peacock or the dogs giving a sign. They came to a hollow tree with holes in the stem. This tree had been mentioned as 'Power's look-out', and it was reported that he frequently went into it to survey the country through the holes, without exposing himself. There was plenty of room inside for more than one man, and the natural holes formed by the decay of the tree had been added to by augur holes bored at a convenient height for spying through. They examined it, but it was empty.

All round was a dense growth of cherry and wattle scrub through which they cautiously pushed their way, and peeped into a small clearing. A gunyah of bark stood in the middle of this space and before it a fire was burning. Creeping cautiously up, the police saw a man's leg sticking out from under the gunyah. One of them seized it and drew the man out on his back. It was Harry Power. He had been lying asleep under the impression that he was perfectly safe. He gave a loud howl on being thus rudely awakened, and then asked, 'Who are you?' 'The police,' was the reply. 'No fear,' said Power; 'you couldn't have got past Quinn's; the dogs and the peacock would not have let you.' 'We did,' replied Inspector Nicholson; 'the dogs and the peacock never saw us, but there were several men there and Quinn himself — they saw us.' 'You've given us a great deal of trouble, Power,' said Inspector Hare, 'but we've got you at last.' 'I'm sorry I didn't hear you,' remarked Power; 'I'd have dropped some of you if I had.'

**Harry Power (real name, Henry Johnson) shortly after his capture. It was claimed that Power was 'the man who taught Ned Kelly'. Kelly was arrested at Greta in May, 1870 and charged with having assisted Power, but he was acquitted.**

In the gunyah were a government revolver, stolen from the police, loaded and capped; a double-barrelled gun, hanging from the ridge pole, loaded ready for use; and a loaded pistol lying close beside the sleeping bushranger. There were also a box of slugs, a powder flask, two boxes of caps not quite full, a carpet-bag full of clothes, and a saddle and bridle. The bed was a very comfortable one, with a good supply of blankets.

The police informed Power that they had been out in the ranges for more than a week and were starving. They had not had a mouthful of food for more than twenty-four hours and were anxious to get back to town. 'There's plenty of tucker here,' said Power. 'Where?' asked the police. 'In that tree,' replied Power. They went to the tree and saw a bag hung up among the branches, as is common in the bush. In this 'bush safe' they found part of a large home-baked loaf, some potatoes, tea and sugar, and a piece of fresh beef. 'Golly, what a —— feed we'll have,' cried Donald the black tracker, when he saw the food. The police cut the beef into steaks and fried them and had a good meal. In their search they found £15 4s. 6d. in bank notes and money.

They mounted Power on the horse ridden by the black tracker, while Donald mounted behind Sergeant Montford, and left the camp. They reached Wangaratta at 7 p.m. on Sunday 5 June 1870, eleven days after the death of Captain Thunderbolt in New South Wales. The news of Power's capture had already spread in the district, and numbers of people who were out for their Sunday evening ramble, crowded the streets of Wangaratta to see the noted bushranger. Power waved his hand in response to their cheers, and cried, 'They've caught poor Harry Power, but they caught him asleep.'

On Tuesday the 7th, Power was removed to Beechworth jail, and a number of men and women in carriages, buggies, spring carts, and other vehicles, or on horseback, went along the road to meet him and escort him into the town. The procession as it passed over Newtown Bridge was quite an imposing one as the majority of the residents who had neither horse nor vehicle had collected there. Power was sitting in a police cart and bowing right and left to the crowd as if he had been some high potentate. He wished the people 'Good morning,' and continually repeated his formula about having been captured asleep. On his arrival at the jail he greeted Mr Stewart as an old friend, and hoped they would never fall out. He made a short speech, in which he publicly thanked the police for the kind and considerate manner in which he had been treated since his arrest.

The *Ovens Spectator* at this time said: 'Henry Power, alias Johnson, is a hale, hearty-looking man, although past the meridian of life, with grizzly hair and beard, and certainly not of such an appearance as one would expect a bushranger to have.'

On 2 October Henry Power was tried on four

Superintendent Hare, together with Superintendent Nicolson, Sergeant Montford and a black tracker called Donald, was responsible for the capture of Power. Hare was also a prominent figure in the hunt for the Kelly gang.

charges of highway robbery. On 7 May 1869, he had bailed up Arthur Woodside a squatter at Happy Valley, as he was riding towards Bright. The robber had taken a horse, saddle, bridle, and spurs, giving in exchange a knocked-up horse, a broken saddle, a bridle tied up with string, and one rusty spur. While Mr Woodside was giving his evidence Power exclaimed, 'Speak up, young man. You spoke different to that when I met you on the road.'

The mail coach from Beechworth had been bailed up at the same time. Power had asked the driver, Edward Coady, to throw out the gold. Coady replied, 'There is none'. 'I was told there was', exclaimed Power. 'Any parcels?' Coady threw down two which Power opened. There was only one passenger, a Chinaman, and Power asked him for the key of his carpet-bag. At first the chinaman said 'No savvy', but on the revolver being pointed at his head, he handed over the key. Power searched the bag, but took nothing out. This was the first case.

On 28 August, the same mail had been bailed up. At that time there were three passengers — Mr Hazleton,

Ellen Hart (a servant), and Mrs Li Goon. A boy also got on to the coach at Boyd's for a ride down the hill. The coach had just passed the gap when the driver had to put the brake on and pull up because the roadway was blocked with logs and saplings. Mr Hazleton exclaimed 'Who did this?' when Power stepped out from behind a tree and replied 'I did. Put up your hands.'

The passengers were made to alight and turn out their pockets. Hazleton made a step forward to hand his watch and chain to the robber, but Power cried out 'Stand back', and raised his revolver. He then told Hazleton to put the watch on the ground and retire, and when this had been done Power went forward and picked it up. Mrs Li Goon said she had no money, but when Power threatened to shoot her she gave him fourteen shillings. 'It's all I've got and I'll want a cup of coffee', she said. 'All right', returned the bushranger, 'take this', and he gave her back one shilling.

The robber took £2 13s. 6d. out of Coady's pocket-book. There was also a threepenny-piece in it and Power told the coachman to give it to the boy. Mrs Boyd came down the hill on horseback and was bailed up. She said she had no money. 'I don't see how ladies can go riding round with handsome dresses and fine saddles and bridles without money,' cried Power. 'Here, give me your horse.' Mrs Boyd said if he would allow her to ride home she would bring him some money, but he refused to trust to her promise and took the horse. He stuck up several Chinamen and a white man, and took their money from them. He said to them 'It's a cold day, but I've got a nice fire down there, go and sit by it,' and he pointed down the hill. He was in a good temper and gave the boy a shilling. The little fellow immediately offered to give him the shilling and the threepenny-piece for his sister's horse. Power laughed and gave the horse to the boy to lead to where his sister was sitting. This was the second case.

The third charge was the robbing of John Whorouly. Power had said, 'I don't like robbing a poor man, but I must have money'. The fourth charge was the sticking up of Thomas Oliver Thomas, on the Buckland Road. When called on to bail up, Thomas had wheeled his horse round and Power had shouted 'If you run away I'll fire. My gun will carry three hundred yards.' Power asked for his money, and Thomas replied 'I've got none.' 'That's a lie', cried Power, 'turn it out.' Power had repeatedly threatened Thomas with his revolver.

Power was found guilty on each of the four counts, and was sentenced to fifteen years' penal servitude. He served out his full sentence. At about the time of his discharge the Victorian Government sold the hulk *Success*. The *President* and the other hulks purchased to supply the want of prison accommodation in 'the roaring fifties' had been sold years before. The *Success* had been utilised as a training ship, and had been kept. In the case of the other hulks, it had been stipulated in the terms of sale that they were to be

After the completion of his jail sentence, Power was employed as an exhibit on the *Success*, an old convict prison hulk converted to a touring museum.

broken up. This clause was omitted in the case of the *Success*; consequently she was purchased by some speculators, and fitted up as a representative convict hulk for exhibition purposes and Harry Power was engaged to add interest to the show.

The ship was exhibited in Melbourne, and was then taken round to Sydney. She was visited by a number of people during the two or three weeks when she was berthed at Circular Quay, and she was then taken down the harbour to be fitted for a voyage to London. Here she sank at her moorings. With the appliances in Sydney, so small a vessel was soon raised, but her immersion had damaged the wax figures intended to represent the prisoners who had once been confined in her, and the other exhibits. While these were being replaced or cleaned, Harry Power was sent into the country districts for the benefit of his health. He was fishing in the Murray River near Swan Hill, on 7 November 1891, when he fell in and was drowned. At the inquest held on his body, a verdict of accidental death was returned. The *Success* shortly after left Australia for England without any living representative of the bushranging times on board.

159

# 23 The Wild Scotchman

**Bushranging in Queensland; bushrangers from over the southern border; a bogus Ben Hall; the Wild Scotchman, Queensland's only bushranger; calls for duel with Sir Frederick Pottinger; the Wild Scotchman's escape, recapture and trial.**

There was still another of the Australian colonies which was affected by the bushranging mania inaugurated by Frank Gardiner. This colony was Queensland.

In May 1864, Harry, the mail-man, was travelling along the road between Bodumba and Leyburn, when he was stopped by an old man and a boy, one of whom asked him, civilly enough, which was the road to Warwick. Harry, very obligingly, had pulled up to tell them where to turn off when the old man drew a pistol and ordered him to dismount. Harry protested against this outrage, and said he was a government employee, but this only produced a reiteration of the order with a threat to blow out his brains if he did not obey. He then dismounted and was tied very tightly, the robbers paying no attention whatever to his complaints that the rope was cutting his wrists.

The robbers went through the bags which they left on the ground. When they had finished, the old man mounted Harry's horse, while the boy climbed on to the packhorse, and rode away. Harry, who was left lying on the ground, rolled himself over and over to where there were some jagged rocks by the side of the road. Selecting the one with the sharpest edge, he wriggled about until he got the rope across it, then moved his body backwards and forwards until the strands of the rope which bound his hands together behind his back parted. Having freed his hands, he soon untied the rope round his legs and walked to Goondiwindi, where he reported the robbery to the police.

The *Brisbane Courier* in reporting this robbery said it was the first case of bushranging that had taken place in Queensland, and hoped that the colony was not about to have its peace disturbed as that of the southern colonies had recently been by bushrangers. Of course a rumour was raised that the perpetrator was Gilbert with some of his gang, but the description given of the robbers shows that this rumour was absurd.

About a month later a bushranger named Wright stuck up and robbed a number of people in the Rockhampton district. He was speedily followed by the police and some black trackers, and was shot early in July at Wipend, on the Mackenzie River, a few miles off the Peak downs road. He was riding a race-horse which he had stolen from Mr Cranston, a squatter of that district.

In September a man entered the bar of the Shearers' Arms Inn at Knebsworth, and cried out 'Bail up! I'm Ben Hall!' the proprietor Mr Philip Hardy, took a revolver out of a drawer under the counter. The bushranger, seeing him do this, fired and missed. Mr Hardy returned the fire and wounded the bushranger. The landlord ran round from behind the bar, collared his assailant, and after a struggle thrust him into a back room. Having locked the door and made his prisoner secure, as he thought, Mr Hardy ran to the police station to report. He returned in a few minutes accompanied by a constable, but the bird had flown. The window of the room in which he had been shut was wide open, so that the bushranger had merely to step out and walk away. Probably he was making his way to the bush at the back of the house almost as soon as the door was locked. He lost his horse, however, as the animal was hitched to the veranda post in front and was taken away by the constable.

One or two other cases occurred, but they were all of a paltry character, until the Celtic blood of Alpin Macpherson, alias John Bruce, alias Mar, alias Kerr, alias Scotia or Scotchie, generally known as the Wild Scotchman, was stirred to emulate the heroic deeds of Hall, Gilbert and Co.

Macpherson was born in Scotland and was taken to Queensland when very young by his father. The elder Macpherson worked for Mr McConnell at Cressbrook and was generally respected by those who knew him. His son Alpin was sent to school in the town and was a favourite with his teachers on account of his diligence. When old enough he was apprenticed to Mr Petrie, a stonemason in Brisbane, and was again well-liked by his master and the members of his family. Alpin was a diligent reader and a fluent speaker. He became a prominent member of the Debating Class in the

Brisbane Mechanics' School of Arts. When Mr Lilley, afterwards Attorney-General, was attacked at a political meeting at the Valley with mud, over-ripe tomatoes and other missiles, on account of his Militia Bill which was strongly opposed, young Macpherson defended him bravely, receiving some bruises. Soon afterwards, without any apparent reason, he ran away from his apprenticeship and took to the roads.

He began his bushranging career by sticking up Wills's Hotel on the Houghton River, after the manner popular with the Hall and Gilbert gang. From there he went to New South Wales to 'fight a duel with Sir Frederick Pottinger', the head of the police force in that colony. He announced this decision himself. The records of this portion of his career are somewhat obscure. It is known that he did exchange shots with Sir Frederick Pottinger and some troopers and that he received a slight wound, but it is doubtful whether he ever joined Hall and Gilbert and committed robberies in their company, as he said he did. However, he did not remain in New South Wales very long. He returned to Queensland and robbed the mails, stuck up travellers, stole race-horses, and otherwise endeavoured to work up to the standard ideal of the real Australian bushranger.

He had been bushranging for some months when Mr W. Nott, manager of the Manduran station, saw him in a paddock belonging to the station, and recognized him. Believing that he was there with the intention of stealing some of the horses, Mr Nott hastily collected a party and started in pursuit. The party consisted of Messrs Nott, Curry, Gadsden, and J. Walsh.

They came in sight of their quarry about five miles away as he was travelling along the Port Curtis road. He was riding slowly when first seen, but seeing his pursuers closing upon him, Macpherson let go his packhorse, wheeled off the road, and galloped down the side of a steep range. His pursuers followed. When he reached the level ground at the foot of the range the Wild Scotchman pulled up and began to unstrap the doublebarrelled gun which he carried across the pommel of his saddle. Before he could succeed Mr Nott came close up and cried 'Put up your hands or I'll fire.' The rifle barrel was only a few feet away, and as the other men came up at once with arms ready for use the Wild Scotchman yielded. 'All right', he said, 'I give up.'

I knew you were not policemen', he said later, 'by the way you came down that ridge, but you wouldn't have caught me if my horse had not been done up.' They took his arms away then returned to the station, two of the captors riding with the bushranger between them, while the other two rode close behind. In the pack on the horse which he abandoned, was found a beautifully-fitted case of surgical instruments, with lint and other necessaries for treating wounds. He also carried a pocket compass, an American axe, and some other useful articles. The axe was required for cutting fences or for making temporary stockyards in which to catch horses.

A warrant had been issued for his arrest for his attack on Sir Frederick Pottinger and the police in New South Wales, and the Wild Scotchman was therefore extradited to stand his trial in New South Wales on a charge of shooting with intent to do grievious bodily harm. His arrival in Sydney was coincident with the resignation of that officer. Sir Frederick, however, was summoned to appear against him, and it was on his journey to Sydney for this purpose that the accident happened which put an end to Sir Frederick's life and the prosecution against the Wild Scotchman at the same time.

The Wild Scotchman was returned to Queensland in charge of the police. He was sent from Brisbane to Port Denison, and was there committed for trial and remanded to Rockhampton, the nearest assize town, for that purpose. He was shipped on board the steamer *Diamantina* in charge of Constable Maher. He was put in leg-irons as his hands were so small that he could easily slip them through any ordinary handcuffs. In fact he boasted freely that the handcuffs to hold him 'had not yet been made'.

When the steamer reached Mackay he was seated reading near the galley, but he had behaved so quietly all through the earlier part of the passage that the constable did not think it necessary to disturb him by taking him below. There was the usual bustle while the steamer was at the wharf, and Constable Maher appears to have lost sight of his prisoner and did not miss him until the vessel had been an hour at sea. Then a search was instituted, but no Wild Scotchman could be found, and as the *Maryborough Chronicle* remarked 'Constable Maher reached Rockhampton minus his prisoner.'

How he got ashore and removed his leg-irons was a mystery which was not solved for some time. However his escape did not profit him much. He went to a paddock on the Kolongo station with the intention of stealing a horse to enable him to stick up the mail coach and 'make a rise'. But a party was organized by Mr Hall and he was recaptured without attaining his purpose. This time greater care was exercised by the police to whom he was handed over, and he reached Rockhampton, where he was tried on several charges of highway robbery and sentenced to twenty years' penal servitude.

Queensland's 'only bushranger', the Wild Scotchman, was captured after a brief but exciting career of about eighteen months, and the colony was not troubled by bushrangers again.

# 24 Captain Moonlite

**The 'Reverend Gentleman' turns to bushranging; robs the bank; breaks out of Ballarat goal: a desperate battle with police; young companions in crime; Captain Moonlite sentenced to death; abortive attempt to stick up another bank.**

For nearly six years, from about June 1872 to April 1878, Australia was free from bushrangers. With the exception of two or three robberies in the far west of New South Wales the roads were safe; travellers journeyed in all directions without fear of molestation. The public, as well as the authorities, began to congratulate themselves once more on having at length definitely stamped out the scourge of bushranging. Since the shooting of Thunderbolt and the capture of Power, there had been no sign of a reoccurance of the crime, and bushranging was beginning to be referred to as belonging to a past age.

But this peaceful condition of the country was not to continue. The old leaven of convictism so frequently referred to, had not as yet been as completely eliminated as the public and the authorities hoped and believed. Reports began to spread in 1878 that robberies had been committed in the neighbourhood where Power had so long set the police at defiance; shortly afterwards the name of Ned Kelly began to be associated with them. Ned Kelly is still spoken of as the last of the bushrangers, and as his death closes the story, it may be as well to deal with some other bushrangers who finished their careers before 'the gentleman of the Strathbogie Ranges'. The most remarkable of these was George Scott, alias Captain Moonlite.

Scott was born in the North of Ireland, and emigrated to Victoria. He went to the diggings at a time when agents from New Zealand were endeavouring to raise a corps in Victoria for service against the Maoris. He enlisted and fought through the war in 1861-65, getting wounded in the leg. On his return to Victoria he showed a strong desire to join the Church. As he was well educated and a good speaker he was appointed lay reader at Bacchus Marsh, with a view to his being ordained a minister of the Church of England when the Bishop of Melbourne should consider him worthy of the charge. His duties as lay reader were to travel round the settlement, to read prayers and conduct services, his headquarters being in the town at Mount Egerton. His chief friends here

were the manager of the Union Bank and the schoolmaster. He soon came to be respected and liked in the district.

One night a masked man walked into the living apartments connected to the bank and ordered the manager, who was alone, to bail up. The manager recognized the voice and asked whether this was suitable practical joke for a clergyman. Scott replied that he would soon find it was no joke. He threatened to shoot the manager unless he surrendered and did as he was ordered. He then gagged the manager, took him across the street to the school-house, and compelled him to sign the following statement: 'Captain Moonlite has stuck me up and robbed the bank.' There was no one at the school-house, Scott having apparently timed his visit when he knew the school would be empty. Leaving the paper on the desk in the school-house, Scott took the manager back to the bank, tied him hand and foot, and then took about £1000 in notes and coins from the safe.

The schoolmaster found the paper lying on the desk when he went to open the school next morning and at first did not know what to make of it. He handed it to the police who, on going to the bank, found the manager gagged and tied. Having heard his story the police considered it absurd, and arrested the manager and schoolmaster as having been jointly concerned in the crime. The idea of charging the minister, as Scott was generally called, appeared to be preposterous, particularly as Scott was very active in trying to find incriminating evidence against his former friends.

Being intimately acquainted with the lives led by the two men, he was able to supply the police with several facts, true or false, which were considered strong circumstantial proofs of their guilt. They were committed for trial, and Scott bound over as a witness against them. He did not wait for the trial, however, but went to Sydney, where he put up at one of the leading hotels and spent money lavishly. He represented himself as a wealthy visitor to the colonies

**Andrew George Scott,** *alias* **'Captain Moonlite'**

travelling for pleasure, and spoke of his intention to visit some of the South Sea Islands. For this purpose he purchased a yacht, for which he paid partly in cash and partly by a cheque for £150. This cheque was returned by the bank on which it was drawn as valueless, and the man who had sold him the yacht immediately communicated with the police. Scott had already set sail but the police followed him in a steam launch and caught him just outside the Heads. He was brought back, tried for fraud and sent to jail for eighteen months.

Even the flight of Scott from Mount Egerton did not at first convince the police and others of his guilt in connection with the bank robbery, but without his evidence the case against the bank manager and the schoolmaster was so weak that it broke down, and they were discharged. Later on, a warrant was issued for the arrest of Scott, alias Captain Moonlite, but he was then in jail in New South Wales. On his release he was rearrested, and extradited to Victoria to be tried for the bank robbery.

He was taken to Ballarat, and lodged in the newly-built jail, a most substantial structure of blue-stone. The building stood in a large courtyard, surrounded by a wall twenty-five feet high, also constructed of blue-stone. It appeared to be one of the most hopeless places for a prisoner to escape from imaginable, but Scott had been educated as an engineer and therefore what might have been impossible for another man was not so for him. There was a wooden partition which divided one cell into two. Scott was imprisoned awaiting trial in one portion of the cell, and a man named Dermoodie was in the other portion. Scott cut through this partition, and with the aid of Dermoodie managed to take the lock off the door. The two men walked into the corridor and hid in a dark corner until the warder came round. Scott sprang on him, grasped him by the throat, and with the assistance of Dermoodie gagged and tied him. Scott then took the keys and having shut the warder in the cell with the door closed, so that any other warder in passing it would not notice that it had been opened, he walked down the passage.

With the keys he opened four more cells and liberated the prisoners in them. He made them take the blankets from their beds and follow him, after carefully closing the doors again. He opened the door leading into the great yard and went to a dark corner under the wall where he tore the blankets into strips and tied them together to form a rope. Scott then stood up against the wall. One of the other men climbed up and stood on his, and so on until the last, Dermoodie, was able to take the rope and sit on the wall. With the aid of the rope each man was able to go up in turn to where Dermoodie was, and then be lowered down on the other side. Here they stood on each others' shoulders as before to enable Dermoodie to climb down; the others followed in turn, and they were free.

The south-eastern corner of the jail wall stood near the edge of the hill where the ground sloped sharply down to Golden Gully. The six men went down the slope to a safe distance, then Scott said they must part as they would have a better chance of getting away separately than if they all kept together. The four men liberated by Scott to help him over the wall were speedily caught, some in Ballarat and the others not far away, but as they were not bushrangers we have nothing further to do with them.

Scott and Dermoodie went away together and slept in the bush. Scott said they must have money, and proposed to rob a bank, which he said could be easily done. Dermoodie said he had only been arrested for a small offence, and he had made his case bad enough by escaping; he did not wish to make it worse. Scott called him a coward, a contemptible cur, and said he should never leave that spot alive. He gave him five minutes to say his prayers. He was in a terrible rage, but before the five minutes were over he said that Dermoodie was not worth killing, gave him a few kicks and blows, and ordered him out of his sight, an order which was quickly obeyed.

Dermoodie went back to Ballarat and was recaptured a day or two after his escape, while Scott was found about a week later in a hut near Bendigo. He was tried and sentenced to ten years' imprisonment for the bank robbery, and to one year's imprisonment in irons for breaking jail.

Scott behaved in the most exemplary manner while he was in Pentridge and convinced both the chaplain and the jail authorities that he intended to live 'on the square' in the future. He was allowed all the remission possible under the rules for good conduct and was released in March 1879. He was a forcible and fluent speaker, and he made a living by open-air lecturing in Melbourne on prison discipline and other subjects. About this time the Kelly gang was at the zenith of its career. Suddenly Scott disappeared from his usual haunts in Melbourne. Probably his imagination was stirred by the reports current about the Kellys; perhaps he was prompted by jealousy of their doings; or perhaps by a sudden desire for notoriety. However this may have been he was gone.

On Saturday 15 November 1879, at about 3 p.m., six armed men rode up to Mr C. F. J. Macdonald's station at Wantabadgery on the Murrumbidgee River New South Wales, and bailed up all the men at work there. Nineteen men were collected from various places about the station and marched into the dining-room of Mr Macdonald's house. Mr Miles was then ordered to unlock the door of the store where the robbers selected a quantity of clothing and other goods which they required or fancied. They were packing these on some spare horses when Mr Weir of Eurongilly, and a schoolmaster rode up, and were called on to bail up. The schoolmaster refused and one of the bushrangers loudly declared that he would shoot him. Hearing the altercation, the leader of the gang came out of the

Constable Bowen of Wagga Wagga led the police in the final 'show-down' with Moonlite's gang.

store, seized the schoolmaster by the leg, and dragged him from the horse, saying at the same time, 'You —— old fool, get down and do as you're told. I'm Moonlite.' He pushed the schoolmaster along forcing him to go into the dining-room where the other men were sitting.

Towards evening Mr Baynes, the manager of the station, returned from a back station and was bailed up and conducted to the dining-room. The women had been told that they would not be interfered with, and were ordered to cook dinner. When it was ready it was served in the dining-room, where all partook of the food; the bushrangers sitting down in turn, while two remained on guard. After the meal some grog, obtained from the station store, was served round and Mr Macdonald was permitted to retire to bed. The others remained at the table all night, the bushrangers taking it in turn to sleep like the others with their heads on the table.

Breakfast on the following (Sunday) morning was taken as supper had been on the previous evening. During the meal Mr Baynes said to one of the young bushrangers who was seated near him, 'This is bad work.' Moonlite, sitting on the other side of the large table, heard him and jumped up. He charged Mr Baynes with trying to tamper with his men and swore that he would shoot him. He seemed to be in a paroxysm of rage, flourished his revolver about in a dangerous manner. The women clustered round,

assuring him that Mr Baynes did not mean any harm and begging him to spare him. In a few minutes Scott's rage had evaporated. He sat down again and went on with his meal, apparently oblivious of Mr Baynes's presence.

During the morning several men came to the station and were bailed up and marched into the dining-room. One of these men was leading a young filly which had only recently been broken in. Scott admired her very much and said, 'She'll just suit me.' He led her round and tried to mount her, but she was very skittish and would not let him. This threw him into a passion and he became violent, frightening the filly and making her more ungovernable. At length he swore that if she did not stand still he would shoot her. As she continued to rear and try to get away he drew his revolver and sent a bullet through her head.

When his fit of passion has passed off, Moonlite said he was sorry he had killed the mare, but she should have stood still when he told her. He then ordered Lindon, the groom, to put the horses into the buggy, and taking Mr Alexander Macdonald as a hostage, drive to the house of the superintendent of the station, Mr Reid. Here he obtained a Whitworth rifle and some ammunition. He forced Mr and Mrs Reid to mount the buggy and drove away to Paterson's Australia Arms Hotel, which he stuck up, taking two shot guns and a revolver. He ordered Mr and Mrs Paterson to walk to the station and to ensure their obedience he put their two little children into the buggy and drove away. On the return journey to the station he stuck up seven more men, compelling them to march in front of the buggy to the station and go into the dining-room.

As Moonlite jumped down from the buggy he caught sight of Mr Baynes standing on the veranda. He rushed across to him and charged him with attempting to corrupt his men. He ordered Mr Baynes to be pinioned with a fishing line and had him lifted into the buggy, saying 'I'll drive under that tree and you can tie the rope to the limb, and we'll leave this gentleman hanging there.' A rope was tied round Mr Baynes's neck ready. The women, seeing these preparations for a tragedy, again gathered round Moonlite and begged him to let Mr Baynes go. At first he refused, saying 'The gentleman does not deserve it,' but gradually he became less violent and finally ordered Baynes to be untied. Then he called a muster of all the men in the dining-room and counted thirty-five.

After giving orders about the custody of his prisoners, Moonlite mounted a horse and rode round, going for some distance along the road on each side of the homestead. He met a man coming from the adjoining station, Eurongilly, where he worked. 'Hulloa,' cried Moonlite, 'where are you going with that pistol?' 'To fight the bushrangers,' replied the man. 'By G——,' exclaimed Scott, 'you've found them, here we are. Hand over that revolver and we'll try you for unlawfully carrying firearms.' The man was compelled

to obey and was taken into the dining-room. Moonlite took his seat as judge, having appointed two of his mates and two of the station hands as jury, and the trial was carried out as nearly in the orthodox manner as circumstances would permit. The charge was read by the clerk, witnesses were heard and cross-examined; the judge summed up, and the verdict returned was 'Not guilty'. Scott turned to the prisoner and said, 'You may think yourself —— lucky. If the jury had found you guilty, I'd have given you five minutes to live.' He then ordered the prisoner to be discharged, announcing it was dinner time.

In the afternoon the vigilance of the bushrangers relaxed so much that Alexander Macdonald was able to make his escape. He got a horse and rode to Wagga Wagga, twenty-five miles away. He informed the police of what had taken place and Constables Howe, Hedley, Williamson, and Johns saddled their horses and started back with him to Wantabadgery. They arrived at 4 a.m. on Monday morning.

The robbers were still in possession and the police hoped to find them unprepared, but this was not the case, and the police retreated to Mr James Beveridge's station, Tarrandera Park, where they obtained fresh horses. By this time five more troopers had arrived from Gundagai, sixty-five miles away, and the police decided that they were strong enough to begin the attack. The people who had been detained in the dining-room quickly made their escape and collected on a ridge a short distance from the scene of battle. Other people attracted by the sound of the firing, rode up from the stations round until some three hundred spectators were collected on the ridge; but they left the police to do the fighting unaided.

Constable Bowen, who had already shot a bushranger in the Thunderbolt rising, was the first to

In the final shoot-out (above) two bushrangers and one constable were mortally wounded before Moonlite and his followers were captured.

The trial of 'Captain Moonlite' was an emotional affair lasting four days. Scott pleaded for mercy on account of the three remaining members of his gang and took the entire blame for the death of the constable. Two were given life sentences but Scott and the third were hanged at Darlinghurst jail on 20 January, 1880.

*Opposite:*
James Nesbitt, *alias* Lyons, was a station hand before he became a member of Moonlite's gang and was only twenty-three when he was shot by Constable Bowen in the final fight.
*Right:*
Gus Wernicke was said by some to be only fifteen when he was shot during the last stand of Moonlite's gang. Despite his diminutive stature, he was more likely about nineteen.

The police capture Captain Moonlite

make any impression, and a great cheer went up as one of Moonlite's men was seen to fall. The bushrangers went into the house and the police took shelter in a hut some distance away. They advanced very cautiously. Constable Bowen shot a second man, falling wounded himself almost at the same time. Some time afterwards Constable Carroll, who had crept close up to the veranda in spite of the heavy fusillade which was kept up, shot a third bushranger and soon after the other three came out and surrendered. Moonlite asked Mr Wise to go for a doctor to attend to Nesbit, saying 'Poor fellow! He was shot trying to save me.'

James Nesbit, alias Lyons, who was shot dead, was born in Melbourne and was twenty-three years of age. Augustus or Gus Wernicke (also from Melbourne) aged nineteen, died a few days after the battle. Graham Bennett, also born in Victoria, was twenty years of age. He was wounded in the arm and recovered. Thomas Williams, alias Jones, nineteen years old, was born in Ballarat, Victoria. Thomas Rogan was born at Hay, New South Wales, but had been living for some years in Melbourne, where he became acquainted with Scott. Scott, the leader, was thirty-seven years of age.

Constable Bowen died of his wound on the Sunday following the fight, and the prisoners were tried on the charge of murdering him. The trial took place at Darlinghurst Court House, Sydney, and lasted for four

*Right:*
**The bushrangers Scott and Rogan were hanged at Darlinghurst Jail, Sydney, in 1880.**

days. A verdict of guilty was returned, but the jury recommended Rogan, Bennett, and Williams to mercy on account of their youth and the belief that they had been led into crime by Scott. In consequence of this the sentences on Bennett and Williams were commuted to imprisonment for life. Although some pressure was brought to bear on the Governor, Lord Augustus Loftus, the Executive declined to extend mercy to Rogan. He and Scott were hanged in Darlinghurst jail.

The gallantry of the police in breaking up this gang of bushrangers at so early a stage in its career was duly recognized. The police authorities voted a reward of £100 to Constable Carroll, £75 to Constable Curran, and £50 each to the other constables engaged in the fight. A public monument was erected to Constable Bowen and a pension was settled on his wife, while the Government undertook the care and education of his children. The police were paraded in Sydney; the Inspector General, Mr E. Fosbery, read a letter from the Colonial Secretary (the late Sir Henry Parkes) publicly thanking the police constables for their services. After this ceremony, the purses containing the rewards were presented and acknowledged.

# 25 The Kelly reign

**Horse-stealing in the Kelly country; bush telegraphs; murder of Kennedy, Scanlon and Lonergan; a big haul at Euroa; Kelly gang sticks up the town of Jerilderie; a three-day spree; the Kellys rest for a year, then reappear; murder of Aaron Sherritt.**

In the early years of Australian settlement bushranging was one of the normal conditions in the colonies, and therefore attracted little notice. Even the exploits of such heroes of the roads as Mike Howe, Brady, the Jewboy, and Jackey Jackey are very briefly related in the Press. With the exception of the first-named, about whom James Bonwick wrote a romance, very little has been heard of them since the age in which they lived.

In the next epoch the doings of the bushrangers were dwarfed in the public estimation by the sensational reports of the gold finds, and although in consequence of the growth of population and the great increase in the number of newspapers their actions received a wider publicity than those of their predecessors, the accounts of them are still meagre. The sensational inauguration of the next era by the Gardiner gang — the sticking up and robbing of the Government Gold Escort — attracted wider notice to the bushrangers of that epoch, and some notice of them appeared even in the English Press. But the notoriety of even the most celebrated of the bushrangers of that epoch was nothing compared with that of the Kelly gang, about whom more columns of newspaper matter have been printed than of all the bushrangers together in the earlier epochs.

Several histories of the Kelly gang have been published, and the Kellys inspired more than one drama, although the subject was not a favourite one with moralists, and the representation of bushranging dramas did not meet with favour from a large section of the community. In this connection we may note the influence of technology. The stage of the performances of the earlier bushrangers was confined to their own locality. They were rarely heard of outside the colony in which they appeared. In the next era the telegraph carried news of their performances all over Australia, and occasionally a stray newspaper paragraph was quoted in England. With the Kellys, however, it was different. Notices of their exploits were sent across the ocean by cable, and the British public naturally wanted to hear more of these daring robbers. Extracts

*Below:*
Mrs Ellen Kelly served three years in jail for the attack on Constable Fitzpatrick. Her second son, Jim, pictured with her some years after the deaths of Dan and Ned, was serving a sentence during the 'Kelly outbreak' and later lived with his mother at Greta until he died in 1946, aged eighty-seven.

*Top:*
The Kelly home near Greta

*Below Right:*
Dan, the youngest of the Kelly boys, was not as physically impressive as his brothers but a fine horseman. He first appeared in court when he was fifteen and died at Glenrowan when only nineteen.

*Opposite Right:*
Jim Kelly was devoted to his brothers and would have undoubtedly accompanied them on their exploits if he had not already been in jail. He was six feet tall and weighed twelve stone.

from the newspapers of Australia appeared more frequently in the English Press than at any former epoch. Consequently we can reconstruct the history of the Kellys more easily than that of any other bushranging family.

The father of Ned Kelly was transported from Ireland. The maiden name of his wife was Ellen Quinn. The eldest son, Ned, was born at Wallan Wallan in 1854. Jim was born in 1856, and Dan in 1861. There were four daughters — namely, Mrs Gunn, Mrs Skillian, and Kate and Grace Kelly. In 1871 the second son, James, then about fifteen years of age, was sentenced to five years' imprisonment on two charges of horse-stealing. After his discharge in 1876 he went to New South Wales and stuck up a number of people. He was captured almost immediately and sent to jail for ten years.

Edward, commonly known as Ned Kelly, was arrested in 1870 and charged with having assisted Power in one of his numerous bushranging exploits, but was acquitted, as none of the witnesses could swear to his identity. It is said that on more than one occasion he took care of Power's horses while that bushranger was engaged in robbing. In 1871 he was sent to jail for three years for horse-stealing.

Horse-stealing appears to have been the principal industry of the district, as cattle-duffing had been of the Wedden Mountain district, and of Monaro. The Kellys, the Harts, the Byrnes, and others in this district were quite as adept in 'faking' brands as the Lowrys, the O'Meallys, or the Clarkes had been. But science had made advances even in these mountains since the era of the Gardiner gang. In earlier times the brands of horses and cattle were 'faked' (altered so as to represent something different from what they were intended to do) by branding over them and adding to them. There were some expert blacksmiths among the cattle-duffers and these would make a brand to fit over an old brand and completely change its character. For instance, a simple A brand might have a circle burned round it thus — (A), or it might have another letter conjoined to it thus — A-B. The manner in which brands might be faked was endless. When it was impossible to fake a brand it was 'blotched', or burned over, so that the original design could not be recognized.

The Kellys and their companions in the Warby and Strathbogie ranges, however, did not go to the trouble of making special brands to fake other brands. They obtained the same results by the use of iodine which burned such marks into the skins of the stolen animals as were desired. The plan adopted was to make raids into distant parts, collect a mob of horses, drive them into an inaccessible ravine in the mountains, fake their brands and keep them until the sores had healed and the brands looked old. Then the animals, fattened in the meantime, were driven to market and sold without fear of detection. Horses stolen in the north — some

**Ned Kelly at sixteen: a photograph from his police file**

even from across the New South Wales border — were driven south to Melbourne, Ballarat, Geelong, or some other large town, and sold openly in the public saleyards; while those stolen in the south were driven to some northern market, sometimes being taken as far as Sydney.

In 1876 Daniel, the youngest of the Kelly boys, was sent to jail for three months for having taken part in a house-breaking robbery in conjunction with the Lloyds, who were connected by marriage with the Kellys. In the following year, 1877, warrants were issued for his arrest on six charges of horse-stealing, but he could not be found. On 15 April 1878, Constable Alexander Fitzpatrick, having learned that Dan Kelly was at home, went to the Kellys' hut at Greta, to arrest him. 'This hut,' said the *Benalla Standard,* 'was a well-known trysting-place for the bushranger Power.'

The constable rode up and seeing Dan standing at the door said to him, 'You're my prisoner.' 'All right,' replied Dan nonchalantly. The constable dismounted and was hitching his horse to a sapling when Dan said that he had been riding all day and had had nothing to eat. After some conversation the constable agreed to wait while Dan had some food before taking him to Benalla, so Dan went in and sat down. As he did so Mrs Kelly said to Fitzpatrick, 'You won't take Dan out o' this to-night.' 'Shut up, mother,' exclaimed Dan, 'it's all right.'

The old woman continued to grumble in an

undertone while she placed bread and meat and tea on the table. Presently she asked the constable, 'Have you got a warrant?' 'I've got a telegram, and that's as good,' replied Fitzpatrick. The constable was standing at the door and Dan, who took his arrest coolly as if it were a mere matter of course, told his mother not to make a row about it as it did not matter. He then invited the constable to take some food. Fitzpatrick accepted the invitation and went in.

As he seated himself Mrs Kelly remarked, 'If my son Ned was here, he'd throw you out of the window.' Dan was looking out of the window at the time and he exclaimed, 'Here he is.' Fitzpatrick very naturally turned to look, and Dan pounced on to him. Mrs Kelly seized a heavy garden spade which had been used as a fire shovel and was damaged and struck Fitzpatrick a furious blow on the head, making a dint in his helmet. Fitzpatrick fell down, and several people heard the noise and rushed in. Among them were Ned Kelly, William Skillian (husband of one of the Kelly girls), and William Williams, alias Bricky.

Ned Kelly held a revolver in his hand which was still smoking, and Fitzpatrick was wounded in the arm. Ned said, 'I'm sorry I fired. You're the civilest —— trap I've seen.' He offered to cut the bullet out and bind up the wound, but Fitzpatrick refused to let him touch it. Then Ned said that the constable could not be allowed to go away until the bullet was cut out and he had promised not to tell how he got wounded. 'You can say your pistol went off by accident,' he said, 'Tell him if he does tell he won't live long after,' cried Mrs Kelly. The old woman was again told to 'shut up'.

Fitzpatrick, knowing the men he had to deal with, promised not to say who had wounded him and took his knife from his pocket. He cut a small gash, over where the bullet was, and squeezed it out. Then he twisted his handkerchief round the wound and said it was 'all right'. Ned Kelly picked up the bullet and put it away on a shelf and a few minutes later the constable was allowed to mount his horse and go.

On the following day a party of troopers went to Eleven Mile Creek and arrested Mrs Ellen Kelly, William Skillian, and William Williams. A search was made for Ned and Dan Kelly, but they could not be found. Skillian and Williams, when brought up for trial for their share in this assault, declared that they only came in after the shot was fired and had taken no part whatever in the scrimmage. However they were sentenced to six years' imprisonment while Mrs Kelly was sent to jail for three years.

It was generally understood that Ned and Dan Kelly were in hiding somewhere in the neighbourhood, and some twenty-five troopers with black trackers were sent off to search for them. Fourteen men, residents in the neighbourhood, were arrested under the Outlawry Act, on suspicion that they had harboured or aided and abetted the bushrangers. They were remanded from week to week for some three months, while the police

By the time he was twenty-two Ned looked more like an outlaw, according to this police photograph taken in 1877.

The newspapers presented Ned in a different light. This is how he was portrayed by the *Australasian Sketcher* after his capture at Glenrowan in 1880.

were seeking for evidence against them. Mr Zincke, who appeared at the police court on behalf of the prisoners, protested against this arbitrary act of the police and urged that it was illegal to detain as prisoners persons against whom no specific charge had been made. 'If the Kellys were caught,' he said, 'these men would be told to go about their business.' He stated his belief that the Outlawry Act would not warrant these proceedings and that the law was being strained in a dangerous manner.

The magistrates on the bench listened to his pleadings with exemplary patience and then granted the remand asked for by the police. There can be very little doubt that Mr Zincke was perfectly justified in saying that these proceedings were illegal, but the magistrates of Beechworth and other parts of the disturbed district had learned by experience that as long as the sympathizers and bush telegraphs were at liberty the police had very little chance of capturing the bushrangers.

During the whole time that the Kelly gang was in existence, a number of people were kept locked up because they were suspected of giving food or assistance to the outlaws and, more important than all, of giving the bushrangers information as to the movements of the police. The number of persons thus held under restraint varied from month to month. Sometimes a few were discharged while others took their places. The largest number in the police cells at any one time was thirty-five. But the authorities only acted in a half-hearted and inefficient manner. They arrested only men and boys, while the women and girls were left free to assist the bushrangers as they pleased. The women were quite as active and quite as efficient in according assistance and information to the bushrangers as the men could have been.

On 26 October 1878 one of the parties of police in search of the outlaws went into camp at Stringy Bark Creek, about eight miles on the King River side of the Wombat Range. Sergeant Kennedy was supposed to have received information from a friend of the Kellys as to their whereabouts, and to have penetrated nearly to their hiding-place. The friend who had informed the police, however, also told the Kellys of their approach.

The country was densely covered with stringy bark trees and scrub and was almost impenetrable. Sergeant Kennedy and Constable Scanlan had gone into the scrub to try and discover the whereabouts of the two Kellys, while Constables Lonergan and McIntyre were left in charge of the camp. Lonergan was employed in making tea, ready for the two who were away, when four men on horseback came up and cried, 'Bail up! Put up your hands.' Lonergan made a jump to get behind a tree, putting his hand to his belt for a pistol at the same time, and was shot. He cried out, 'Oh Christ, I'm shot,' and fell dead. Constable McIntyre was sitting down. He jumped up but having no weapon upon him at the time, he surrendered. Ned

Kelly walked to Lonergan's body and examined it. Then he rose, and said, 'What a pity! Why didn't the — fool surrender?' He afterwards said that it was all Constable Fitzpatrick's fault. 'He'd no right to lag my mother and brother-in-law for nothing.' Ned Kelly ordered Constable McIntyre to sit down as if nothing had happened, and warned him that he would be shot at once if he 'gave the office' to the sergeant. The bushrangers then hid themselves behind the trees.

Sergeant Kennedy and Constable Scanlan rode up some time later, unconscious that anything had happened. When they came close McIntyre said, 'Sergeant, we're surrounded. You'd better surrender.' Scanlan laughed, and put his hand to his belt, when Ned Kelly fired at him and missed. Scanlan jumped off his horse and made for a gum tree but was shot dead before he reached it. Kennedy wheeled his horse round and started at a gallop, but had gone only a few yards when he was brought down with a rifle bullet.

His horse, frightened at the noise and the fall of its rider, dashed through the camp and as it passed Constable McIntyre threw himself across its back. He got into the saddle and was urging it forward when it was brought down by a rifle bullet through the heart. McIntyre fell clear and crawled into a patch of scrub. He found a wombat hole near at hand. He crept into it

The bodies of Constables Lonergan and Scanlan were found the next day where they were shot, but Sergeant Kennedy's inert form was not discovered until four days later because of the impenetrable scrub in the area.

*Left:*
The day after the bloodthirsty incident at Stringybark Creek, Inspector Pewtress came from Melbourne by special train with a party of police to investigate.

*Right:* Sergeant Kennedy

and lay there, hearing the bushrangers walking round searching for him in the scrub and swearing that they would 'do for' him when they caught him. When it was quite dark he crawled out of his hole and walked twenty miles to Mansfield to inform the police of what had taken place.

Inspector Pewtress, with a party of police, started from Melbourne on Sunday the 27th in a special train, and soon reached the camp in the ranges. The bodies of Lonergan and Scanlan were lying as they had fallen not far from where the fire had been lit, but that of Sergeant Kennedy could not be seen from the camp. It was not found until the 31st, owing to the density of the scrub around the little cleared patch where the camp had been pitched. Three bullet wounds were found in it, the body and a cloak had been thrown over the face to protect it from dingoes or the weather. It

Fitzgerald said to him, 'This is Mr Kelly. He wants some refreshments.' By this time Ned had his revolver in his hand. Fitzgerald grasped the situation and replied, 'Well, if the gentleman wants refreshments he'll have to have them.' Ned gave a whistle and the other three bushrangers came forward and Dan took their horses to the stables.

Joe Byrne took care of the Fitzgeralds, while Ned and Steve Hart went round and collected all the men at work on the station and locked them up in the storeroom. Shortly afterwards a man named Gloster, who had a store in Seymour and who frequently travelled round with a spring-cart loaded with goods for sale at the farms and stations, came to the station for a bucket of water to make tea and Ned ordered him to bail up. Knowing that Gloster was of a determined character Fitzgerald shouted to him advising him to 'give in'. 'What for?' asked Gloster. 'I'm Ned Kelly,' exclaimed the bushranger. 'I don't care a —— who you are,' returned Gloster. At this moment Dan Kelly came up and threatened to shoot Gloster, but Ned forbade him and Fitzgerald persuaded Gloster that resistance was useless and prevailed on him to surrender.

When Macaulay, the manager, came home he was also bailed up. 'What's the good of your sticking up the station?' he asked, 'you've better horses than we have and anything else you require you can have without all this nonsense.' Ned said he had a purpose. After some conversation, during which Macaulay said he had no intention of interfering with them, he was permitted to remain free, but was closely watched to prevent him from sending for the police. The bushrangers then searched Gloster's cart, selected suits of clothes for themselves and made very free with the bottles of scent and other small articles.

On the following day, 11 December 1878, Messrs McDougal, Dudley, and Casement, in a spring-cart, were about to pass through the gate over the level crossing of the railway close to the station. Mr Jennant who was riding, dismounted to open the gate for the cart to pass through, when Ned Kelly on horseback, cried, 'Surrender, or you will be shot.' Another bushranger, Joe Byrne, walked down quickly from the station to assist his mate if necessary. Mr McDougal, taking them for troopers as they carried handcuffs in

was said that Ned Kelly had ridden to his camp to fetch the cloak to cover Kennedy with, because he considered him to be the bravest man he had ever met.

Rewards of £100 each had been offered by the Victorian Government for the capture of Ned and Dan Kelly. Now the rewards were increased to £500 while similar rewards were offered for Steve Hart (twenty years of age) and Joe Byrne — referred to in some reports as 'Byrnes' — (nineteen years of age).

It was reported that on 31 October 1878 the Kellys had stuck up and robbed Neil Christian and other persons at Bungowanah, near Baumgarten's on the Murray River, but as the whole of that country was under water because of a flood in the river at that time, this was discredited. The police asserted that the Kellys were somewhere in the mountains but they searched the 'Rat's Castle' and other hiding places without success.

On 8 December a rough-looking bushman called at Younghusband's station on Faithfull Creek, and asked if the manager, Mr Macaulay, was about. An old man named Fitzgerald, employed on the station, replied that the manager was away and would not return till morning. He asked the man if he could do anything for him. The traveller replied, 'No, it's of no consequence.' He walked to the house and said to Mrs Fitzgerald, 'I'm Ned Kelly. You needn't be frightened, we only want food for ourselves and our horses.' Seeing the man talking to his wife, Fitzgerald went to them, and Mrs

**The handsome Joe Byrne (left) was the son of a gold-miner, a crack shot with a rifle and better educated than his companions.**

**Constables Scanlan (top right) and Lonergan (top middle) were shot dead by the Kelly gang at Stringy Bark Creek, in the Wombat Range, but Constable McIntyre managed to escape.**

*Opposite:*

**Kennedy and Constable Scanlan were not at the camp when the Kellys first surprised Constables Lonergan and McIntyre, shooting the former almost immediately when he went for his gun. When the two missing police rode in soon afterwards, they were greeted by the Kelly guns and McIntyre urging them to surrender.**

their hands, asked what right they had to arrest them in this manner. Ned replied, 'Shut up. I'll shoot you if you give me any cheek.' 'You wouldn't shoot an old man unarmed,' exclaimed McDougal. 'Not if you surrender quietly,' replied Ned. They said they surrendered and Byrne opened the gate and told them to drive to the homestead. As they came up a station-hand who was standing at the store door said 'Gentlemen, allow me to introduce you to Mr Edward Kelly.' McDougal and his companions were not very surprised, as they had already begun to perceive that their captors were not troopers in plain clothes as they had at first thought. The prisoners were taken into the store, the bushrangers telling them that the horses would be looked after.

The store-room was a long wooden building situated about twenty yards from the house. It had only one door and one window, both close together, so that it could easily be guarded. With so many men confined in it the air soon became foul and the prisoners were allowed to come out in small batches to obtain some fresh air. Only the men were locked up; the women were left free and were not molested in any way.

At about three o'clock Ned Kelly asked Mr Macaulay for a small cheque. Mr Macaulay gave it to him. It was for £3. Joe Byrne was left in charge of the station while the others started away, Ned in Gloster's cart, Dan in McDougal's and Hart on horseback. At about half-past four there was a knock at the door of the National Bank at Euroa. When it was opened a man requested that a cheque might be cashed for him. The manager, Mr Robert Scott, said it was after hours, and he could not open the bank again till the morning. The man said it would inconvenience him greatly to have to call again as he did not live in the town. He begged so hard that at length the manager consented to give him the money to oblige him. the manager opened the bank door and as soon as they were inside the man said, 'Put up your hands. I'm Ned Kelly.'

Taken by surprise, the manager was compelled to obey. He was forced to open the safe door and to hand over £1942 0s. 6d. in notes, gold, and silver, thirty-one ounces of smelted gold, five bags of cartridges, and two revolvers. There had been rumours that the Kellys intended to stick up a bank, and arms and ammunition had been sent from the head offices in Melbourne to most of the country branches. The National Bank at Euroa had been thus furnished, but because of the cunning of the bushrangers the arms were useless. Mr Scott had a loaded revolver on his table when Ned Kelly asked him to cash the cheque but he was so unsuspicious of the character of his customer that he left it there when he went into the bank chamber.

Having obtained all the money he could get, Kelly turned to enter the private apartments when Scott said, 'If you go in there I'll strike you whatever the consequences may be.' Steve Hart put his revolver to Scott's face and said, 'Keep back.' Kelly laughed and

The National Bank at Euroa was on the opposite corner to the local State School.

walked through the door. He went along the passage and looked out of the back door into the yard. Then he returned and told Scott to go and put his horse into the buggy. 'That's the work of the groom,' said Scott, 'but he happens to be away just now.' 'I'll do it myself,' returned Ned, and went into the yard.

When the horse was harnessed, Kelly said he was going to take the family out for a drive. He made Scott get into Gloster's cart and Mrs Scott and the child into the buggy. Dan Kelly and Hart came on behind. When they had gone out of the little street Scott asked Ned where they were going. 'To Younghusband's,' was the reply. 'I'll drive,' said Scott, 'I know the road.' 'All right,' replied Ned, handing him the reins. 'But if you try any pranks, look out.' Ned Kelly treated Mrs Scott with such politeness that she said that she could never believe he was the bloodthirsty villain he had been represented to be.

The telegraph wires had been cut on each side of the station soon after their arrival, and while the main body of the robbers were at Euroa a train stopped close to the station to set down a line-repairer named Watts. As the railway station was some distance away it was thought that the train had brought the police and Byrne prepared to defend himself. He shut all the men in the store, charging them to keep quiet. When Watts came to the station to inquire how the break in the line had occurred and to obtain assistance, Byrne

turned to Scott and said, 'That looks like a —— good watch. Let's see it.' Scott handed him the watch and the robber put it in his pocket. This was a signal to the other bushrangers. One took Macaulay's watch and another asked McDougal for his. McDougal took it from his pocket and said, 'I should be sorry to lose it. It is a keepsake from my dead mother.' 'Is it,' said Kelly, 'then we'll not take it.' Ned Kelly warned Macaulay that he held him responsible for the men. 'If you let them go before the time,' he replied, 'I'll shoot you like a —— dingo the first time I see you.'

Shortly afterwards the bushrangers mounted their

Steve Hart (below), Dan Kelly's best friend, was a superb horseman of local renown and lived on his father's farm on the outskirts of Wangaratta. He met Joe Byrne and Aaron Sherritt in 1876 whilst serving a twelve-month sentence in the Beechworth jail. It is said that when the Kelly boys asked him to join them, he rode off with them saying, 'Here's to a short life and a merry one.'

bailed him up and told him that he could repair the line later on. Nothing else happened after this until the return of Ned and his mates with the bank manager and the money.

During their drive together Ned Kelly told Scott that he was —— sorry that Sergeant Kennedy had been shot. He was a brave man. 'But,' he added, 'I couldn't help it. The police ought to surrender when they are called on.' He showed Scott the presentation gold watch which had once belonged to Kennedy and which he had taken from the body 'to remember him by'.

Soon after this return to the station they all had tea, Ned Kelly telling his prisoners that he would not detain them much longer. The meal was barely over when a train drew up opposite the station and whistled. Ned Kelly shouted, 'Hullo, boys, here's a special with the —— bobbies. We'll fight 'em. We're ready for 'em, however many there may be.' The driver waited for a few minutes and then the train went out. It was soon ascertained that Watts, the line repairer, had arranged for the train to pick him up after he had had time to repair the break. Owing to his being shut up in the station store he had neither repaired the line nor been able to inform the engine-driver of the reason for the delay.

At about half-past seven, the prisoners were mustered and told to remain in the store for three hours. Scott took out his watch and asked, 'Eleven?' 'No,' replied Ned, 'half-past. If anyone leaves before, I'll hear of it and make it —— hot for him. I'll track him down and shoot him dead. You can't escape me.' Byrne

**Steve Hart**

horses, which had been feeding in the stables during the time the station was held, and rode away. The men were released from the store but were kept at the station for about three hours. Mr and Mrs Scott returned to Euroa in their buggy and telegraphed the news of the robbery as soon as possible, which was not before the next morning. Gloster rode off to inform the police at the nearest town, and the news of this daring outrage was spread about by others who had been robbed.

After the bank robbery the 'gentlemen of the Strathbogie Ranges' again retired to their mountain hide-outs. Occasionally a paragraph in one of the local newspapers recorded the movements of the police or furnished a story about the black trackers, but these notices were necessarily very meagre, as the police declined to furnish any information as to their proceedings or intentions because this would be of more use to the bushrangers than to anyone else. For more than a month nothing reliable had been heard of them. Even the reports of the arrest and detention of numbers of bush telegraphs failed to attract any attention and the Kelly gang had almost ceased to be spoken of, when suddenly the whole country was roused by the news that the bushrangers had stuck up the town of Jerilderie, in New South Wales.

Jerilderie is situated on the Yanco Creek, not far from its junction with the Billabong. At that time it contained about 300 inhabitants, a bank, four public-

houses, a post and telegraph office, and several churches, schools, and other buildings. The local police station and lock-up was near the outside of the town and there were two officers — Constables Devine and Richards — stationed there.

At midnight of 8 February 1879, a man roused Constable Devine from his bed informing him that a row had taken place at Davidson's Hotel and a man had been killed. He urged the constable to 'come quickly'. Constable Devine woke Constable Richards and both dressed as hastily as possible. When they came out they were confronted by Ned Kelly, revolver in hand, and ordered to bail up. Not having their arms on them and being taken completely by surprise, the two constables surrendered at once and were locked up in the cells. The bushrangers then compelled Mrs Devine who had also partially dressed, to hand over all arms and ammunition. They took possession of the lock-up, remaining quietly there till morning; their horses were housed in the police stables at the rear.

It was Sunday morning, and as the Catholic church had not yet been finished, the court house had been rented for religious purposes. Mrs Devine had been accustomed to clean up the place, set the temporary altar, and place the forms and chairs ready for Mass. The bushrangers told her to perform her task as usual, after having extorted a promise from her that she would not mention their presence to anyone. To make certain of her keeping her word, one of them dressed as a constable, went with her to the court house and stayed while she swept the floor and prepared the room. Then they returned to the lock-up, which was about one hundred yards from the court house, and remained there all day. The bushrangers, arrayed in the constables' uniforms, sat quietly in the guard-room. No doubt numbers of people passed and saw them, but no one had any suspicion that the bushrangers were in charge instead of the police.

Early on Monday morning Byrne took two horses to the blacksmith's shop to be shod. The blacksmith, feeling some doubt as to the bona fides of the pseudo trooper, made a note of the brands on the horses. At about 10 a.m. Ned and Dan Kelly, accompanied by Constable Richards, went to the Royal Hotel, the largest hotel in the town, where Richards formally introduced them to the proprietor, Mr Cox. Ned informed Mr Cox that he required the use of some rooms as the gang intended sticking up the bank. He selected a large and a small room on the ground floor near the bar, and conducted the few men about at the time into the large room, where they were ordered to remain until given permission to depart. Dan Kelly was placed on guard at the door to keep order and prevent anybody from escaping, and was instructed to shoot the first man who refused to do as he was told.

On Mr Cox giving his word as a gentleman not to mention their presence to anyone who should come in, he was permitted to take charge of the bar as usual, and was given to understand that he would be held responsible for the discretion of the women and servants. Any one of them whom he could not trust was to be sent into the large room. The preliminaries were arranged so unostentatiously and quietly that no rumour of the presence of the bushrangers had yet been heard. As customers dropped into the hotel they were taken into the big room and told to remain on penalty of death.

Having made these arrangements, Ned Kelly walked into the hotel yard to reconnoitre. There was a detached kitchen there, and the rear of the bank of New South Wales was only a few yards from the rear of this kitchen. As the bank faced on another street there was no dividing fence between the yard at the back of the bank and the hotel yard. Hart was placed on watch near the kitchen while Byrne entered the back door of the bank.

Mr Living, the teller, was in the bank chamber. He was not surprised to hear a man enter by the back door as Mr Cox and other customers frequently came in that way, it being a short cut from the hotel. Suddenly Byrne came to the counter, pointed a revolver at Living's head, and cried out, 'I'm Kelly, keep quiet.' Living held his hands above his head. 'Where's your pistol?' asked Byrne. 'I've got none,' replied Living. Byrne then ordered Living and the accountant Mackie to 'Come over to the hotel'. They came from behind the counter and did as they were told, Byrne following them. When they reached the door of the large room, Dan Kelly inquired, 'Where's Tarleton?' 'In his room,' replied Living. 'Then go and fetch him and no —— nonsense,' said Dan. Living went back to the bank, but being unable to find the manager in his rooms, began to fear that something might have happened to him.

He was about to return to the hotel to inform the Kellys that he could not find the manager, when he heard a splashing. He went to the bath-room and knocked. Tarleton had just returned from a forty-mile ride that morning and was having a wash. When he opened the door and was informed that the town was in possession of the Kelly gang and the bank was stuck up, he laughed heartily, believing it to be a huge joke. Living assured him that it was not a laughing matter but he was still incredulous. However he dressed and went to the hotel, where he soon discovered that what he had deemed impossible had come to pass. The three bank officials were placed in the large room. Tarleton, who took a seat next to Constable Richards, whispered, 'I can knock Hart down. Shall I?' 'What's the good?' replied the constable, 'Dan Kelly's there, and he'd shoot you down at once.'

Ned Kelly had hitherto been walking round as a sort of inspector-general of the proceedings and giving orders. He now entered the room and ordered drinks to be served all round. Then he made a speech in which he blamed Constable Fitzpatrick for all that had

The Kellys hold up the Jerilderie police station at midnight on 6 February, 1879.

occurred. 'I wasn't within a hundred miles of Greta when he was shot,' said Ned, 'and up to then I'd never killed a man in my life.' He went on to say that he had stolen 280 horses from Whitby's station, and had sold them at Baumgarten's. He took out a revolver and exclaimed: 'This was Lonergan's! I took it from him. The gun I shot him with was a crooked, worn-out thing, not worth picking up. I shot him because he threatened my mother and my sister if they refused to tell where Ned Kelly was. The police are worse than the —— black trackers. I came here to shoot Devine and Richards, and I'm going to do it.' The men at the table began to intercede for Richards, who was sitting quietly among them and who did not speak, but Kelly exclaimed dramatically, 'He must die.'

Ned got the key of the bank safe and took £1450 worth of notes and money from it. He also took £691 from the teller's drawers. While thus employed, Messrs Gill, Hardie, and Rankin came in on business in the ordinary course and were ordered to bail up. They turned and ran. Ned Kelly followed and caught Rankin, but the others got away. Ned was furious at this escape. He said that news of their presence would be all over the place in a few minutes, and he swore he would shoot Rankin in revenge. He took Rankin to the hotel, stood him up against the wall in the passage, and flourished his revolver about. The men in the room pleaded that Rankin might be spared and urged that he could not have prevented Gill and Hardie from running away.

While this was going on Byrne came in with Mr Hardie and said that they could not find Gill, the proprietor of the local newspaper, who had not returned to his office. Ned Kelly then let Rankin go and declared that he would burn the newspaper office. It is said Mr Gill went out of the town and hid in a clump of trees by the side of the river till evening. Ned walked down to McDougall's Hotel and 'shouted' for about thirty men who were in or about the hotel at the time. On his return to the Royal Hotel he was informed that Hart had robbed the Rev. Mr Gribble of a gold watch. He called Hart up and asked indignantly, 'What right has a thing like you to rob a clergyman?' He swore a good deal and compelled Hart to give the watch back. Complaints were made that he had stolen a new saddle and a bridle from a saddler's shop, and some other articles from other places. Ned called him a — thief, and ordered him to return everything he had taken.

Ned Kelly paid more than one visit to the post and telegraph office to 'see how things were going on'. The robbers had cut the wires on either side of the town before their entry and had chopped down seven telegraph posts in the main street near the office. They had given orders to Mr Jefferson, the telegraph master, that no repairs should be attempted until permission was given, and Ned took care that these orders were obeyed.

The robbers held the town for three days, in imitation of the manner in which the Hall and Gilbert gang had held Canowindra. Jerilderie was at this time slightly larger than Canowindra at the time when it had been stuck up and held, but there was less traffic through it and consequently less connection between it and the outer world than with Canowindra. The road running through Jerilderie led from Conargo to Narrandera. Jerilderie was about thirty miles from Conargo and sixty-five from Narrandera. All round were huge sheep and cattle stations, with only a few men employed on them except at shearing or mustering time. All through the remainder of the year the traffic was inconsiderable. There was in Jerilderie, however, a large wool- washing and fellmongery establishment which employed a fair number of workmen. Canowindra, on the other hand, was a wayside town on the main road from Bathurst to Forbes and the traffic was considerable all the year round. There were also several small diggings settlements not far away, and the residents of these frequently came to purchase articles from the stores at Canowindra.

It was far easier, therefore, to isolate Jerilderie for three days than it had been Canowindra in the earlier days of bushranging. The Hall and Gilbert gang also robbed everybody except the landlord of the hotel they took possession of. The Kellys, on the other hand, robbed no one outside of the bank. Jerilderie also was

THE KELLY GANG—
Steve Hart.                           Dan

a much more compact town than Canowindra, the latter consisting of one long straggling street with only a few houses outside this line, while Jerilderie had several cross streets with at least two parallel with the river.

The robbers held the town from midnight on Saturday, until about 4 p.m. on the Wednesday following. Shortly before the men were allowed to leave the Royal Hotel, Ned Kelly gave Living a paper which he said gave a history of his life and the truth about what he had done. Living promised that he would do his best to get it published and handed it to Mr Gill, who read it and forwarded it to the Government.

This long, rambling statement, which was not published in the manner Kelly wished, came to be known as the celebrated 'Jerilderie Letter'. Parts of it were almost incoherent and patently false, and there were passionate passages of Irish rebellion and hatred of the police. The statement gave, among other things, Kelly's version of the Stringybark Creek incident, and railed against what Kelly believed to have been the harrassment of his mother by the police, described in one emotional outburst as 'a parcel of big ugly fat-

original Photograph.
Ned. Kelly.

This postcard of the 1880s claimed to reproduce an early photograph of the Kelly gang, although its authenticity is dubious.

necked wombat headed big bellied magpie legged narrow hipped splay-footed sons of Irish Bailiffs or English landlords which is better known as officers of Justice or Victorian Police . . .'

At about four o'clock Byrne left the town in the direction of the Murray River. He was riding his own horse, and had the money stolen from the bank packed on one of the police horses, which he was leading. A minute or two later Dan Kelly and Steve Hart mounted their horses, and galloped several times up and down the main street, flourishing their revolvers and shouting, 'Hurrah for the good old times of Morgan and Ben Hall.' Then they left the town along the main road. Ned Kelly, mounted on his grey mare and leading a second police horse, left some minutes later. Before going, he rode from the police station to the Royal Hotel and told the men detained in the large room there that they were free.

The bushrangers had left the town by different routes, probably to prevent any information as to the road they had travelled from being furnished to the police, but no doubt they had arranged where they should meet outside at a safe distance. Late in the evening they rode up to Wannamurra station, about twenty-five miles from Jerilderie, where Ned Kelly asked Mr A. Mackie whether his brother was at home yet? Mr Mackie replied that he did not know. 'I'm going to shoot him for giving horses to Living and Tarleton to ride to Deniliquin for the traps,' said Ned. They all went to the station together, but evidence was soon brought forward to prove that the bank employees had not obtained horses from Mr Mackie.

At length Ned exonerated that gentleman for what he called 'his treachery', but forcibly expressed his intention of shooting Living. 'I gave him back his life policy,' he said, 'and I only burned two or three of the bank books instead of the lot to oblige him. He asked for them, and I treated him as fair as I could, and now he takes advantage of my kindness to betray me.' He walked up and down on the veranda of the house for several minutes swearing at Living, and more than once said he had a good mind to go back and 'settle him' at once. His rage, however, soon subsided, and the gang proceeded on their way, no attempt being made to detain them.

Jerilderie lies about one hundred and fifty miles, as the crow flies, from where the bushrangers were supposed to have been hidden in the Strathbogie Mountains. When the news of the bank robbery at Jerilderie was telegraphed all over the country, everybody wondered how the robbers had crossed this terrain, some of it thickly populated, without being noticed. The skill with which the robbery had been planned, the boldness and completeness of the arrangements, and the apparent ease with which it had been accomplished, made the Kelly gang the principal topic of conversation.

The New South Wales Government issued a proclamation declaring Ned and Dan Kelly, Joe Byrne and Steve Hart outlaws, and offered a reward of £3000 for their capture, dead or alive. The associated banks of the colony supplemented this reward by another of £1000. The Victorian Government increased the rewards already offered to the same amount as was offered by the New South Wales Government, while the banks in that colony added another £1000; thus making the total reward offered for the capture of the four members of the gang £8000. Two thousand pounds per man was the highest reward ever offered for the capture of bushrangers in Australia.

For some time the police of New South Wales scoured the country round Jerilderie and the plains between that town and the Victorian border, while the Victorian police were quite as active on their side of the Murray River, until at length it was definitely ascertained that the bushrangers were safe back in their mountain hide-outs.

The paragraphs published from time to time in the

Beechworth, the Benalla and the Wangaratta papers, and in local papers even farther afield from the home of the Kellys tend to show that although the black trackers failed to follow a trail in the mountains with the certainty and skill displayed by them in leveller country, they still kept the outlaws in a continual state of fear of capture. Ned Kelly is reported to have called them 'those six little black devils' and to have sworn to shoot them if ever he 'got the chance'. 'Those —— trackers,' he cried, 'I'd like to shoot 'em. They're no —— good in this country. They can't track in Victoria. I can track as well as they can out on the plains. I can run an emu's trail for miles as well as them. They may be good in Queensland or the plains, but they're no good in the mountains.' Nevertheless they worried him, as his frequent complaints of their activity prove. The district was no doubt a difficult one to track in. None but a first class horseman could ride through it with any degree of certainty, and no one but an aboriginal or a white man born in the district could cross the ravines and gullies unaccompanied by a guide without getting hopelessly 'bushed'.

The arrests and detentions of Kelly's sympathizers continued with increased vigour. 'Wild' Wright and his brother Tom, relatives of the Kellys, Frank Hart, brother of the bushranger, the Lloyds and others, passed a considerable portion of their time in the cells of the various lock-ups round the district. Robert Miller was arrested and detained because his daughter, a daring horsewoman, was observed to go into the mountains at night with what were supposed to be provisions for the bushrangers. She was followed more than once, but eluded her pursuers by plunging up or down a steep mountain, or across an almost impassable gully. She never started twice in the same track, sometimes going up one spur or ravine, and next time choosing a different one, leading even the black trackers astray.

The newspapers frequently pointed out the folly of detaining the father while the daughter was left free to furnish the outlaws with food and news. The fact is that, special laws having been applied, there should have been no exceptions. In this case the women were far more active and reliable partisans of the Kellys than the men. As there can be little doubt that the Outlawry Act was strained, to put it mildly, by the police and the local magistracy with the connivance of the Government, another turn of the screw would not have made the actions of the authorities any more illegal; it might have made them efficient.

It was about this time that the name of Aaron Sherritt was first heard of in connection with the bushrangers. Sherritt was the son of an ex-policeman. He was about twenty-four years of age and had settled in the district some time earlier. He selected one hundred and seven acres of ground on the Woolshed Creek, and the Kellys and Byrnes helped him to fence it in and clear part of it. He had recently sold his farm

**Aaron Sherritt**

to a Mr Crawford of Melbourne, and had built himself a hut at Sebastopol, about two miles away, until he could take up another selection. He was engaged to be married to a sister of Joe Byrne and was regarded as one of the family.

Sherritt was suspected of having taken a share in some of the extensive horse-stealing raids in company with the Kellys and their friends, so consequently was an object of police suspicion and supervision. This was the man to whom the police made advances. They succeeded in winning him over to their side by promising him the whole of the eight thousand pounds reward offered for the capture of the bushrangers on condition that it should be through his aid and assistance that this capture was effected.

Sherritt led Superintendent Hare and a party of police into the innermost recesses of the mountains, pointing out several camps where the bushrangers had been; but in each case, the bushrangers appeared to have received warning and to have moved on before the police came. Some thought that Sherritt was playing a double game and that he let the bushrangers know when the police might be expected to arrive. There appears to be no foundation for this opinion as it delayed his chance of obtaining the reward.

At first he was careful not to be seen in company with the police, but their association could not be kept secret for long, and Sherritt soon became suspected by the Kelly family. One day Mrs Byrne openly accused him of trying to betray her son. There was a row; Sherritt was ordered from the house and his engagement with the daughter was broken off. After that Sherritt appeared only openly in company of the police, parties of whom were constantly watching the

After Dan Kelly convinced Joe Byrne of Aaron Sherritt's treachery, they both went to Sherritt's house with a neighbour, Antoine Weeks (also recorded as Anton Wicks) whom they handcuffed and ordered to call out to Sherritt. When he opened the door, Byrne shot him dead without a word.

homes of the four bushrangers on the chance of capturing them should they visit their parents or other relatives. Sherritt married the daughter of another settler in the district and all communications between him and the families of the bushrangers were broken off. Sherritt, instead of being a friend, was considered an enemy of the bushrangers.

During the latter half of 1879 and the first half of 1880 nothing of any importance was heard about the movements of the bushrangers. More than once it was reported that they had left the country, sometimes it was said for New Zealand, and at other times for America. These reports were invariably contradicted within a few days, and the Kellys were said to be still somewhere in the ranges. Sometimes it was said that the money stolen from the Jerilderie Bank must be all expended and that the Kellys would be forced to leave their hiding-place shortly, but frequently during the twelve months following that raid, nothing would be heard of the bushrangers for weeks, and the public almost forgot that there was such a gang in existence. Then suddenly came the news that the robbers had shot Aaron Sherritt on 27 June 1880.

For some weeks a party of police had been secreted, as much as possible, in Sherritt's house, for the purpose of watching Byrne's mother's house, and four of them were quietly sitting in the inner room at the time of the murder. The particulars of the murder were as follows:

A German market-gardener named Antoine Weeks

was living on the Woolshed Creek, not far from Sherritt's and Byrne's houses. He was walking home on the evening of the day mentioned when he was met by Dan Kelly and Joe Byrne. 'Do you know who we are?' asked Dan. 'No,' replied Weeks. 'Well, we're the Kellys,' said Dan; 'you do as we tell you and no harm will come to you.' They handcuffed the German and led him along the road to Sherritt's house. Here Dan told him to shout 'Aaron.' Weeks did so, and when Aaron Sherritt came to the door to see who wanted him, Byrne shot him dead without a word. The bushrangers took the handcuffs off Weeks and told him to go home. Then they went to the door of the hut, called Mrs Sherritt out, and told her that she had better send some of the —— traps in her house out to bury her husband, because 'we've shot him for being a traitor'.

The Kellys were fully aware that the police were in the house, and called on them to come out and 'fight like men'. If the constables had come out as invited they would have been courting almost certain death. A bright wood fire was burning in the hut and the front room was as bright as day, while all outside was as dark as possible. Had the police left the shelter of the inner room and entered the front apartment they would have been shot down before they could have seen their enemies, whose whereabouts could only have been guessed at from their shots or from the flash of their revolvers.

The bushrangers raged round the hut calling the police the most opprobrious names and threatening and taunting them in hopes of inducing them to come into the light. The police kept quiet and made no reply whatever to their taunts, so the bushrangers swore that they would 'burn 'em like rats in a trap'. They fired through the windows and doors, but they appear to have been just as unwilling to enter the well-lit room as the police were.

In fact neither party would give the other a chance. The robbers remained round the hut at this labour of hate until 2 a.m., when they departed. At daybreak one of the troopers went to where the horses were kept and rode to Benalla to give information of the reappearance of the Kellys, while the other three followed on the tracks of the outlaws.

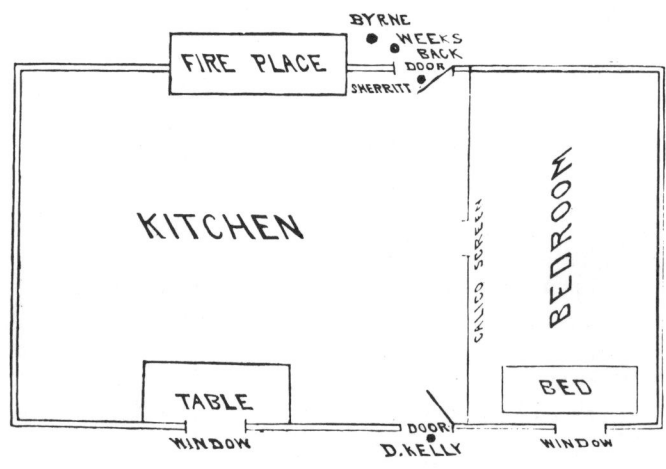

*Top:*
**Ned's grey mare, sketched at the time of Sherritt's murder.**

*Centre: Below:*
**Exterior and floor plan of Sherritt's hut.**

A rare photograph of Aaron Sherritt. He had attended the same school as Joe Byrne and the two had carried out horse-stealing raids together. His parents were respectable Beech-worth people. Although Sherritt did not actually take part in the Kelly gang exploits, he was active in assisting them as a 'bush telegraph'.

# 26 Drama at Glenrowan

**Drama at Glenrowan; attempt to wreck the police train; the Kelly gang's last stand; Ned Kelly in armour; the inn is burned; end of the Kelly gang; trial, conviction and death of Ned; the Kelly Show; decrease of crime in the colonies.**

As soon as the news of this fresh outrage was telegraphed to Melbourne, Sub-inspector O'Connor of Queensland, with his six black trackers, Superintendent Hare, Inspector Pewtress, and several other officials of the Victorian police, a number of newspaper correspondents, and a few other favoured persons, started by special train for the scene of disorder. Eight troopers were picked up at Benalla, and at 3.25 a.m. the train was stopped near the Glenrowan platform by Mr Curnow the local schoolmaster, who stood on the line waving a red scarf. He informed those on the train that the robbers had torn up the rails a short distance ahead with a view to wrecking the train, and that they were waiting near to shoot the police or any one else who might be sent to capture them. A consultation was immediately held to decide as to the next step.

While this was going on, Constable Bracken, the local representative of the police force, arrived and reported that the bushrangers had taken possession of the Glenrowan Inn, not much more than a hundred yards away and that he had just made his escape from them.

The Glenrowan Inn was built on the Sydney Road, about half-way between Winton and Wangaratta, shortly after the discovery of gold at the Ovens River in 1853. The glen was then a camping-place for teams travelling between Melbourne and the diggings. A second hotel was constructed later, and a small township grew up on the little flat at the gap in the hills, locally known as the Futter's Range, a spur jutting out from the larger Strathbogie Range. For some years Glenrowan was quite a flourishing little town due to the large amount of traffic to the diggings. When the Great Northern Railway was opened in 1873 the village began to dwindle away. The railway carried the trade past it to the more conveniently situated and larger towns on either side; consequently the population left for these towns. The two hotels remained and there was also a store, a blacksmith's shop, and a few other houses. These depended for their support on the fruit growers, market gardeners,

**Mr Curnow stops the special train**

**Inside the press carriage on the special train**

188

and farmers who cultivated the rich alluvial flats interspersed around the lower spurs of the mountains. The railway platform had been constructed by the Government to accommodate the trade in fruit, vegetables, and other produce which formed the staple industry of the district in 1880.

The Glenrowan Inn was a long, low, weatherboard building, with a wide veranda along the front. It stood some distance back from the road, with a large trough hewn from the stem of a tree in front for horses and bullocks to drink from. Near this was a sign-board with the names of the hotel and the proprietor on it:

THE GLENROWAN INN
**ANN JONES**
BEST ACCOMMODATION

The robbers, it appears, did not go very far when they left Sherritt's hut. They were aware that when the news of the murder reached Melbourne and other centres, an attempt would be made to follow them, and they seem to have made up their minds to a final effort to conquer the police force of the colony.

They went to the camp of the line repairers and roused them up. James Reardon, on coming out of his hut, was ordered to get his tools as the robbers were determined to rip up the line and wreck the train which they expected to arrive. Reardon at first refused but when threatened with death he gave in. Although he said that the tools were locked up and that he could not get them till morning he was told that the chest would soon be broken. His mate, Sullivan, was also held, and at length they agreed to do as they were told. They went to a bend in the road, a short distance north of the platform, under the impression that the

Repaired section of railway ripped up by the Kelly gang on the north side of the Glenrowan station

During the siege at Glenrowan, many spectators lined the nearby railway station in order to get a good view of the shoot-out at Jones' hotel, pictured in the background.

train would arrive from Wangaratta or Beechworth. They ripped up a number of the rails and piled them across the track. Then they marched Reardon and his wife and child and Sullivan to the Glenrowan Inn and took possession.

They collected sixty-two people in the township, including Mr John Stanistreet the station-master, and escorted them to the hotel. Among the prisoners was Constable Bracken. Ned Kelly walked about telling the people that the train would 'soon be here' from Rushworth with the black trackers and 'a lot of other —and we're going to kill the lot.' There was some confusion owing to the fears of the women and children, and while the bushrangers were engaged in restoring order, Constable Bracken managed to get hold of the key of the front door. He watched for an opportunity, opened the door and ran out. He reported later that three of the troopers who had been hidden in Sherritt's hut had followed the bushrangers. They had watched all their proceedings but had not ventured to attack them, as their ammunition was short, and they were not strong enough.

Presently a man came out on to the veranda and the police, recognizing him as Ned Kelly, fired a volley. Ned laughed, and shouted 'Shoot away, you ——, you can't hurt us.' At this juncture Mr Stanistreet came out of the house and walked from the hotel to where the police were, at the imminent risk of being shot, as he was between the two firing parties. He escaped, however, and reported that although Miss Jones, aged fourteen, and several other of the prisoners in the hotel had been wounded by the police fire, none of the bushrangers had been hurt. Superintendent Hare had also been severely wounded by the bushrangers; a bullet shattered the bones of his wrist. He was taken to the railway station-master's house and attended to.

At about 5 p.m. Mrs Jones, the landlady of the hotel, appeared on the veranda, wringing her hands and weeping. She called the police murderers, saying that her son had been killed and her daughter wounded. The police ceased firing and the boy was brought out. He was still alive and was sent off at once to the Wangaratta Hospital where he died the next day. An old man named Martin Cherry was also said to have been killed. Mrs Jones and her children and servants, and the men and women who had been made prisoners by the bushrangers, left the hotel after dark during a truce, after which firing was kept up during the night.

About daybreak another party of troopers arrived from Benalla, Wangaratta, and Beechworth, making the attacking party about thirty strong. There was a lull in the firing for a time while the newly-arrived men were being placed in positions, when suddenly a revolving rifle and a cap known to have belonged to Ned Kelly were found a hundred yards from the hotel at the rear of the attacking party. The rifle was stained with blood.

The police were still discussing this find and

speculating how the articles could have got there when they were fired at from behind a tree. The next moment an extraordinary figure marched across the space between two trees. The figure looked like a tall, stout man with a nail can over his head. Sergeant Steele,Constable Kelly, and Railway-guard Dowsett fired at it simultaneously, but the bullets appeared to rebound from the body of the figure. Steel then fired at the legs. At the second shot Ned Kelly fell, crying out 'I'm done for.' The police rushed forward, but Kelly raised himself on his elbow and fired, howling like a wild beast and declaring that they should never take him alive. He continued shooting but the bullets 'went wild' and as he was weakening through loss of blood he was soon grappled with and handcuffed.

**Constable Bracken, the Glenrowan policeman, gave the alarm after escaping from the inn.**

*Top Right:*
**Sub-Inspector O'Connor (second left) and Sergeant King (far left) with a party of black trackers were the first police to arrive at Glenrowan. When Superintendent Hare was shot in the wrist during the first volley, he retired to Benalla and telegrammed Captain Standish, the Chief Commissioner (far right) , who boarded another train with Superintendent Sadlier (second right) .**

*Right:*
**The Wangaratta contingent of police who were present at the siege of Glenrowan**

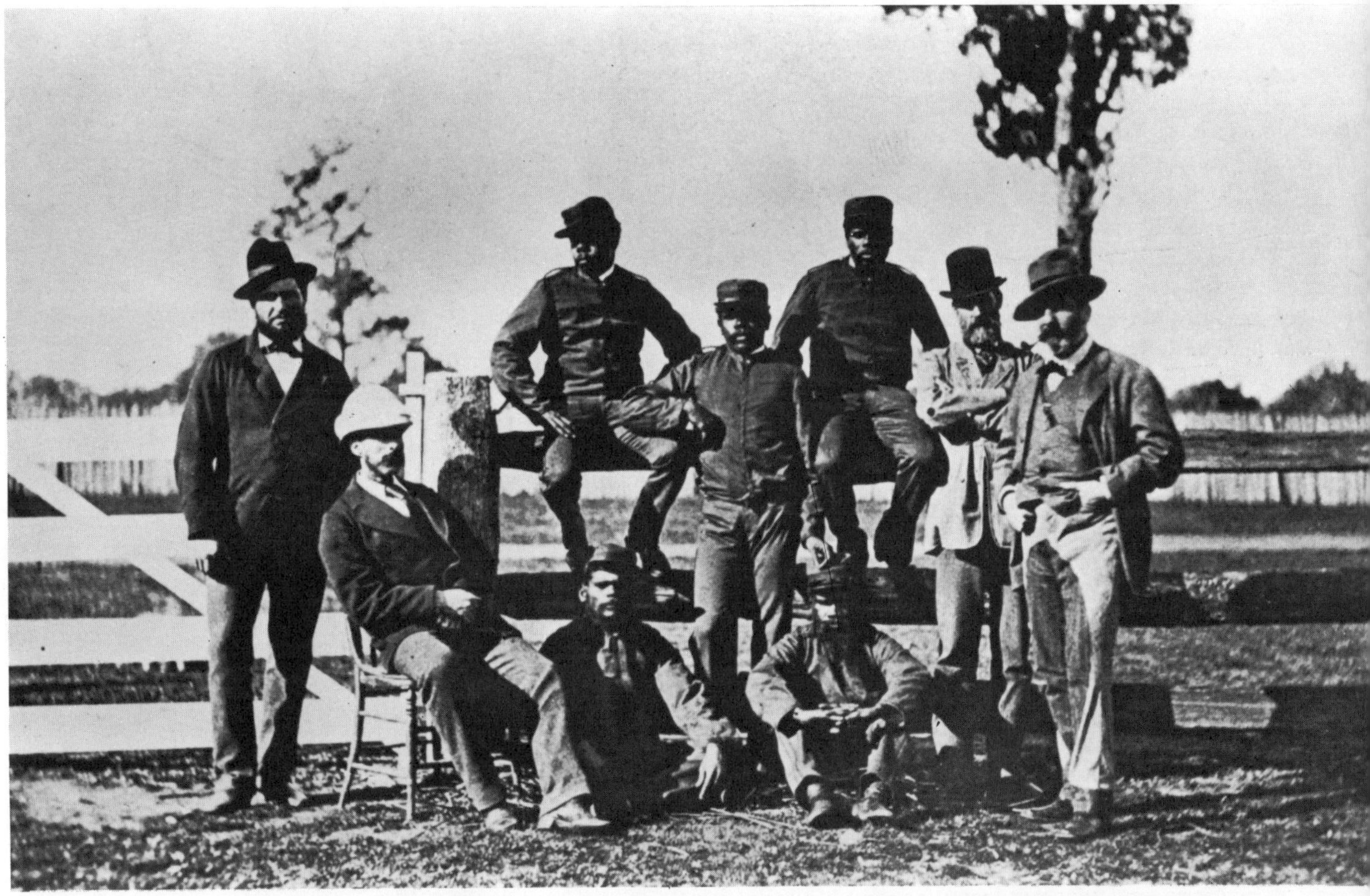

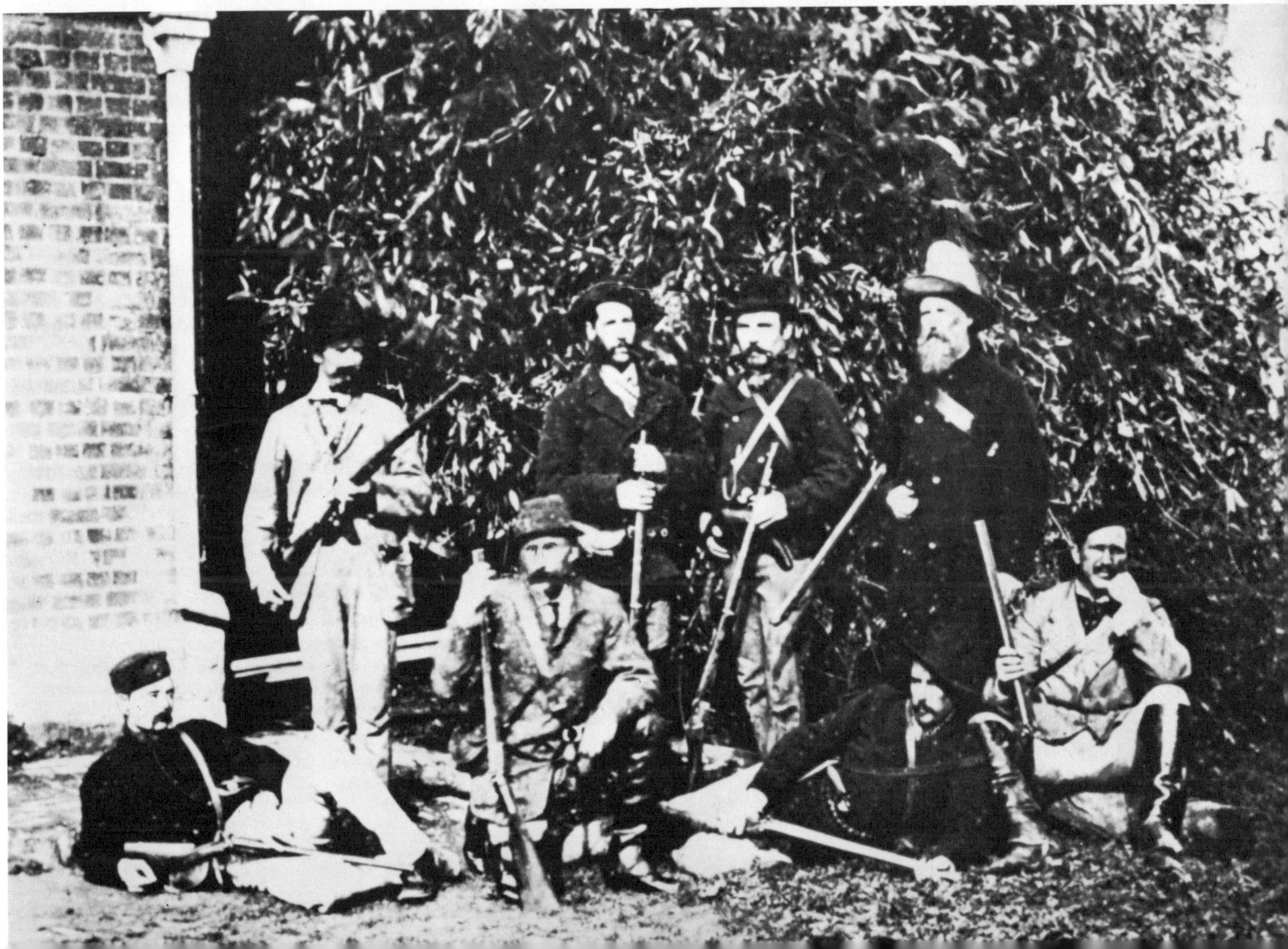

**Above:**
Before the shooting began, those imprisoned in the inn enjoyed themselves. Dancing and gaiety were punctuated by harangues from Ned Kelly.

**Left:**
Superintendent John Sadlier, in charge of the north-eastern police district, tracked the Kellys after the shooting of Constable Fitzpatrick.

**Top Right:**
Sub-inspector Stanhope O'Connor came from Queensland with a party of black trackers to help in the Kelly hunt.

**Top Far Right:**
The Kellys firing at police from the inn.

**Opposite:**
The armour used by the Kellys was recorded at Glenrowan by the *Australasian Sketcher*.

WEIGHT
97 pounds

The armour worn by Ned is said to have been made from stolen plough-shares by a local blacksmith, who also made similar 'suits' for other members of the gang. It consisted of a helmet shaped like a nail can and coming down to the shoulders, with a slit in it to enable the wearer to see; a breastplate, very long, with shoulder plates and back guard. The steel averaged nearly a quarter of an inch in thickness and the weight of the suit worn by Ned Kelly was ninety-seven pounds. The breastplate showed several dints where it had been struck by bullets, but it had not been pierced. However Ned had received two wounds in the groin and one each in the left foot, right leg, right hand, and right arm.

Kelly was immediately removed to a safe distance and placed under medical care. Despite the loss of one of their small number, the bushrangers kept up a brisk fire from the hotel. At one time a report was circulated that Joe Byrne had been shot dead while drinking a glass of brandy in the bar, but as there was no apparent slackening in the fire this was discredited.

At 3 p.m. Constable Charles Johnson, under cover of a volley from the besiegers, rushed up to the side of the hotel with a huge bundle of straw which he placed in position and set fire to. The straw blazed up well but soon died out, and the crowd of spectators pronounced the attempt to fire the building a failure. It was at this time that Mrs Skillian, a sister of the Kellys, rode up, dressed in a well-made black cloth riding habit and a Gainsborough hat. She advanced boldly towards the hotel but was stopped by the police and warned of the danger she was courting. She replied that she was not afraid, but wanted to persuade her brother Dan to surrender. A consultation was held as to whether she should be permitted to try, but before a decision was reached flames burst out of the roof of the building.

It may be as well to explain here that the wood of the district was principally stringy bark, and that the timber of these trees will not burn. Apparently when the straw was ignited against the wall of the building, the calico sheeting with which the rooms were lined, and the ceiling, caught fire and burned, while the stringy bark weatherboards resisted the flames and only charred through slowly. However this may be,

The police firing at the Glenrowan Inn were puzzled by a ringing sound on the cold, misty, early morning air. Then Kelly appeared in armour, a huge figure, beating his metal helmet with the butt of his revolver and roaring, 'You —— dogs, you can't shoot me.' In the panic of fear and confusion, random shots bounced from Kelly's armour until Sergeant Arthur Steele (left) got behind the bushranger and fired into his legs. The police did not know until the helmet was removed that it was Ned Kelly, who had slipped out of the hotel some time before. Steele, stationed at Wangaratta, had led many abortive attempts to capture Kelly. He kicked the helpless outlaw in the groin and thrust his pistol into Kelly's face but was restrained by Constable Bracken who said, 'You shoot him and I'll shoot you. Take him alive.'

the furniture and other fittings burned fiercely and the whole building was in a blaze.

At this time the Rev. Father M. Gibney, a Roman Catholic priest from Perth, Western Australia, who was on a visit to the Benalla district at the time, walked up to the front door holding his crucifix in his hand. He was followed by a number of the police. When they entered the front door they saw the body of Joe Byrne lying in the bar, in such a position as to make it probable that the report which had been spread as to his death had been true. The body was dragged out slightly scorched. Dan Kelly and Steve Hart were found dead in a small parlour off the bar. From the position in which they were lying it was thought that they had either committed suicide or that they had simultaneously shot each other.

There was no time to decide whether these conjectures were true. As Father Gibney was about to stoop down to examine the bodies, a gust of wind swept the flames towards him and compelled him to retire. The building was thoroughly alight at last, and the priest, police and others who had entered were forced out by the fierce heat. A very short time afterwards the house collapsed. Nothing was left but a heap of ashes, the sign post and trough in front, and the detached kitchen at the rear. In this kitchen was found old Martin Cherry, severely wounded. He was carried out and placed under the doctor's care but died before night. Close beside the kitchen was the body of a dog which had been wounded by the attacking party and had crawled between the two buildings to die.

Some time before the attempt to fire the building had been made, a telegram had been sent to Melbourne to ask for a small cannon to blow the house down with. Now a telegram was sent to say it was not required. Consequently the 12-pounder Armstrong gun with the requisite number of men of the Garrison Artillery which had been sent off by special train was stopped at Seymour and sent back.

When the fire had burned down sufficiently for an examination to be made, the two mounds of ashes which were all that remained at Dan Kelly and Steve Hart were given to Mrs Skillian for burial, while the body of Joe Byrne was reserved for an inquest to be

The siege at Glenrowan continued (top) until Monday afternoon when Constable Johnson set fire to the inn (centre). The building burnt slowly at first but in the final blaze it was impossible to remove the bodies of Dan Kelly and Steve Hart and only the charred remains (top left) were found later. It was thought that they had committed suicide.

held. Two other suits of armour similar to that worn by Ned Kelly were found, the lightest being ninety-two pounds.

During the fight 'Wild' Wright, Tom Wright, Frank Hart, Kate Kelly, several of the Lloyds and the Byrnes, and other relations and friends of the bushrangers, had been stationed on a ridge a short distance away to see the fun. There was also a large number of other and perhaps more disinterested spectators, some of them from Melbourne or Beechworth or other even more distant localities.

After the inquest the body of Joe Byrne was given to his friends for burial. Ned Kelly soon recovered from his wounds and was tried, convicted and sentenced to death for the murder of Sergeant Kennedy. In conversations with Inspector Sadlier and other police officials before his trial, he said that the bushrangers had known of every movement of the police. They were aware that the police had been hiding in Sherritt's hut for more than a week, hoping to catch Joe if he visited his mother. The police had no right to stop a man from going to see his mother. When the special train arrived the intention of the bushrangers had been to rake it with shots as soon as it reached the place where the rails had been removed. 'But,' exclaimed Sadlier, 'you would have killed all the people in the train.' 'Yes, of course, God help them,' replied Ned, 'they'd have got shot, but wouldn't they have shot me if they could?'

Kelly said that Steve Hart had visited his mother at Wangaratta, and 'didn't we laugh when we saw it in

The partly charred body of Joe Byrne was strung up outside the Benalla police station for photographers and newspaper artists. (Julian Ashton, sketchbook under arm, is on the far left.) After a hurried inquest, Byrne was buried quietly at night in the Benalla cemetery.

the Wangaratta News afterwards. It was true, too, though the police didn't believe it.' He also said that he had been told that after the sticking up of the banks at Euroa and Jerilderie, all the branch banks in Victoria sent their receipts to Melbourne almost daily. They were not going to stick up any more banks. It wasn't worth it. What they had intended to do was to stick up a railway train, and they'd have done it, 'only those little black devils were always about.'

Kelly's trial was begun at Beechworth, but after the prosecution had protested that it would be impossible to obtain an impartial jury in the locality, it was transferred to the Central Criminal Court in Melbourne.

The trial commenced on 28 October 1880 before Mr Justice Barry and by the second day Kelly had been found guilty. Asked if he had anything to say before the death sentence was passed, the outlaw replied:

Well it is rather late for me to speak now. I thought of speaking this morning and all day. But there was little use. It's no use blaming anyone now. Nobody knows about my case except myself, and I wish I had been allowed to examine the witnesses myself. If I had examined them, I'm confident I could have thrown a different light on the case.

It is not that I fear death. I fear it as little as to

196

Ned Kelly, watched by Sergeant Steele, is taken by train to Beechworth.

*Left:*
Thomas Carrington, staff artist of the *Australasian Sketcher*, made these drawings of the Glenrowan siege during the encounter:
1 Firing the Glenrowan Inn.
2 Civilians emerging from the inn with their hands in the air.
3 The body of Joe Byrne lying where it fell in front of the bar.

Interior of the Beechworth courthouse where the trial of Ned Kelly began.

drink a cup of tea. On the evidence that has been given, no juryman could have given any other verdict. That is my opinion. But as I say, If I'd examined the witnesses, I'd have shown matters in a different light . . .

For my own part, I don't care one straw about my life, nor for the result of the trial; and I know very well from the stories I've been told, of how I am spoken of — that the public at large execrate my name . . . But I don't mind, for I'm the last that carries public favour or dreads the public frown. Let the hand of the law strike me down if it will; but I ask that my story be heard and considered . . .

After some further exchanges between the prisoner and the bench, Sir Redmond Barry proceeded to pass sentence, saying: '. . . I cannot hold out any hope to you that the sentence I am about to pass will be remitted. I desire not to give you any further pain or to aggravate the distressing feelings which you must be enduring.' When he concluded with the formal injunction: 'May the Lord have mercy on your soul', Kelly replied: 'Yes, I will meet you there.'

On 5 November, a mass meeting was held in the Hippodrome in Stephen's Street, Melbourne, with Mr Hamilton, President of the Society for the Abolition of Capital Punishment, in the chair. The principal speaker was Mr David Gaunson, M.L.A., and a resolution was unanimously carried to the effect that the case of Edward Kelly was a fit one for the exercise of the

Despite the odd bullets still coming from the direction of the inn, the capture of Ned was greeted with celebration, and sightseers and police posed proudly near the spot where Ned was taken.

Ned Kelly in remand at Pentridge jail. Constable McIntyre, the only survivor of the Stringybark incident, is shown standing on the extreme right.

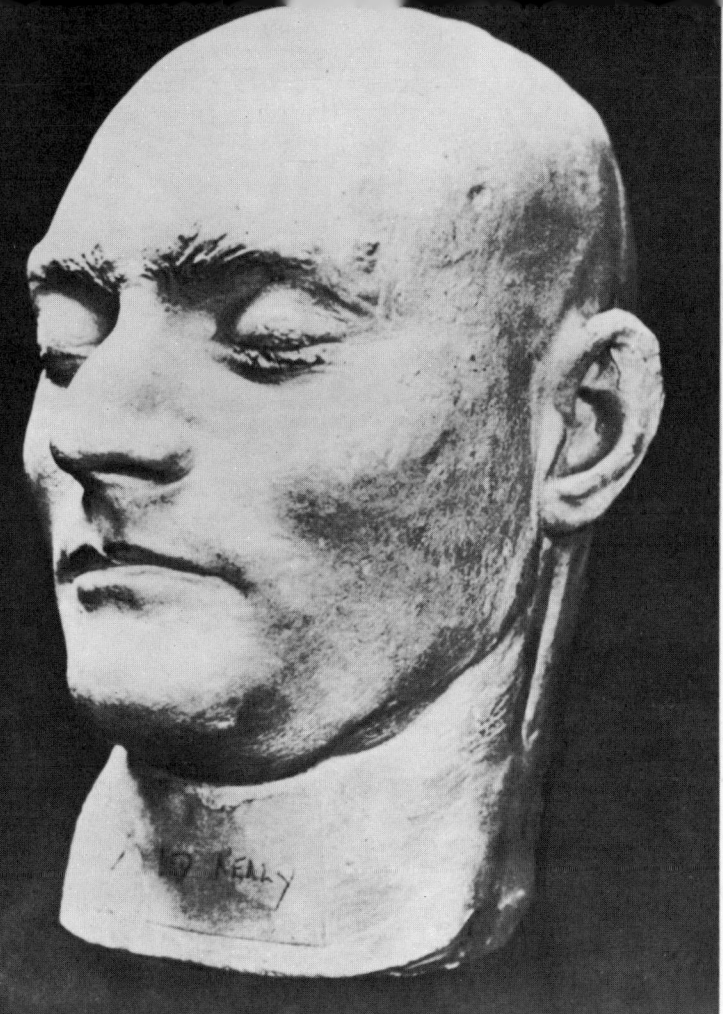

**The death mask of Ned Kelly**

Royal Prerogative of Mercy. The Melbourne *Argus* said that 'those present belonged to the larrikin classes', but the attendance was estimated at 4000 people (including 300 women) inside the building, and about 2000 outside who could not obtain admittance. Similar meetings were also held in Ballarat, Bendigo, Geelong, and other towns, but these efforts were of no avail. Ned Kelly, 'the last of the bushrangers', was hanged in the Melbourne jail, on 11 November 1880.

Twenty-two official witnesses were present at the hanging, and Kelly was attended by Dean O'Hea and the Roman Catholic chaplain at the Melbourne jail, Father Donaghy. The bushrangers' last words were the subject of dispute: according to some reports he made the memorable observation, 'Such is life'; others attributed to him the more prosaic reflection, 'Ah well, I suppose it had to come to this'.

After the execution Ned Kelly's head was cut from his body and shaved for study. A death mask was made and later the skull was kept by a government official. Kelly's remains were buried in an unmarked grave in a section of the old Melbourne jail which has now been built over.

Within a few days of the execution, a show was opened in Melbourne with Kate Kelly, one of the sisters of the dead bushrangers, 'mounted on Ned Kelly's celebrated grey mare'. A suit of the armour

used in the last great fight at Glenrowan, several guns, pistols, and revolvers alleged to have been used in the various raids committed by the bushrangers, some handcuffs and other articles which had belonged to, or were used by them, were exhibited, and some particulars of their careers were given in the form of a lecture. The police authorities soon interfered and the show was closed. It was reopened in Sydney, but was suppressed there almost immediately as 'tending towards immorality' and the Kellys returned to the obscurity of private life.

Thus ended the last act in the great tragedy which had supplied much of the romance in Australian history. Bushranging had been spoken of as 'the national crime of Australia', but, as I have shown, there was very little bushranging outside the three colonies of New South Wales, Van Diemen's Land, and Victoria. It was an excrescence on, rather than a development of, Australian character.

It has been estimated that the bushrangers in the colonies from the date of the great outbreak inaugurated by Frank Gardiner in 1861, to the death of Ned Kelly, never exceeded 300 people, the story of their exploits shows how even so small a party can disturb a whole country when the rebels are reckless and determined. It may be said in conclusion that crime steadily decreased in Australia from the cessation of transportion. At first, while the gold fever raged, the improvement was very slight, but from the date when the population settled down to steady work the criminal statistics, which were very complete in the colonies, showed a steady diminution in crimes against person or property. There was an increase in the years during which the Ben Hall and Gilbert gang, and their imitators in New South Wales and Victoria, were most active; even this did not materially affect the general result and was speedily compensated for after the death of Thunderbolt and the capture of Power. In this last epoch of bushranging, the Moonlite and Kelly gangs arrested the movement to some degree, but far less sympathy was exhibited for them than in the earlier epoch. Their deeds did not inspire so many young men with the desire to go and do likewise, as those of Hall and Gilbert had done. In fact bushranging had ceased to be popular, so that the retrogression was small in comparison.

Numbers of jails were then closed or converted to other uses. There was a time when every little town in New South Wales had its jail. By 1890 many of these jails had been converted into factories or stores, or used for municipal or other purposes. In Victoria the jails were fewer but larger and several of these were closed, while others once full were almost empty.

**Ned Kelly's last stand was drawn on the spot by T. Carrington and published soon after by the *Australasian Sketcher*.**

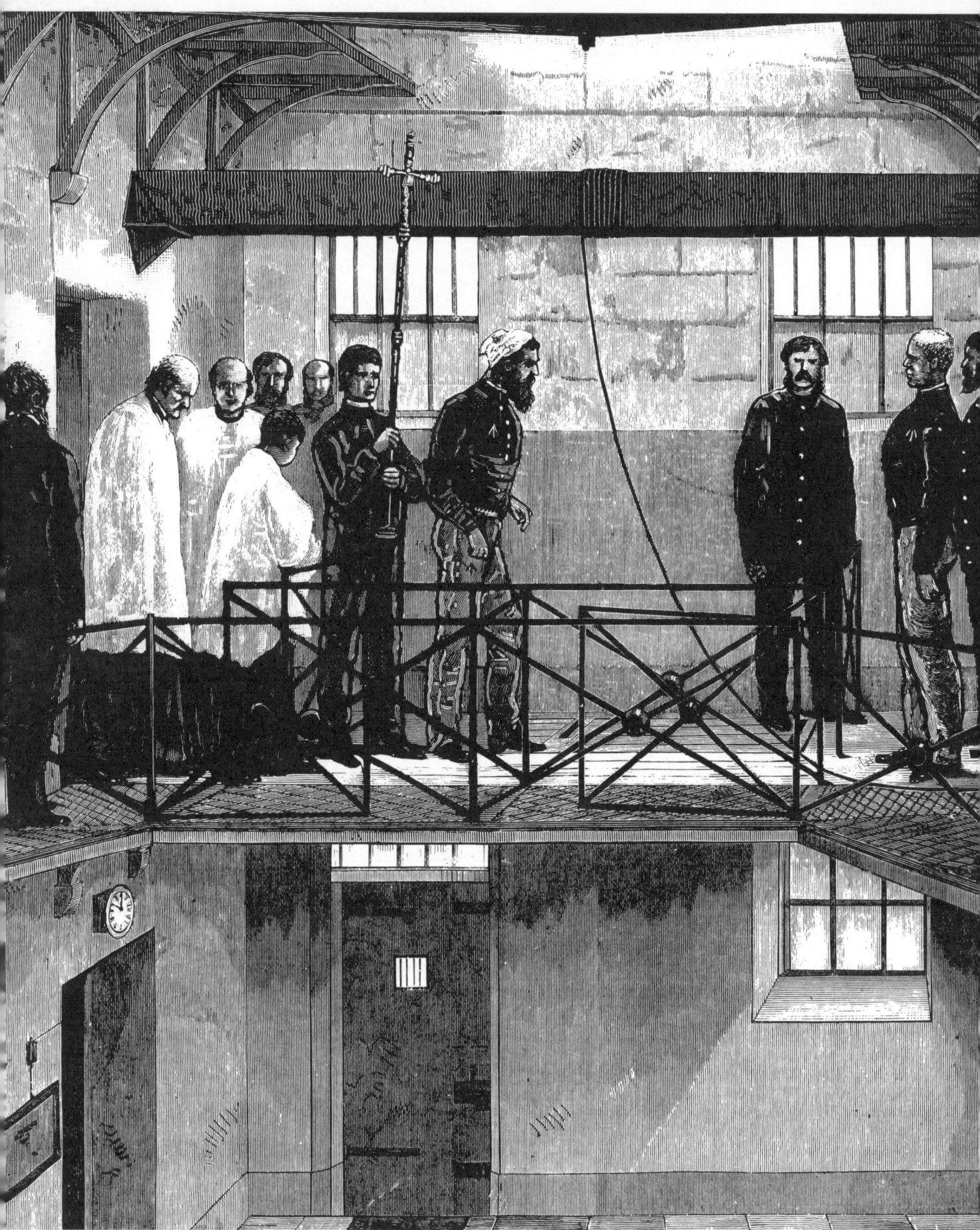

Twenty-two official witnesses were present at the hanging of Ned Kelly at 10 a.m. on 11 November, 1880. Among them were Dean O'Hea, Father Donaghy and eight journalists.

*Right:*
Although the suit of armour worn by Ned on that fateful day at Glenrowan was (and still is) held by the police, sisters of the dead bushrangers opened a show in Melbourne displaying another suit used in the fight and various guns used by the Kelly gang on their raids. Police soon closed the exhibition.

*Below:*
The Colt revolver used by Ned Kelly as he advanced on the bewildered police at Glenrowan is now held in the Police Museum, Melbourne, with his armour and other Kelly relics.

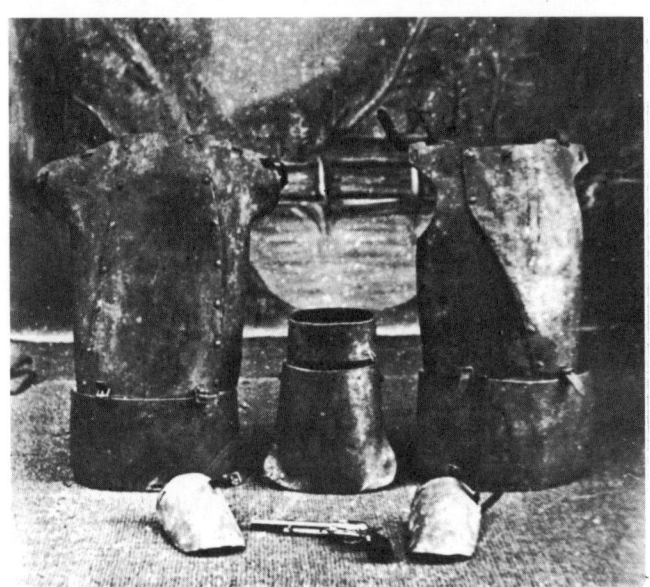

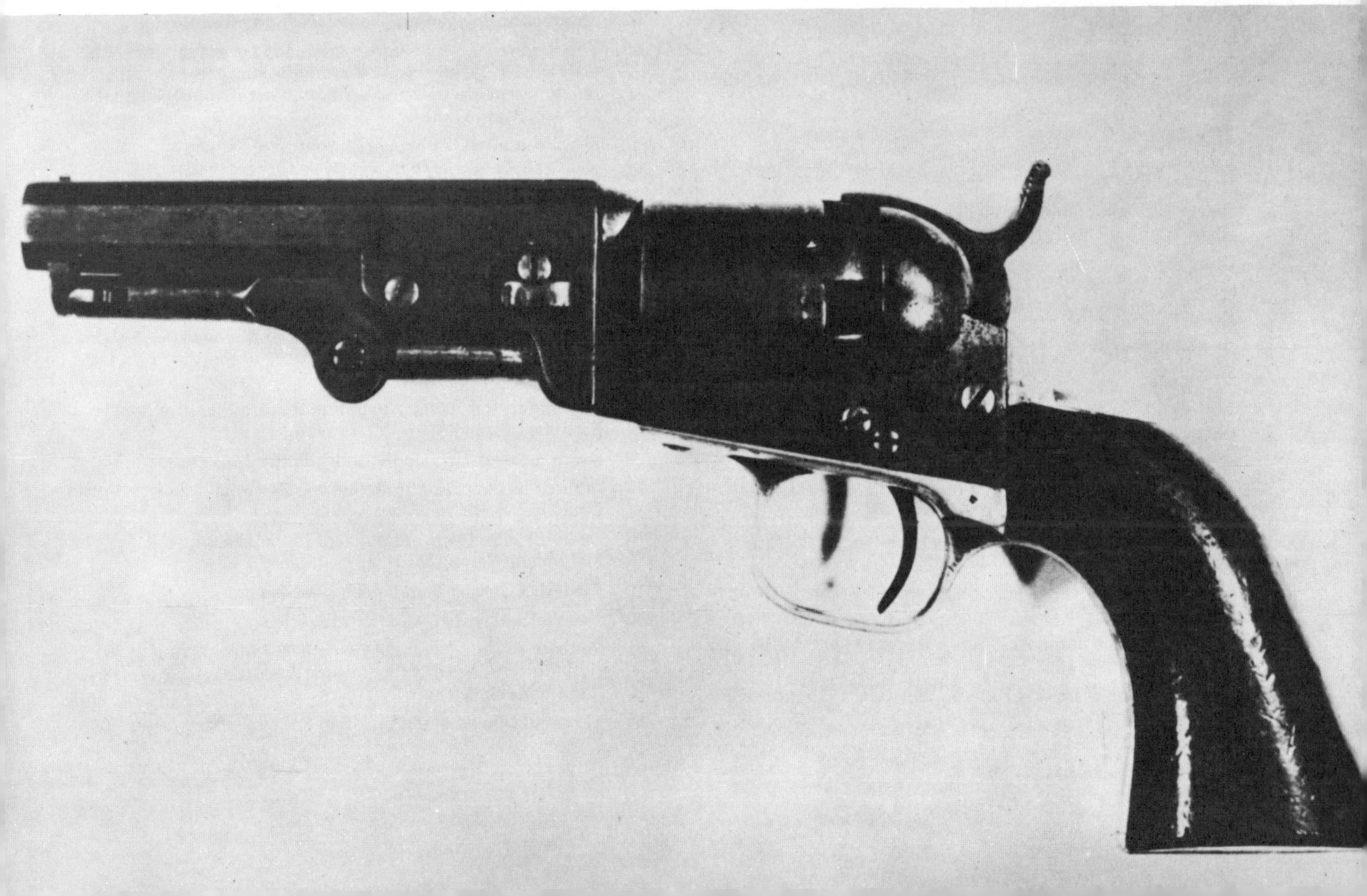

# Picture Sources

The illustrations in this book have been supplied by a variety of private and public sources to which acknowledgement is made below. The publishers express their particular thanks to the staff of the Latrobe Library historical collection, and to Sergeant John Ward of the Police Museum, Victoria Police, Melbourne.

Illustrations and their sources are listed below by page numbers, in the order in which they appear.

# Reference Notes

BIBLIOGRAPHY: BOOKS AND OFFICIAL SOURCES

Reports of the Select Committees of the House of Commons on Transportation, Sessions 1837 and 1838.
Report of the Special Commission of Enquiry into the state of the Colony of New South Wales by John Thomas Bigge, 1822 and 1823.
Dispatches of Governors Macquarie, Bourke, Sorell, Arthur, Franklin, Denison, Latrobe, etc., to the Colonial Office.
Anon., *History of Van Diemen's Land, from 1820 to 1835*.
Mackay, George, *History of Bendigo*.
Bonwick, James, *The Last of the Tasmanians*.

BIBLIOGRAPHY: NEWSPAPERS

*Spectator; Hobart Town Gazette; Hobart Town Courier and Murray's Review; Colonial Times; Cornwall Chronicle; Launceston Advertiser; Launceston Examiner; Sydney Gazette; Sydney Monitor; Sydney Australian; Sydney Morning Herald; Melbourne Argus; Port Phillip Herald; Geelong Advertiser; Melbourne Herald; Melbourne Age; South Australian Register; Brisbane Courier.*
The quotations from numerous provincial papers acknowledged in the text have been taken at second hand, principally from the metropolitan papers of the colony referred to, and which are included in this list.

CHAPTER 1

1 Evidence of Sir Francis Forbes, Chief Justice of New South Wales; Report of the Select Committee of the House of Commons on Transportation, July, 1837.

2 Despatch from Governor Macquarie to Earl Bathurst, June 28, 1813.
3 *Sydney Gazette*, November 20, 1830.
4 Commission of Enquiry into the state of the colony of New South Wales, 1822.
5 Report of the Select Committee of the House of Commons on Transportation, July, 1837.
6 Report by Captain Maconochie, forwarded to the Colonial Office by Sir John Franklin, October 7, 1837.
7 Select Committee of the House of Commons on Transportation, August, 1838.
8 Ditto.
9 Dispatch to Colonial Office, entitled, 'Administration of Justice at Norfolk Island, November, 1838'.
10 *History of Van Diemen's Land from 1820 to 1835*.
11 *Sydney Gazette*.
12 Dispatch of Governor Bourke to the Colonial Office, 1835.
13 Select Committee of the House of Commons on Transportation, July, 1837.
14 Commission of Enquiry into the state of the colony of New South Wales, 1822.

CHAPTER 2

1 *History of Van Diemen's Land, from 1820 to 1835*.

CHAPTER 3

1 Report of the Select Committee of the House of Commons on Transportation, 1838.
2 The first supply of horned cattle for Australia was obtained from Capetown, South Africa, big-boned, slab-sided animals, with enormous horns. These animals are much more active than the fine-boned, heavy-bodied, short-horned, or other fine breeds, but they can never be properly tamed. It is always unsafe to milk one of these cows unless her head is fastened in 'a bail', and her leg tied. When driving the cows into the bail it was the custom to order them to 'bail up'. It was also

usual for bullock drivers when yoking their teams to call out 'bail up' to the bullocks, although no bail was used for this purpose. The words were in constant use all over Australia, and were adopted by the early bushrangers in the sense of 'stand'.

3 History of Van Diemen's Land in the *Launceston Advertiser*, 1840.
4 *Hobart Town Gazette*, 1826.
5 *Hobart Town Gazette*.

## CHAPTER 4

1 Select Committee of the House of Commons on Transportation, July, 1837; Major Mudie's evidence.

## CHAPTER 9

1 The *Colonial Times*.

## CHAPTER 10

1 'Mr Lachlan McLachlan, or 'Bendigo Mac', as he was more familiarly styled, administered the law with a vigour and severity which brought upon him censure from many quarters . . . but "desperate evils require desperate remedies." . . . When an old hand happened to be among the prisoners, he would be terrified by the fierce reprobation of Bendigo Mac, or by the glare which shot from that inevitable eyeglass. . . . At other times he would say to a prisoner, "This district is not big enough for both you and me. One of us must leave — which shall it be?" The prisoner would feel, of course, that there was very little doubt about the matter, and would promise to make himself scarce, requesting probably a couple of days' grace to wash up a bit of washdirt.' *History of Bendigo*, by George Mackay, Chap. III.

# Index

## Principal bushrangers, their pursuers, and other participants